Ten Minutes to Deep Meditation

Deep Meditation

Techniques that Reduce Stress and Relieve Anger, Anxiety & Depression

Michael J. Cavallaro

TEN MINUTES TO DEEP MEDITATION: TECHNIQUES THAT REDUCE STRESS AND RELIEVE ANGER, ANXIETY & DEPRESSION

Copyright © 2014 Atlantic Publishing Group, Inc.
1405 SW 6th Avenue • Ocala, Florida 34471 • Phone 800-814-1132 • Fax 352-622-1875
Website: www.atlantic-pub.com • E-mail: sales@atlantic-pub.com
SAN Number: 268-1250

Library of Congress Cataloging-in-Publication Data

Cavallaro, Michael J.
  Ten minutes to deep meditation : techniques that reduce stress and relieve anger, anxiety & depression / Michael J. Cavallaro.
      pages cm
  Includes bibliographical references and index.
  ISBN-13: 978-1-60138-586-4 (alk. paper)
  ISBN-10: 1-60138-586-2 (alk. paper)
  1. Meditation--Therapeutic use. 2. Stress management. I. Title.
  RC489.M43.C38 2014
  155.9'042--dc23
                            2014018663

Lane E. Buchner: Hand model, Chapter 4, pages 109-111

Printed on Recycled Paper

Printed in the United States

A few years back we lost our beloved pet dog Bear, who was not only our best and dearest friend but also the "Vice President of Sunshine" here at Atlantic Publishing. He did not receive a salary but worked tirelessly 24 hours a day to please his parents.

Bear was a rescue dog who turned around and showered myself, my wife, Sherri, his grandparents Jean, Bob, and Nancy, and every person and animal he met (well, maybe not rabbits) with friendship and love. He made a lot of people smile every day.

We wanted you to know a portion of the profits of this book will be donated in Bear's memory to local animal shelters, parks, conservation organizations, and other individuals and nonprofit organizations in need of assistance.

– *Douglas & Sherri Brown*

PS: We have since adopted two more rescue dogs: first Scout, and the following year, Ginger. They were both mixed golden retrievers who needed a home.

Want to help animals and the world? Here are a dozen easy suggestions you and your family can implement today:

- *Adopt and rescue a pet from a local shelter.*
- *Support local and no-kill animal shelters.*
- *Plant a tree to honor someone you love.*
- *Be a developer — put up some birdhouses.*
- *Buy live, potted Christmas trees and replant them.*
- *Make sure you spend time with your animals each day.*
- *Save natural resources by recycling and buying recycled products.*
- *Drink tap water, or filter your own water at home.*
- *Whenever possible, limit your use of or do not use pesticides.*
- *If you eat seafood, make sustainable choices.*
- *Support your local farmers market.*
- *Get outside. Visit a park, volunteer, walk your dog, or ride your bike.*

Five years ago, Atlantic Publishing signed the Green Press Initiative. These guidelines promote environmentally friendly practices, such as using recycled stock and vegetable-based inks, avoiding waste, choosing energy-efficient resources, and promoting a no-pulping policy. We now use 100-percent recycled stock on all our books. The results: in one year, switching to post-consumer recycled stock saved 24 mature trees, 5,000 gallons of water, the equivalent of the total energy used for one home in a year, and the equivalent of the greenhouse gases from one car driven for a year.

Disclaimer

This publication does not offer medical advice. Any content presented in this publication is for informational purposes only, and is not intended to cover all possible uses, directions, precautions, drug interactions, or adverse effects. This content should not be used during a medical emergency or for the diagnosis or treatment of any medical condition. Please consult your doctor or other qualified health care provider if you have any questions about a medical condition, or before taking any drug, changing your diet or commencing or discontinuing any course of treatment. Do not ignore or delay obtaining professional medical advice because of information presented herein. Call 911 or your doctor for all medical emergencies.

Dedication

This book is dedicated to Jean Arlotta

Table of Contents

Chapter 2: Considerations Before You Get Started 45

Chapter 3: How to Create a Regular Meditative Practice 63

Chapter 7: Finishing Core Meditation with Lovingkindness 161

Chapter 8: Divine Meditation 181

Introduction

How do you really feel about life? Are you someone who believes you are unfortunate and that other people are to blame for your troubles? Do you have overwhelming stresses or frustrated ambitions? Is your self-image full of hidden fears and hurtful resentments? If you are reading this book, something in your life is not working and you have come to the point, probably after years of suffering, where you have had enough and finally want to do something about it by learning meditation. Meditation is the devotional exercise of training the mind to connect with the body, which creates a higher consciousness that yields some intended life benefit. In order to examine these questions further, think back to when you were a child and ask yourself if you had a mindset. A mindset is the sum total of your conscious and subconscious programming directly formed by the events of your individual lifetime. When a child enters this world, it enters with the pure loving light of creation, free of judgments and attachments. It understands nothing of the petty and serious conflicts that entangle this world. However, as the child gradually encounters the successes, failures, joys, and miseries that accompany modern life, the light of pure creation slowly dims within the child. Over time, it develops a *type of mindset* based on those experiences, which then determines the physical, intellectual, emotional, and spiritual and quality of its life. Once fully grown and subjected to the various influences that formed the mindset, the individual then wrongfully comes to associate suffering as part of some maturation process. He or she never questions whether this suffering was intended, or whether there may be something very wrong with this widely accepted belief.

Whatever mindset you have developed in life (optimism, pessimism, fear, determination, confidence, anxiety, self-loathing, etc.) your ego was the source of consciousness that created it. Through the development of your mindset, you perceive your sense of self in relation to the world around you. The ego drive, therefore, is the impulse that serves to satisfy what the formulated sense of self thinks it needs. It manifests in our thoughts, our actions, our emotions, and even our bodies. For example, when you ardently defend your own beliefs, behave in certain ways toward others, or compete against others as a form of fulfillment, your ego drive is working to protect the self it individually created. Over the past few centuries, the ego drive has been useful in shaping life to meet many of society's physical and emotional needs. Consequently, it also has been the source of physical and emotional stresses created by its own evolving maneuvers. Worse, it has removed our connection to something more satisfying than what the ego-driven material world has

to offer. While the ego-driven material world continually strives to devise solutions to the sense of lacking it creates, these solutions ultimately prove artificial as a healing remedy.

If you are like most people, your ego drive created some type of mental or emotional turbulence that you are either consciously or unconsciously aware of, and it ultimately has lead to your own suffering. If you can begin to understand that a mindset was programmed into you as you aged, you can begin to understand that it is a false construction, capable of being changed, and that none of it has its origin in the spiritual dimension. This book will help you shed your past mental and emotional conditioning so that you can begin to achieve whatever intention you set out for yourself as you move forward in your life. People turn to meditation because scientific and historical research shows that meditating at least ten minutes a day can dramatically alter the way the body responds to stress. It can also change brain chemistry to correct bad habits, support physical healing, and improve task performance in everyday activities. Since having an intention plays an important role in helping you continue a meditative practice once you have started, this book can help you find and explore a specific intention if you do not already have one. No single prevailing reason for meditation exists, but the most common reasons for why people meditate include a desire to reduce the stress in their life; a desire for physical, emotional, or spiritual healing; a desire to improve their relationships; and a desire to improve their life's work. While these may seem like egocentric reasons, we face the daunting challenge of finding the best way to function and live a meaningful life in an egocentric world. In actuality, meditation will teach you that the way to achieve what you want out of meditation (and out of life) is to release yourself from the egocentric experiences that may have adversely formed your mindset and altered your consciousness.

This book has been divided into ten chapters arranged in a chronological way so as to help you understand how to begin your meditative practice and deepen it further by adding new techniques. Starting with an explanation regarding the history and science of meditation, this book will move toward getting you started by helping you further identify and explore a specific intention for continued meditative practice. From there it moves toward defining the three core meditations, including an overview of the techniques and exercises that correspond to each core meditation. Once you understand what you will need to begin your regular meditative practice, chapters 5, 6, and 7 will each include exercises for putting together a ten-minute meditation. There is nothing wrong with using meditation for even the smallest or most common of reasons if you feel it will add something to your life. If reducing stress, relieving emotional turbulence, or improving some other aspect of your everyday well-being is your only goal, you may skip chapters 8 and 10. If your intention for meditating includes increasing your spiritual connection to nature and mysticism, you are encouraged to read the entire book.

The information contained here also will include case studies from meditation teachers sharing their personal wisdom. Their insight will help clarify how the information applies to the development of your practice. Last, consider using the resource and appendix information at the end of this book as a complement to the subjects covered in each chapter. We hope you are excited about the possibilities of improving your life through meditation. The door to greater well-being awaits you.

Chapter 1

The History and Science of Meditation

ost of us probably will agree that the world is deeply troubled. If even you live a relatively comfortable life, you probably sense something degenerative about the way society is "progressing." It is no secret that many people today are physically, intellectually, emotionally, and spiritually imbalanced. Physically, more people than ever suffer heart attacks, develop cancers, and die of stress related diseases. Intellectually, the mass media seems more interested in dumbing down the content of information by flooding us with "junk news," celebrity obsession, and shallow movies that express nothing truthful about life. Emotionally, our hatreds, fears, resentments, and jealousies disconnect us from love, leaving us spiritually empty. The good news is that you can counteract these internal disturbances brought on by the outside world, and the answer is through meditation.

The word for meditation in Sanskrit is *shamatha*, which translates as "peacefully abiding." In his book, *Passage Meditation: Bringing the Deep Wisdom of the Heart into Daily Life*, Eknath Easwaran defines meditation as the end of sorrow and mastery of the art of living. The goal of meditation is to return the mind to its natural resting state. Without meditation, the mind is often a mass of untamed and scattered confusion. Meditation allows us to develop internal peace and well-being while giving us the emotional resources to protect against turbulent states of mind. The simplest way to define meditation is to think of it as an experience that makes it possible for us to transform the mind. Beginning meditators should expect to practice:

1. Correct posture
2. Relaxed but deep breathing
3. Attention to thoughts, objects, or sensations
4. Mindfulness of distractions
5. Present moment thinking
6. Open, nonjudgmental attitude

What Disturbs Wellness?

While technological advances have increased life expectancy and made life more convenient, human beings find themselves in a faster-moving world bombarded by too much information, too much conflict, and too many choices. Excessive lifestyles have diluted our values and led to moral ambiguity. Technological progress has triggered widespread hunger, war, and political strife in Third World countries exploited for land or geopolitical purposes. In his controversial manifesto, *Industrial Society and Its Future*, criminal mastermind Ted Kaczynski (more famously known as the Unibomber) described society as an endless power process that can never satisfy the desires it creates. As an example of this, Kaczynski writes, "Consider the hypothetical case of a man who can have anything he wants just by wishing for it. Such a man has power, but he will develop serious psychological problems. At first, he will have a lot of fun, but by-and-by he will become acutely bored and demoralized. Eventually he may become clinically depressed. History shows that leisured aristocracies tend to become decadent because power is not enough. One must have goals to exercise one's power…Consistent failure to attain goals throughout life results in defeatism, low self-esteem, or depression."

Years after Kaczynski's 1995 publication and subsequent arrest, the debate over his social commentary still continues. In 2013, Fox News contributor Dr. Keith Ablow wrote, "While Ted Kaczynski was rightly imprisoned for life in 1998…[his ideas] cannot be dismissed, and are increasingly important as our society hurtles toward individual disempowerment at the hands of technology and political forces that erode autonomy. Watching the development of Facebook® heighten the narcissism of tens of millions of people, turning them into mini-reality TV versions of themselves, I would bet he knows with even more certainty that he was on to something. As we witness average Americans 'tweeting' about their daily activities as though they were celebrities—with fans clamoring to know their whereabouts—he must marvel at the ease with which technology taps the ego and drains the soul."

The truth of Ablow's statement leaves one to wonder why our society remains so determined to encourage self-indulgence and things it knows only creates more unhappiness. The next time you turn on the nightly news, ask yourself why you need to hear so many negative stories about the current human condition. When all they do is report about murders, rapes, robberies,  and corruption, does it make you any wiser and more informed, or does it simply destroy your outlook and cultivate your sense of despair and powerlessness? We all know that many reasons contribute to why the world exists as it does; however, you accomplish nothing when you attempt to resist what you cannot control. If you slam your hand on the horn in the middle of a traffic jam, you are not going to ease your frustration. If you complain that your boss increased your workload without giving you a raise, it will not increase your job performance. In short, none of your negative responses to an unjust world will do you any good, especially if those responses carry harmful effects.

Harmful Effects of Stress, Bad Habits, Anger, Anxiety, and Depression

Meditation works because it restores the body's metabolic balance to where all its biological systems operate at functional levels. Stress, on the other hand, attacks and gradually destroys these systems, leading to a number of health-related issues and life-threatening problems. The regulatory systems affected by stress, bad habits, and emotional turmoil include:

1. The nervous system
2. The immune system
3. The cardiovascular system
4. The gastrointestinal system
5. The musculature system
6. The lymphatic system

A body out of balance is very resilient. In fact, most people are living proof that the body is capable of functioning under the rigors of everyday modern living. Over time, however, these regulatory systems begin to fail if they remain stressed for too long. The nervous system is the body's regulatory agency that maintains and manages your stress and relaxation responses to external events. When something stressful occurs in your life, your nervous system activates its stress response as a means of adjusting the body's functions to the situation. For example, when you are under stress, your nervous system will activate its *stress response* by raising the body's adrenaline levels. The stress response is the body's transition from a resting state into a state of increased biological activity. During the stress response, adrenaline gives the body an enormous burst of energy, which allows it to function at a higher rate than normal. As adrenaline rises, muscle tension and blood pressure increase. Metaphorically, your body is in a state of high alert and preparing to do battle with whatever has triggered the stress response. However, this heightened state of activity burns energy in your body very rapidly, so the nervous system stops digestion in order to reallocate that energy to its hyperactive state.

When the stress in your life decreases, the nervous system activates the *relaxation response* by lowering your body's adrenaline levels, softening your muscles, and decreasing blood pressure. The relaxation response is a physical state of deep rest that the body strives to achieve. Though the nervous system exists to help you deal with adversity, it strives to return the body to its natural resting state. When stress becomes chronic, when we cannot meet the constantly reinforced pressures and demands of society telling us who to be, what to think, and what to want, the body never lowers its stress response, and we carry tension into every aspect of our lives. The effects of the stress response eventually will manifest in our physical and emotional appearance, eventually radiating out into our personal and professional relationships.

Physical Ailments

Research shows that chronic stress and hypertension at roughly ten percent above the body's normal resting state can lead to stress-related diseases as early as middle age. When life's circumstances keep the body in a state of chronic stress, blood pressure remains high and the risk of heart, kidney, and respiratory failure increases. This happens when the body's stress response pressures the cardiovascular system to increase delivery of blood, causing blood to thicken with fatty acids and glycogen. As breathing becomes more

constricted, so do the body's muscles, veins, and arteries, causing tiny rips in the lining of the arteries as greater amounts of blood and fatty acids are forced through narrower passageways. With time, blood clots break loose and block arteries, causing blood cells to die. The greater the blood clot, the greater the risk of a heart attack or stroke. When your muscles remain tense, you risk developing severe back pain. Since relaxed muscles help move oxygen throughout the body and move out waste products, they are vital in supplying every cell in your body with nutrients. When muscles tighten, reduced oxygen supplies and immobile waste products begin to poison the body.

If your digestive system slows for too long, saliva and juices dry up. Hydrochloric acid production jumpstarts and you increase the chances of having gastrointestinal problems such as ulcers, heartburn, gas pain, or constipation. When your body burns energy at unsustainable levels, you risk other types of cell damage. For example, when the immune system becomes hyperactive, it begins to destroy healthy tissue, causing arthritic conditions and autoimmune disorders. According to registered holistic health practitioner of alternative medicine, Dr. Alka Khurana, "Meditation strengthens the immune system and cellular activity by enhancing the telomerase enzyme that protects genetic material during cell division." When the musculature system tightens from stress, the lymphatic system (responsible for regulating the immune system and moving waste products) becomes impaired, causing lymph glands to shrink and white blood cell count to drop. Diseased lymph glands are commonly associated with various types of cancers resulting from the immune systems inability to fight arising pathogens. Meditation provides the body with a counteraction to all of this by reducing blood pressure, breathing rates, muscle constriction, and adrenaline levels. In short, it acts to assist the body in returning to its natural resting state where it can begin to heal itself from the effects of long-term hypertension and chronic stress.

Mental Ailments

If you have ever heard the yogic term "mind-body connection" you probably can figure out that it refers to the connection between the body and mind and how they influence one another. Our thoughts and actions can have a powerful, influential, and resonating effect on the body's physical well-being due to the stress/relaxation response. How you think and act creates a reaction in your body that brings either harmony or discord to the entire biological system. The same holds true for mental diseases and disorders that afflict the brain. Research shows that biological symptoms typically begin to surface when the brain shows an abnormal balance of neurotransmitters, which help nerve cells in the brain communicate with each other. When chemicals that regulate neurology become unbalanced, the brain does not receive messages well. Likewise, certain infections can cause brain damage. Since stress tightens the musculature system and causes the blockage of waste products, your body begins to hold toxins for long periods. These toxins become poisonous and create bacterial infections that eventually damage the brain. For example, researchers have linked Pediatric Autoimmune Neuropsychiatric Disorder (PANDA) to the development of obsessive-compulsive disorders in children. Septicemia, which accounts for the presence of bacteria in the blood stream, is also associated with other infections in the body, including infections in the lungs, abdomen, urinary tract, central nervous system (meningitis), heart (endocarditis), and bones (myelitis).

Research also links poor nutrition and substance abuse to anxiety, depression, and paranoia, which in turn play a role in the development of mental illness. Here is where negative emotions create actions destructive to the body. Negative emotions create blockages in the energetic openings of the body. These energetic openings, called *chakras*, assist in releasing emotions that cause chronic stress and keep the biological systems in a continual state of hypertension. Meditation unblocks the energetic openings, which then restores the mind/body connection and gets the biological systems of the body working again. In a study conducted at Massachusetts General

Hospital, researchers found that individuals who meditated for about a half hour a day through eight weeks showed an increase in gray matter located in the higher brain called the neo-cortex. Research on these same individuals concurrently showed a decrease in the size of the amygdala, the area of the brain that helps regulate anxiety and stress. Not only does meditation stimulate gray matter, it also accelerates white matter fibers, which facilitate connectivity between different biological systems, thus reducing age-related brain atrophy.

Bad Habits

In addition to studies on the brain's physical reaction to meditation, research also shows that meditation can serve to improve bad habits. In a 2013 study published by the *Proceedings of the National Academy of Sciences*, researchers investigating the effects of meditation on smoking cessation found that smokers who meditated were 60 percent less likely to smoke than those only taught to relax various part of the body. According to lead researcher Michael Posner, "Resting-state brain scans showed increased activity for the meditation group in the anterior cingulate and prefrontal (or neo) cortex — brain areas related to self-control. These results suggest that brief meditation training improves self-control capacity and reduces smoking….One reason for addiction to tobacco may involve a deficit in self-control. Self-control is important because the level of childhood self-control predicts long-term outcomes, including mental health, substance abuse, financial independence, and criminal behavior. Individuals at risk for substance abuse typically have deficits in self-control. Dysfunction of the prefrontal cortex, including dorsolateral PFC, anterior cingulate cortex, and medial orbitofrontal cortex, play a key role in addiction."

Depression, Anxiety, and Procrastination

If you consider how the body's biological systems regress under prolonged periods of stress, it should come as no surprise why depressed people feel unmotivated. When people suffer from chronic stress, they tend to inflate the difficulty of small tasks while allowing larger challenges to paralyze them. Likewise, depression can lead to avoidance behavior expressed as problems with concentration and feelings of inadequacy. A mind focused on fear and anxiety prevents the mind and body from solving problems and properly responding to the obstacles of life. Therefore, once the mind becomes quiet at the beginning of your daily practice, the ensuing goal of meditation is focus. Focus serves to counteract the mind's desire to return to thoughts and emotions that create noise and foster symptoms of depression. You might be surprised to learn that multitasking is actually *less* efficient than focusing on one thing at a time. *The Journal of Experimental Psychology* found that multitasking requires more time when it comes to concentrating on difficult or unfamiliar tasks because of the extra mental effort needed to break "flow state" (discussed further in Chapter 9) and shift back and forth between different tasks. Humans have become so accustomed to multitasking that they never give their full concentration to *anything*, and the mind resorts to half measures as a means of solving its problems.

This is why chronic anxiety has become an epidemic in modern society. The more the mind worries, the more overwhelmed and entrained to a pattern of thought the mind becomes. It is for this reason that fourth edition of the *Diagnostic and Statistical Manual of Mental Disorders* (DSM-IV) has classified generalized anxiety disorder as one of the most common forms of chronic stress in modern society. When the mental condition is not the result of a chemical substance, medical issue, or part of another diagnosis, a person meets the criteria for generalized anxiety disorder when symptoms include:

1. At least six months of excessive anxiety
2. Difficulty controlling anxiety
3. Significant muscle tension and restlessness

4. Fatigue
5. Irritability
6. Lack of Concentration
7. Lack of Sleep
8. Dysfunction in in daily life

Most people across a variety of backgrounds have struggled against depression, anxiety, and procrastination at one time or another. Few, however, are aware that they meet the criteria as someone with general anxiety disorder. If you suffer from the symptoms listed above, or if you have come to this reading with some other intention, this book will show you how a daily ten-minute meditation can lead to a variety of life sustaining benefits.

How Meditation Fosters Physical, Mental, Emotional, and Social Well-Being

Daily meditation reduces production of epinephrine and norepinephrine, commonly referred to as "the stress hormones." When a person experiences stress on an ongoing basis, these stress hormones reduce immune system function, can lead to elevated cholesterol levels, and increase heart rate. No matter what short-term or long-term intention you set for your

meditative practice, you eventually will begin to see improvements in your overall physical, mental, emotional, and social well-being. Using concentration techniques, you will notice improvements in mental focus if you previously suffered from a wandering mind. If you suffer from an addiction, meditation can help you overcome your physical and mental compulsion. You will experience reduced anxiety about the future if you are someone who tends to obsess about the unknown.

Hurtful and regretful events of the past will no longer have dominion over your mindset. You will enjoy greater intimacy with friends and relatives as your sense of isolation and disconnection to others dissolves. Your mind will be free and clear to think problems and challenges through, thus improving your life choices. In short, gaining control over the mind involves a process whereby the meditator learns exactly how the mind works.

When meditation quiets the mind, it becomes willing to receive both blissful and uncomfortable thoughts, emotions, and sensations without replaying the chatter that has formed its mindset. The chatter in the mind is the "life story" that the neo-cortex interprets and fabricates out of the experiences that occur over an individual lifetime. When the mind buries the root causes of inner discord deep within the unconscious, the individual begins to act out these root causes on the conscious level in an unexamined way. If you never examine or take time to understand the thoughts and actions that control you, you can never hope to free yourself of them. It is for this reason that meditation involves techniques that cultivate mind quieting and present moment awareness, which forces the root causes of inner discord to the surface.

Meditation does not support avoidance behavior. It is a means of confronting inner turmoil in order to reduce its power over the mind, not a means of escaping pain. When the mind becomes quiet through meditative practice, the voice of judgment begins to settle down until eventually it stops talking. Now you are ready to move into a state of mindfulness whereby you simply can observe whatever thoughts or emotions come into the mind without judgment. In this heightened state of consciousness, the mind is able to examine everything from a position of greater clarity and take the proper steps to repair its insecurities and learned behaviors of helplessness, blame, pessimism, judgment, and so forth. Meditative techniques are coping skills used for cultivating positive emotions and mind states that prevent negative and distracting thoughts from harming the mindset further. Mental clarity improves the mind's ability to make important distinctions between thoughts and emotions that previously ran rampant and went un-examined. Through concentration, awareness, and mental clarity, you will begin to see more deeply into your true self and unravel the habitual patterns that need healing. The process of healing the mind/body connection is gradual; it takes time, and more important, patience. If you become frustrated when you set an intention that does not immediately manifest in your consciousness or everyday life, do not get discouraged or feel you are doing something wrong. The frustration you feel is merely the beginning of the mind's resistance to letting go of the mindset that no longer serves you well. That you remain focused on the concept of success and failure in meditation is the first sign that your mind is still talking to you. Over the course of this reading, different techniques will address and provide solutions for the most common roadblocks and challenges encountered along the meditative journey.

The History of Meditative Practice

Archeological findings trace meditative practice as far back as 5,000 years when wandering holy men and women called *sadus* and *yogis* used meditative practice to connect with divinity and wrote scriptures called *Vedas*. Based on the Vedas, Vedic priests performed rites and chants that required

concentration, prayerful meditation, and breathing control. Fueled by Vedic tradition, Yoga, Buddhism, and Tantra were born. While meditation connects these practices to the same ancient root, Yoga aims to merge the physical body into the formless reality of consciousness. Tantra involves centrality of ritual and visualizations in connection to awakening energetic openings called *chakras*, as well as a powerful life energy called the *kundalini*.

Meditation in Eastern Religion

The foundation of Buddhism traces back to the Indian sage, Gautama Buddha, also known as Siddhārtha Gautama Shakyamuni whose name means "awakened one." As a Hindu prince who led a privileged life in the area now known in modern times as Nepal, Gautama felt a profound sense of compassion for human suffering after witnessing the poverty, sickness, and death that existed among the less fortunate. Having resolved to devote himself to uncovering a path to enlightenment that could end human suffering, Gautama ultimately rejected his privileged life. Eventually, he discovered a path to greater enlightenment through an examination of the spirit contained within his body and mind while sitting under a tree. By his late 20s, he became a spiritual teacher of the basic enlightenment principals upon which modern Buddhism now stands. Among Buddha's chief teachings is the belief that people suffer because they:

1. Falsely believe that permanence is real and can be relied upon for happiness
2. Falsely believe that the "self" forms our real identity and is independent of others

Buddhism, like its sister religions, agrees that everything in this world is deeply connected, and that suffering is the result of the perceived disconnection to the union of all things. To liberate oneself from suffering, one must liberate the mind from the negative mindset formed by ego consciousness. It was by the third century B.C. that Buddha's teachings spread beyond the confines of India as other Eastern cultures began practicing the art of meditation. As Buddhism underwent significant changes in Sri Lanka and Southeast Asia, the newly formed approaches to Buddhism mainstreamed enlightenment beyond monks and nuns. From the roots of Buddhism came the practice of Zen, which blended traditional Buddhism with Chinese Taoism.

Meditation in Judeo-Christian Traditions

Meditation, however, is not a religion, but rather a practice used by many religions, including those that originated in other parts of the world. While meditation is not traditionally associated with the Judeo-Christian and Islamic traditions that emerged from the Middle East, it is undoubtedly woven into the fabric of its customs. While you may not recognize its presence, meditation in Christianity takes the form of a contemplative prayer. The book of Matthew tells the story of Jesus as he meditated, fasted, and prayed in the desert before starting his public ministry. When Jesus retreated to the desert for 40 days and 40 nights, he meditated through contemplative prayer as a means of opening awareness to the God. In fact, most modern English adaptations of the Bible contain more than 20 uses of the word "meditate." Joshua 1:8, for example, reads, "Do not let this Book of the Law depart from your mouth; meditate on it day and night." To understand the connection between Christianity and meditation more fully, consider the words of the anonymous author believed to have channeled the voice of Christ consciousness while writing the 16-letter book, *Christ Returns, Speaks His Truth.*

In transcribing the meditative experience that Christ encountered, the author writes, "My six weeks meditating in the desert were a time of total inner cleansing of my human consciousness where all attitudes, beliefs, and prejudices dissolved. I was uplifted into inner radiant light and felt vibrant and wonderfully alive with power. I knew beyond all doubt that this power was from the true Creator out of which all created things had been given their being. This glorious interior harmony, peace, and sense of perfect fulfillment — needing nothing more to be added to the beautiful moment — was the very nature of reality giving life to creation and existence. What I saw, realized, and perceived in the desert [was] another dimension

of conscious perception that enabled me to see the truth concerning life and existence. I saw clearly and lucidly what was real and what was false in man's thinking. I realized this creative power was infinite, filling all space between sky, ocean, earth, and all living things. I saw that it was mind power, the creative power of mind. There was no point where this divine creative power of mind was not."

By 300 A.D., Christian meditators in Egypt and Palestine began to follow Christ's meditative teachings by cultivated awareness of Divine presence. From these desert wanderers came the monks of the Eastern Orthodox Church and medieval Europe who used the scriptures as meditative prayer. In Judaism, interpreters of the Old Testament trace meditation back to Abraham, who entered into altered states of consciousness through fasting and ascetic practices. Even Islam shares a connection to meditative practice, as a group of mystical seekers known as Sufis engage in a meditative practice called *zikr*, which involves chanting a sacred phrase while rhythmically breathing.

In the early 1600s, as secret societies began to form, a German by the name of Christian Rosenkreuz founded Rosicrucianism after studying in the Middle East under various masters. Under his new order, the Rosicrusians blended Christianity with Sufism and spread the knowledge he acquired to prominent the European figures. Following the Age of Enlightenment, a Jesuit from Upper Bavaria founded the Order of the Illuminati (enlightened ones) on May 1, 1776. By the early 1800s, another secret order called Freemasonry, included initiation rituals of symbolic rebirth similar to the Hindu *diksha* and Christian baptism. Such early and well-known American figures such as George Washington and Benjamin Franklin were members of the Freemason society. By the 1840s, writers like Ralph Waldo Emerson were writing meditative stories influenced by the Transcendentalist movement taking hold in the West. In 1875, Helena Blavatsky's Theosophical Society, founded in New York City, provided an offshoot of earlier theosophical ideas, which included concepts from eastern esotericism. However, it was not until an international conference in 1893 between religious world leaders that Asian priests and Zen masters were finally able to share their meditative concepts directly with the westerners. By the 1950s, Western societies began considering meditation as a means of helping citizens deal with the stress, anxiety, and depression caused by modern life. Meditation fully popularized into Western life when *The Beatles* began practicing Transcendental Meditation with the Maharishi Yogi, and Jack Kerouac's book, *The Dharma Bums*, became an international bestseller. Within two decades, researchers began testing the effects of meditation on the human psyche. As further scientific research legitimized the connection of meditation to wellness, more doctors began recommending it as complementary treatment in medical and therapeutic communities. Today's health industry officially recognizes meditation as a complimentary alternative medicine (otherwise known as CAM). Moreover, The National Center for Complementary and Alternative Medicine (NCCAM) reports that the number of meditative studies conducted by its agency increased from seven in 2000 to 47 in 2010. During this same period, the Department of Defense conducted its own clinical studies to treat at least 17 percent of its veterans who suffered from post-traumatic stress disorder after returning from Iraq and Afghanistan.

Modern Schools of Meditation

Mainstream schools of meditation, such as Yoga, Tai Chi, and Qigong, are now commonplace in every town and sports club across the United States and the West. Qigong meditation allows you the flexibility of practicing in a concentrative or mindful style. A concentrative practice provides a particular focus, such as a mantra, color, or breath. As with any mindfulness practice, the goal

is simply to notice or be aware of your breathing. At its core, Qigong is a series of standing or seated movements that release tension and build energy flow. The practice emphasizes the development of mind and spirit through body movement. Tai chi allows you to find inner stillness using outer meditative movement that draws your "chi," or life force, through your body to create a feeling of relaxation, well-being, and balance. Tai Chi can be challenging to learn on your own. If you cannot find a meditative school or class that suits your needs, consider purchasing a DVD to guide you visually through the movements. Yoga involves meditating conjunctively through breathing, exercises, and physical postures. Some of the more traditional forms — based on Hindu philosophy — include Raja, Karma, Bhakti, and Jnana. In the United States, the most popular form of Yoga is Hatha, which places more emphasis on stretching, breath control, and body poses to renew the body's energy source.

The Science of Meditation

Meditation is the practice of reaching an intense state of awareness through the stillness of thoughts. It is a journey into the center of our own being. The word derives from two Latin words: "meditari" (to think or to dwell upon) and "mederi" (to heal). The Sanskrit derivation is "medha," which means "wisdom." Unfortunately, many people who have never used meditation view these kinds of concepts with abject skepticism without realizing that meditation taps into the scientific nature of the physical and metaphysical universe. Over the last 30 years, advancements in the scientific field of quantum physics have led to astounding discoveries about the world in scalar reality, ranging from the smallest measurable units of matter to the universe as a whole. With respect to the topic at hand, scientific research in meditation has focused specifically on the body/mind connection to that scalar reality. Therefore, if one defines the physical world as anything observable and measurable to the five senses (taste, feel, see, smell, and hear) then the metaphysical world requires analysis of two questions: What really exists behind the physical world, and what is its true nature?

The Origins of Research

Scientific research began in the 1960s and 1970s with Transcendental Meditation®. Led by Harvard Professor Herbert Benson, research into the body's physiological changes in body temperature, heart rate, metabolism digestion, and oxygen intake during meditation yielded surprising results. First, Benson examined earlier research on the effects of meditation, such as B. K. Anand's 1961 study of yogis and monks who could lower their oxygen consumption by 20 percent during meditation. Using biofeedback, Benson found that Americans who practiced TM® were able to lower their oxygen metabolism by an average of 12 percent, which represented a greater drop than during sleep. Later studies of test subjects showed a 40 percent decline in oxygen consumption and a 50 percent decline in their respiring rates.

In his 1975 publication, *Decreased Premature Ventricular Contractions Through the Use of the Relaxation Response in Patients with Stable Ischemic Heart Disease*, Benson notes, "After four weeks of regularly eliciting the relaxation response, a reduced frequency of premature ventricular contraction was documented in eight of the 11 patients." That same year, Benson published, *The Relaxation Response*, which garnered acclaim for its unprecedented scientific data on meditation's effects on the body. In 1981, Benson and his colleagues began to work directly with the Dalai Lama to investigate how meditative techniques work as a regulatory tool for the body. Following the study, which appeared in *Nature*, Benson wrote, "Since meditative practices are associated with decreased activity of the sympathetic nervous system, it is conceivable that measurable body temperature changes accompany advanced meditative states.... we found that our subjects exhibited the capacity to increase the temperature of their fingers and toes by as much as 8.3 degrees Celsius."

Benson's medical publications provided the foundation for further research into the effects of deep meditative states. Subsequent independent studies of test subjects revealed a decrease in heart rate by as much as 15 beats per minute, lower blood pressure by as much as 25 mmHg systolic, and cholesterol reduction by as much as 30mg/dl. While limitations of study existed in early research — such as lack of data from random control groups — studies later incorporated subjects who were not experienced meditators and monitored them for short periods to measure the results. During the 1980s, researchers began using electroencephalogram (EEG) technology to record the brain's electrical brain wave activity as a new way of studying the effects of TM. As technology for brain mapping developed further, research shifted from studying the effects of TM to studying the effects of Mindfulness Meditation . Based on the work of molecular biologist professor Jon Kabatt-Zinn, EEG research led to the Mindful Based Stress Reduction (MSRB) Technique, which blended Yoga and present moment awareness. A 2010 study of MSRB conducted by Harvard University neuroscientist Sara Lazar showed that after just eight weeks of MSRB training, the brain scan results of test subjects showed growth patterns in both the hippocampus and neo-cortex. In recent years, the study of tissue, organ, and cellular changes during meditation indicate a new push to study meditative effects on patients with various cancers. EEG recordings from Lazar's research show that meditation improves memory function and reduces stress by activating:

1. The prefrontal cortex or neo-cortex (responsible for decision making)
2. The anterior cingulate cortex (responsible for mental concentration)
3. The amygdala (responsible for emotion control)
4. The hippocampus (responsible for memory)

Vibrational Frequency

Does the universe hear you? Quantum physics tells us that as we move our scientific observations below the subatomic level we do not find any matter, but instead, pure energy. All matter, including our own bodies, exists in a constant state of energetic vibration or motion. However, not all matter in the universe vibrates at the same rate. For example, one rate of vibration causes sound, which the human ear can detect at a range produced from 20 to 20,000 cycles per second. As the rate of cycles per second, or frequency amplitude increases above sound, the vibrating particles begin to manifest themselves in the form of heat. Higher up the scale, vibration becomes light — and at even higher vibrational levels, the power of thought. Since the body radiates electrical impulses generated by the central nervous system, low voltage equals low frequency. This tells us that vibrational frequency is a form of communication among all matter in the universe. The higher the frequency level, the higher the level of communication.

When researchers used voltmeter tests on different age groups, they found that all humans have different millivolts ranges in their system. The average person ranges between 50-100 millivolts, while athletes train to reach 2000 millivolts. Medical conditions like depression have millivolt ranges between 5 and 9 millivolts. Therefore, we also can think of the Law of Vibration as *The Law of Attraction*. If your body is vibrating at a low frequency, your thought communication with the universe becomes inaudible. If your body is vibrating at a high frequency, your thought communication with the universe resonates. Researchers such as Dr. David R. Hawkins, head of the University of Applied Kinesiology, argue that within levels of vibration exists consciousness. To measure the level of vibrational consciousness in humans, Dr. Hawkins created a "vibometer," tracked on scale from 1 to 1,000, illustrated in the chart below.

As this scale shows, when humans exist in low vibratory states of emotion, such as shame, guilt, apathy, fear, guilt, and grief, suffering occurs. Middle vibratory states indicate an emotional state of "getting by" in life. As an individual's vibratory frequency increases, he or she begins to enter a more peaceful state. What vibratory research indicates is that our thoughts and emotions determine our vibratory rate, and if we can increase our frequency, we can generate stronger signals under the Laws of Attraction. If you do not have enough power in your nervous system, the chances of manifesting your reality are much lower. What this suggests is that meditation fosters emotions that raise vibratory frequencies that heal the body.

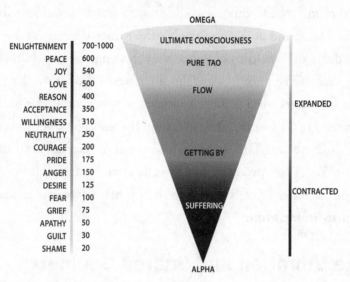

To understand the relationship between frequency and matter further, consider a 1995 study published in the *Journal of Neuroscience Research* involving the effect of electrical frequencies on different types of human tissue. B.F. Siskin *(et.al)* found that:

1.   2 Hertz (Hz) affected nerve regeneration
2.   7 Hz affected bone growth
3.   10 Hz affected ligament healing
4.   72 Hz affected stimulation of capillary formation
5.   25 and 50 Hz created synergistic effects with nerve growth factors

In the *New York Times* bestseller, *The Hidden Messages in Water*, experiments conducted by Dr. Masaru Emoto provides visually documented evidence that human vibrational energy contained in thoughts, words, ideas, and music have a profound effect on the molecular structure of water. Following his experiment, Emoto received some criticism in the scientific field for what others believed were insufficient experimental controls. However, Emoto noted in a 2004 photo essay published in the *Journal of*

Alternative and Complementary Medicine that he chose distilled water as an experimental control because it forms a simple, standard hexagonal shape. In his experiments, Dr. Emoto would subject water to various vibrational frequencies of sound and emotion. He then froze droplets and examined them under a dark field microscope with photograph capabilities. In his *Healing with Water* photo essay, Emoto states, "We wrote the words in different languages onto a piece of paper wrapped around a vial of distilled water for 24 hours. After creating 100 samples, we observed that the worlds 'Love and Thanks' produced beautiful crystals, and the world 'Devil' or 'You Fool' produced no crystals at all." More information and photos of the water crystals can be found on **http://www.masaru-emoto. net/english/index.html**.

Divine Vibration and Sacred Geometry

Famed inventor Nikola Tesla once said, "If you want to find the secrets of the universe, think in terms of energy, frequency, and vibration." Creation occurs only when vibration happens. If you want to be the creator of your own life, you can use meditation to cultivate your own vibratory ascension. Examination of the Hawkins vibrational scale shows the body's vibratory levels of consciousness ranging from the most base level of consciousness (shame) all the way up to the divine consciousness, otherwise known in Christianity as "Christ consciousness." It is the purest form of enlightenment, the highest frequency at which the meditator achieves a sense of union and communication with God and all of life. If you wish to deepen your meditative practice beyond the flow states of peace on Hawkins vibrational scale, Chapter 8 will discuss the process of meditating toward enlightenment. For now, it is important to understand the fundamental principles of creation. The physical world derives its structure from something called *sacred geometry*. If you begin to look around, you will find its patterns in nature, religious monuments, and even on corporate logos. In order to create something out of nothing, creation must begin with the existence of three dimensions called *space*. In the first stage of space creation, the creative spirit of divine vibration points a beam of consciousness from a central point in six directions — front, back, left, right, up, and down in equal measure, as illustrated in the figure below.

With six points drawn from the central point, the void must define boundaries around these points in order to complete the process of creating space, because if no boundaries exist, then relative movements of spirits remain impossible. To create boundaries, the creative spirit then connects the end of every point to each other, as illustrated in the figure below.

The six points connected forms the shape of an octahedron so the single points of consciousness can now move around *in space* from the central location. In sacred geometry, straight lines are the male life-generating principal, and curved lines are the female creative principal. In the next step, the creative spirit spins the octahedron, which creates the parameters of a perfect sphere, or spherical membrane, with curved boundaries, as illustrated in the figure below.

With the curved boundary created, the creative spirit creates a genesis pattern by moving the boundary of the spinning sphere, which projects another identical sphere, as illustrated in the figure below.

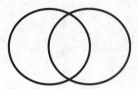

The formation of two spheres in the genesis pattern form a unique pattern in the middle called the vesica piscis, illustrated in the figure below.

This shape exists as a pattern in two parts of the human body: behind the eyes (your "third eye") and in the lens of the eye which adjusts the focus of light. This symbol also exists in various religious and corporate symbols, as illustrated in the figures below.

To repeat the genesis pattern, the creative spirit moves the Piscis and creates a central point for a third sphere. Having created a third sphere, the genesis pattern repeats again, this time creating more circles within the innermost points to prevent the formation of a chaotic pattern. The genesis pattern creates seven spheres in a structured, vortex-like motion. The result is a perfectly symmetrical pattern called the Seed of Life (illustrated below) which lays the foundation for the creation of matter and the universe.

The seed of life, however, is not the complete pattern of creation. The creative spirit builds further by creating six more circles, known as the second vortex motion, on top of the existing seed of creation. The second vortex motion is then followed by a third vortex motion, which establishes the complete pattern (illustrated below), known as the Flower of Life.

SEED OF LIFE   FLOWER OF LIFE

When the creative spirit adds two more additional layers to the Flower of Life, the pattern reaches the complete and final layer called the Fruit of Life. The Fruit of Life is the template for the creation of all living things, which encapsulates two things, structure and consciousness. When the creative spirit creates life, it removes several circles from the Seed of Life and uses this form in the embryonic creation process (illustrated below) for every single form of life on this planet. Nature uses this form because it is the most balanced and harmonious geometrical form in existence.

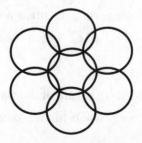

To create dimensionality between time and space, nature extracts the following 13 circles from the Fruit of Life, and the result is the holy archetype (illustrated below) known as Metatron's Cube.

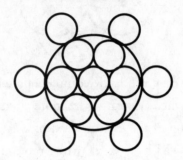

Nature then uses the parameters of this pattern to extrapolate four different hypercubes (illustrated below), which allows nature to create even more dimensionality in space and time. Science refers to the four hypercubes created from this pattern as Platonic solids. The Platonic solids are the geometrical figures, which represent the four classical elements: earth, air, fire, and water. However, there is one more element derived from these patterns — a fifth element. Named after Plato's philosophical musings on the mathematics of creation, Plato noted that the fifth element represented among the Platonic solids, "was used for arranging the constellations on the whole heaven." The fifth element, therefore, is *spirit*.

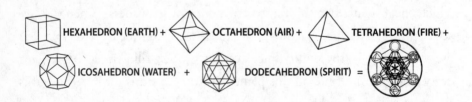

Using these geometrical dimensions, scientists are able to mathematically calculate the golden ratio (x = 1.618), which measures the geometric *relationship* of all things.

Think back to the geometrical structure of the water crystals that appeared as a more beautiful expression when higher, more loving vibrational frequencies began interacting with it. Now consider how the geometrical structure of the water crystals broke apart at lower, more negative frequencies. Are you beginning to see how your own vibratory energy is in direct communication with everything around you? If you ever find yourself asking if the universe hears you, stop and remember the relationship between vibrational frequency and sacred geometry, because the answer to your question is yes! The creative expression of life is geometrically perfect and universally interconnected. The next time you go on a nature walk, examine the different plants in the wilderness that resemble these patterns. What you will find is the creative spirit's wonderful expression of sacred geometry in the biological world.

CASE STUDY: PRACTICING TRANSCENDENTAL MEDITATION

Glenn Murray
Zen Center of Georgia
Radagast97@gmail.com
www.zen-georgia.org
(404) 680-7983

When I was in my 20s, I began experimenting with transcendental meditation. When I was 40, I started taking Aikido and Zen meditation. I also currently practice Zen meditation in the Rinzai tradition and attend retreats three times a year. I train under my teacher Zen Master Miller Roshi, who is the Bishop of Daiyuzenji in Chicago. I now run our local school. I have no religious title or rank, other than as a student.

I do not really have a typical sitting session. If I had to describe the experience, I would use words such as "quiet," "meditative," and "centering." Sometimes the meditation comes very easy and deep; sometimes I struggle with it. The benefits of meditation depend on the individual. Sometimes, the outcome can be as simple as something that calms and reduces tension. Some meditators just want to reduce blood pressure and enhance their well-being. Some meditate to increase concentration. Some do it for religious reasons.

Meditation centers me and helps me to understand myself better. Perhaps one day it will lead to enlightenment, but that is not the reason I sit. I appreciate the way meditation enhances my ability to live in the moment and accept things as they are. I am Buddhist, so meditation is my primary religious practice. If feel it also makes me a better person. What people look for from meditation varies. Ultimately, meditation is personal in practice, both in its benefits and in its goals. The advice I would offer to someone beginning a meditation practice is simple: Do not be too hard on yourself. As simple as meditation is to learn, it is not easy to master. Learning to accept that you cannot be perfect from the beginning is part of learning to accept yourself as you are.

Environment is also an important consideration for beginners. Initially, a quiet environment free from distractions is important to learning how to meditate. As one gets more skilled, the environment becomes less important. Personally, I can mediate while hearing the noises from an Aikido class in the next room without it affecting my concentration. Ultimately, I would want to be able to enter any situation with complete equanimity. As beginners are developing a meditation practice, a guide or teacher can be helpful in offering feedback on breathing and posture. At the more advanced levels, it is important to develop a more mindful practice to deal with distractions created by the mind's ego.

Considerations Before You Get Started

Before you commit to a daily meditative practice, it is important to understand several things about meditation beforehand so that preconceived ideas do not get in the way of your intentions. The first thing to understand about meditation is that it occurs in three stages: relaxation, internalization, and expansion. Relaxation is the first and most important stage of meditation because it helps the mind release itself from stored thoughts and emotions. If you cannot relax your body, the rest of the process will become difficult. The body relaxing techniques discussed in Chapter 5 will help you reach the first phase of meditation. Internalization is the meditative stage whereby the body experiences the release and flow of energy. The body disconnects from the outside world and all energy directs inward. This energy refocuses the mind, increases intuition, and oxygenates the cells. In the expansion stage of meditation, the perceived self dissolves into an expanded consciousness and new understanding of who we are. The most important thing to understand about the stages of meditation is that it takes time and practice to reach these states, and you should not think about your progress along the path when you meditate.

The second thing to understand about meditation is that it involves a process that requires two character traits: patience and non-judgment. If you expect results too quickly, if you expect results different from the ones you feel you wanted, or if you begin to judge and evaluate your progress, then you immediately will begin to defeat your own intentions. Many beginning meditators who prematurely quit their practice do so because no one has set them straight about what to expect or what not to expect as they progress. Those who do not shed their preconceived ideas and expectations about meditation are the ones most likely to ruin their commitment and discontinue their practice. This state of mind is what meditation gurus call *the beginning mind*. The beginning mind involves examining what attitudes you must shed and what attitudes you must adopt before you meditate. Therefore, this chapter will explore the necessity of understanding how the beginning mind creates the very anxieties, frustrations, and evaluative judgments that work to counteract the meditative process and eventually destroy the will to keep going. The purpose of understanding your state of mind is to cultivate the kind of mindfulness that identifies negative attitudes and judgments as they arise and to bring your focus back to meditation. The second consideration explored in this chapter is determining your motivation for beginning a meditative practice. As a third consideration, this chapter will provide an overview of the three core meditations and their corresponding techniques, as well as the aspects of well-being each one cultivates.

Pitfalls of Beginning Meditation

If the meditation process requires the character traits of patience and non-judgment, the easiest way to understand the beginning mind and the pitfalls of starting meditation is to examine the character traits of the beginning mind. The beginning mind tends to bring an established attitude containing disharmonious aspects of the outside world into a harmonious practice. Using these attitudes, the beginning mind allows the unquiet inner dialogue that has been talking for most of the individual's life to form judgments destructive to the practice. Therefore, it is important to understand that inner conflict at the beginning, and throughout various stages of meditative development, is inevitable. The best way to deal with inner conflict is to understand when and why inner conflict occurs during meditation, that it is part of meditation's natural process, and be willing to let it go. A beginning meditator who encounters the first stage of inner conflict often misinterprets this conflict as failure to follow directions, failure of the instructor to give directions, or failure of practice to do what it claims.

Meditation involves a very simple instruction: *just sit and be*, yet the process can be very difficult and the experience very complex. Beginning meditators who come to their first session expecting immediate physical or emotional results often find themselves frustrated when they fail to achieve them. What they fail to realize is that any evaluation of the experience in terms of success or failure is the first sign of an active, unquiet mind blocking progression. Some beginning meditators may find the initial results pleasing, only to encounter negative thoughts and emotions they neither wanted nor expected during subsequent sessions. Such meditators cannot rectify these negative experiences with their preconceived notion that meditation should not ever produce such inner turbulence. These meditators fail to realize that negative thoughts and emotions are the result of meditation opening up the energetic blockages pent up over years of suffering. When beginning meditators evaluate their sessions and think in terms of results, they fail to understand the attitude necessary to achieve results. To successfully begin and continue a meditative practice, the beginning meditator must first:

1. Examine his or her present attitudes
2. Discard all expectations
3. Reserve all judgments
4. Learn to quiet the inner dialogue in his or her mind
5. Become open to whatever arises or does not arise
    during meditation

The easiest way to examine your present attitudes is to reflect on your life. To examine your present attitude, you have to examine your established core beliefs and examine the impact of those beliefs on your past actions, thoughts, and decisions. Doing so will enable you to determine what attitudes you must shed versus what attitudes you must adopt before you meditate. You can make this your first meditative exercise by taking a few deep breaths, closing your eyes, and reflecting on past events important to you, or you can reflect by writing down your thoughts. There are no right or wrong answers to derive from this exercise; simply imagine your life as if it were a movie unfolding. Start with your early years, continue through the various stages of your life and note how the events in between have shaped your beliefs about yourself, about others, and about the world around you. As you play this movie in your head, think about accomplishments you feel good about, what makes these moments memorable, and what feelings they conjure. Once you have finished replaying your life up to the present moment, consider how you might have lived life differently with the knowledge you gained from your life experience. (Do not read further until you have completed this exercise).

Now that you have completed this exercise, look at your answers to the question about what you might change about your life if you could do it all over again. The point of this exercise is to measure your sense of happiness about life without actually conjuring any negative thoughts. The larger the list of things you would change in your life, the more likely you are to have an unquiet, judging mind and an unhealthy attitude. In other words, this preliminary exercise is a way of predicting how your mind will react when finally asked to calm and quiet down. It also will serve as a barometer for the attitudes you must shed versus the attitudes you must adopt for your meditative practice. Gaining a sense of your mindset should not discourage you from practicing meditation or give you a false sense of confidence. It is merely a way to prepare you for the challenges beginning meditators sometimes face. The table below lists the character traits of a mind prepared for beginning meditation versus a mind unprepared for beginning meditation.

Prepared for Pitfalls	Unprepared for Pitfalls
Ability to understand that difficult thoughts and emotions are part of the process	Over-reaction to difficult thoughts and emotions and inability to understand them as part of the process
Nonattachment to thoughts, memories, and emotions	Tendency to dwell on thoughts, memories, and emotions
Ability to quiet mind chatter	Inability to quiet mind chatter
Feeling a sense of connectedness	Feeling a sense of isolation
Ability to let go of external distractions	Inability to come back to focus
Present moment awareness	Preoccupation with past and future
Acceptance of reality	Resistance to reality
A mind that relinquishes its tendency to judge and compare	A mind that judges and compares
Cultivated optimism	Cultivated pessimism

According to prominent Yogi scholar Tsultrim Gyamtso Rinpoche, "Being led by the thoughts is a waste of time in meditation… his continuous stream of thinking is *samsara* (perpetual wandering). Many people believe that since samsara is of such great suffering, we should try to leave it behind and try to obtain nirvana. They imagine that after practicing, one day will come when they see nirvana or emptiness and they will think, 'Now, I have attained realization and have been liberated.' In this way, they pursue and hope for some kind of appearance or phenomenon. Thus, in their meditation, they will always have a sense of waiting and expectation…these people are always pursuing some kind of meditative state and waiting for some state to appear…In general, people who are in [these] situations will be very tense in their meditation and have very strong attachments."

Exploring Your Motivation

Motivation is an important part of meditation. It not only establishes your reason for coming to your first practice, but also for continuing your practice over a period of weeks, months, and years. More important, motivation can make a difference between a halfhearted practice and a deep meditative experience. Keep in mind, there is a difference between expectation and intention. Expectations are desires and beliefs that the ego-driven will tries to force into reality by its will. Intention is the focused attempt to accomplish something without the burden of attachment to success or failure. To explore your motivation, think about your deepest aspirations. At this point, it is permissible to be honest and admit that your deepest aspiration might concern your own well-being rather than others. You might want to stop feeling depressed or worried. You might want to reduce the stress resulting from your job. You might want to kick a bad habit or addiction that causes problems for you. Spiritual leaders call these desires "lower intentions" because they are not the true intentions buried deep within your spiritual essence, but rather, artificial desires constructed by the ego drive. You should not be concerned with drawing a higher intention at the beginning. Meditation eventually will reveal the higher intention.

For now, focus on your lower intentions with the understanding that it is all right to have them. The natural energies you release during meditation will not judge your lower intentions; they simply will do what they do: respond to your intention and improve your life. If you have a higher intention, such as developing genuine compassion for others or reaching higher levels of spiritual understanding, take that intention to your practice along with your lower intentions. To explore lower intentions, ask yourself what is lacking in your life and declare your desire to improve this aspect as your lower intention. Your lower intention might take the form of:

1. Stress relief
2. Improving performance in your daily activities
3. Improving your health
4. Improving your creativity or concentration

Higher intentions are more difficult to name because the beginning mind is rarely aware of its true nature. Some people intuitively sense a hidden universal truth, so they seek to penetrate the mysteries contained in esoteric knowledge. They ask, "Who am I?" or "What is the meaning of life?" The answer given by the most enlightened meditators is quite simple: Attainment of the true self occurs when ego consciousness fades and you begin to identify with everything in being. Thus, higher intentions might take the form of:

1. Searching for meaning
2. Accepting and loving yourself/others
3. Expressing your inner perfection
4. Communication with the divine
5. Awakening others

Among all the higher intentions, Buddhists consider awakening others to be the most important intention of all. This higher intention, known as *bodhichitta*, is a selfless aspiration that accelerates the process of well-being because it offers a spiritual antidote to the ego-drive's need to acquire things for the self. Seeking the higher intention, the body and mind begins to radiate with love and affection for others and a genuine desire for their well-being. This is how the higher and lower intentions entwine. By connecting with your higher intention, you *amplify* the realization of your lower intentions. Staying with a lower intention is all right, but it is for this reason that you are encouraged to develop a deeper practice as you go along.

Overview of different practices

This book identifies three core meditations and more than 20 meditation techniques that any meditator can apply to their practice. Both the techniques and the core meditations serve to elicit very specific benefits. As you read about the core meditations, you will discover that some overlap exists between the intentions they cultivate, so you might use one technique to serve two or even three core meditations. For example, if you want to enter a formless state of being, you first have to remove mind chatter. A mind quieting technique might serve to build your focus and concentration, which paves the way to a deeper meditative state. The purpose of this section is to define the three core meditations and provide an overview of the techniques that serve them.

Core Meditation is the meditative practice that empowers you to shift your mental and emotional state as well as improve all areas of your life. These include the ability to relax and concentrate, to detach from limiting thoughts and feelings, and to visualize, feel, and sense your inner guidance. Core Meditation will help relax, energize, release negative emotions, increase your positive outlook, clear and focus your mind, and strengthen your spiritual connection. What benefits you get depend on your motivation, intention, and depth of practice. Higher intentions lead to deeper practices, which raise the body's

vibratory level. Core Meditation derives its roots in Qigong, Tao, and Kriya Yoga. The three core meditations are:

1. Concentration Meditation
2. Mindfulness Meditation
3. Lovingkindness Meditation

Core Meditation #1: Concentration Meditation

Concentration Meditation is the art of eliminating internal distractions so the mind can quiet the inner dialogue that clouds insight into the meaning of things. Internal distractions, for example, may take the form of past regrets and mistakes. People spend so much time focusing on the past that they never fully appreciate what they actually have, or they tell themselves they have nothing. They miss the gift of the beautiful moment happening right now. Hall of Fame football coach Mike Ditka once said, "You live in the past, you die in the past." Perhaps replaying the past has you already thinking about the things in life that you cannot go back and change. Perhaps the past is something you long to have back because you felt happier back then. This is when the ego controlling the inner voice starts chattering. The ego's desire to protect the self it constructed may be well intentioned, but it only serves to cripple you in the present and beyond. Life experience demonstrates that when the mind dwells in past regrets, it begins to live in fear of the future. It also demonstrates that when the mind lives in reverie of the past, it seeks to duplicate those experiences in the future. A mind dwelling in the future might think, "I cannot let this happen again" or "What if I can't get back what I used to have?" Now fear controls the mind and the ego defense protecting it begins to imagine frightful scenarios where history repeats itself. The ego controlling the inner voice starts chattering. For example, it might say, "Avoid this situation at all costs." In this sense, people who dwell in past regrets bypass the present by moving directly from past to future. People who use the past to springboard into the future live in a perpetual state of postponement. The art of concentration allows the mind to quiet the inner voice by eliminating its concentration on past or future scenarios that detract from present moment awareness.

Deep concentration also serves to eliminate external distractions that can disrupt a deep state of meditation. Beginning meditators tend to have more mind chatter to go along with a diminished ability to concentrate. Losing a meditative state to an abrupt noise from the outside world can be one of the most frustrating experiences for beginning meditators. They become so aware that they have lost a meditative state that the inner dialogue begins to work its way back into the fold. The mind begins replaying old stories about regret and fear. For example, it might say, "I lost my concentration because I'm easily distracted," and then it reverts to some past event where this mindset formed. If unchecked, the mind chatter jumps to the future and envisions a future where it fears the same habitual patterns of distraction will renew old hurts. When you develop strong concentration, you allow your awareness to expand into thoughts and emotions with a more penetrating insight because the mind chatter controlling judgments remain absent. A more penetrating insight into the meaning of thoughts and emotions will help dismantle habitual patterns and lead you on a journey to self-discovery. Concentration occurs at the relaxation stage of meditation when you employ techniques such as body scanning, which helps the body relax and releases the mind from stored thoughts and emotions. Concentration also may occur at the internalization stage when you employ techniques such as the Breath Wave, which directs energy inward. The techniques used to cultivate the core practice of concentration include:

1. Mind quieting technique
2. The counting technique
3. Breath Wave technique
4. Breath motion synchronization technique
5. Naming technique

6. Releasing thoughts technique
7. Auditory technique
8. Thought release technique

Core Meditation #2: Mindfulness Meditation

The fact that concentration cultivates aspects of relaxation and internalization explains why some techniques for concentration also can cultivate mindfulness. Mindfulness is the second core meditation practice. It refers to the process of bringing nonjudgmental attention to the internal and external experiences that exist in the present moment. Since mindfulness deals with present moment awareness, you must achieve a meditative state whereby your internal dialogue is not constantly returning your thoughts to past or future events. This is why concentration comes before mindfulness as a core meditation. Nonjudgmental attention to internal and external experience may include sensations, thoughts, bodily states, consciousness, and the environment, while simultaneously encouraging openness, curiosity, and acceptance.

The best way to cultivate and improve mindfulness is through the regular practice of meditation. In recent years, health care practitioners have adopted Mindfulness-Based Stress Reduction (MSRB) as an official Complimentary Alternative Treatment (CAM). CAM Treatments describe practices recognized by doctors as effective treatments used in conjunction and cooperation with conventional medicine. During mindfulness, a meditator should not ignore distracting thoughts and feelings that arise during Concentration Meditation. Rather, the meditator is encouraged to acknowledge and observe them in a nonjudgmental manner as they arise. In this manner, the individual detaches from internal and external thought in order to gain insight into what they represent. One key element of mindfulness includes the ability to stay in present moment awareness regardless of the emotional or mental content observed. In other words, Mindfulness Meditation does not block anything; it requires that you let anything in, even thoughts, feelings, or sensations you might consider very unpleasant. By exercising the quiet mind, concentration gives you the tools to observe the experience without the mind chatter triggered by an emotional reaction. The techniques used to cultivate the core practice of mindfulness include:

1. Body scan technique
2. Muscle tensing technique
3. Expanding to sensations technique
4. Walking technique
5. Drinking tea technique
6. Everyday activity technique
7. Thinking technique
8. Positive emotion technique
9. Self-inquiry technique
10. Habitual pattern technique

Core Meditation #3: Lovingkindness Meditation

Concentration and mindfulness share aspects of the internalization stage of meditation. The expansion stage of meditation occurs during the third core practice: lovingkindness. When self-concern dissolves into a feeling of genuine love and compassion for all living things, the meditator has entered a state of expanded consciousness beyond the "I." As the mediator radiates love outward, the body raises its vibratory state of communication with a universe that is now listening and ready to respond. The techniques used to cultivate the core practice of lovingkindness include:

1. Mantra (or chanting) technique
2. Altar technique
3. Compassion technique
4. Walking in nature technique
5. Third eye technique

Finding or Joining a Meditation Group

At this point you may be wondering if it easier to learn and practice meditation in an individual or group setting. The answer depends on you. Some people feel more comfortable beginning a meditative practice alone; others prefer practicing with a group. Learning to meditate by yourself is not hard if you follow the principles outlined in this book. Where meditative sessions occur is not as important as the overall ambience of the meditative space. Creating a meditative space at home only works when few distractions exist. If your home is located in a noisy neighborhood, or if you have children running around all the time, these familiar and comforting environs could become more of a distraction than a respite. If so, joining a meditation group could be a great opportunity to network with other like-minded people, especially if you are someone more motivated when working in a group setting and enjoy sharing experiences with others. Indian scriptures use the word, *satsang*, which means "in the company of other truth seekers," and espouse the idea that the collective energy flow of a group amplifies the experience.

In the opinion of integrated energy therapist Wil Langford, "The benefit of group meditation is that you are encouraged by the participation of the other people in the group. Some may help you by giving suggestions based on their own experiences. During meditation, the energy changes, and a group that is meditating together may help to increase each other's energy.

It is also less expensive to join a group than it is to hire a private teacher or meditation guide. On the other hand, experiencing the energy radiated by a group may not be so

good if the group has many negative members or people who are experiencing high stress due to their life styles and circumstances."

Group meditation classes have become a mainstream pursuit, so finding a local class has become easier than ever. The most popular places to find group sessions are in community recreation departments, sports clubs, local colleges, places of worship, meditation centers, and private studios. If you already belong to a sports club such as L.A. Fitness®, your membership may include free Yoga sessions. Many meditation centers also offer free sitting instruction. For example, the Shambhala Meditation Center of Atlanta offers day and evening instruction twice a week. These instruction sessions are wonderful for beginners who have questions about posture, wandering minds, or even shifting position in the middle of a sitting session. For a list of meditation centers across America, go to **www.freemeditationinfo. com/places-to-meditate/north-america/usa.html**. If you feel that Buddhist monastery will have more experienced meditators, you can find a listing in 23 American states at **www.brandbharat.com/english/religion/ buddhism/buddhist_temple/usa_buddhist_temple_list.html**. If you feel more comfortable with a more mainstream setting, private studios offer Yoga classes that often blend meditation with Yoga. LuluLemon, for example, is a meditation outfitter that offers free sessions once a week, courtesy of local instructors who volunteer their time to lead classes. To find a meditation class in your area, go to **www.lululemon.com/stores/** and ask for a schedule. However, before you contact any of these places, consider the following pros and cons of meditation classes to decide if group meditation is the right choice.

Pros of Meditation Classes

1. More likely to reduce stress in a shorter span of time
2. More likely to continue practice if motivated by others
3. More likely to receive encouragement

4. More likely to progress faster toward deep meditation with instruction

5. Less risk of sustaining physical injury from certain body poses with instructors present

6. Increased energy flow from collective meditation

7. Opportunity to network and socialize with like-minded people

8. Instructors can answer questions, provide added guidance, or correct issues that create roadblocks

9. Many sessions are free

Cons of Meditation Classes

1. More likely to face frustration if you begin looking around and comparing your efforts to others

2. More likely to lose focus due to external distractions

3. More likely to feel self-conscious if you are too concerned about your appearance

4. More likely to skip sessions and eventually discontinue practice if you have to travel more than five miles

5. You may not like the instructors teaching style or technique

6. The schedule may conflict with some of your other commitments, disrupting your practice or causing you to discontinue

What to Look for in a Meditation Teacher

A third option is seeking a private teacher. Hiring a private meditation teacher works if you want individualized coaching and might feel self-conscious or distracted by other group members. The meditation teacher you choose should

be a reliable person, and the method used to help you to learn meditation should be within the guidelines for your own personal belief system. An ideal coach will take a student-centered approach. This type of teacher will ask what the student wants to get from meditation before giving any instruction and is sensitive to any fears, doubts, or insecurities the student might have. A good teacher also makes suggestions without pressuring the student to accept them. If you decide to get a private teacher, you also have to decide what type of teacher you want. Do you want an instructor, a mentor, a pandit, or a master? An instructor teaches meditative techniques and offers troubleshooting advice. A mentor may not have the same level of experience as an instructor but may offer personal encouragement and be willing to teach certain techniques they learned from others. A pandit may not have meditative experience but may be a scholar with knowledge of ancient spiritual texts who can offer spiritual guidance. A master is someone who has practiced meditation for years and is the most advanced type of meditative teacher.

Beginning meditators are likely to encounter different scenarios with each type of instruction, so it is important to make a quick determination of your teacher's credentials. An instructor may request payment for instruction time, whereas a mentor may simply offer time and advice free of charge. Making these distinctions is important because you will need to know exactly what to expect out of this person's instruction. For example, if you come across a mentor, you may expect more than wind-up receiving. If you contact an instructor, you may be looking for spiritual advice that only a master can give. When contacting someone, it may seem apparent as to what type of instructor this person offers. If not, there is no harm in asking.

Meditators who start off meditating alone or without instruction sometimes encounter recurring emotions they find difficult to handle without guidance; others suffer from procrastination. These types of meditators usually need a teacher to coach them through the beginning practice. Finding the right teacher involves more than just determining their level of experience.

The search should be highly personalized because in addition to needing the right kind of instructor, you want someone you can trust. Here is where your intuition becomes important. Searching for a guru is a lot like searching for a soul mate. You want to find someone who emulates the kind of qualities you admire, the kind of qualities that make you feel at ease. Does this person's beliefs appear to match their mannerisms, or do they appear to say things that do not correspond to their behavior? Does this person encourage new ideas, or do they rigidly cling to certain methods of practice? The best way to determine what kind of teacher exudes the right qualities is to get a referral from a friend, relative, or colleague. Short of that, you might start by evaluating a prospective instructor by sitting in on a class.

CASE STUDY: FROM TAKING CLASSES TO TEACHING CLASSES

Jim Malloy
Merida, Yucatan, MX, 97130
jmalloy@meditationcenter.com
www.meditationcenter.com
052-999-272-8968

I came to the practice of meditation relatively early in life. I had just graduated from high school and a good friend suggested we go to a lecture on meditation. The speaker appeared very peaceful and said that meditation would change our lives in many wonderful ways. So we signed up, learned how to meditate, and sure enough, it did. I started practicing mantra meditation, but after about ten years, I started following more of an intuitive path where I found myself drawn to meditations that aligned with whatever phase of spiritual growth I happened to be in at the time. After practicing Transcendental Meditation for seven years, I spent ten months on the southern coast of Spain, where Maharishi Mahesh Yogi trained me. After teaching within the TM organization for a few years, I began teaching independently.

Sitting sessions for students often vary. For most, it is relaxing and peaceful. I teach students how to find deep states of inner quietness known as Yoga nidra, which generally feels like sleeping or dreaming. Some struggle with mental distractions until they come to accept that it is not necessary to fight thoughts or try too hard to stay focused. I think the need for relaxation and stress reduction is very important. However, what I believe is even more important is learning to elevate one's vibratory consciousness, which reconnects one with the innermost self or spirit. Nowadays, most people come to meditation looking for relaxation, stress reduction, improved health, and better sleep. Only a small percentage of students in my classes seek spiritual development. My advice for someone just beginning a meditation practice is simple. Put aside all your expectations about what you want to happen and what you think is supposed to happen when you meditate and simply accept whatever does happen.

Also, commit to staying with it. If you are just beginning a meditation practice, it is helpful to give careful thought to the environment. It helps to have a quiet place with no potential interruptions. Having a place specially designated for meditation helps with one's practice and tends to build up the peaceful energy generated through meditation. However, after someone has been meditating for quite a while, the environment becomes less important. I believe it is very helpful for most people to have a teacher to help them get started, but I do not think it is essential for everyone. Some individuals can develop new abilities well on their own.

How to Create a Regular Meditative Practice

*M*editating in the private space of a home or office is a great way to begin a practice if you decide not to pursue a group practice or teacher. To create a regular meditative practice, it is important to select one or more core practices and then customize that practice with the techniques that fit your needs. When thinking about what you hope to get out of meditation, contemplate or re-read the core meditation overview provided in Chapter 3 after finishing this book. After deciding which core meditation to use, consider or re-read the corresponding techniques described in greater depth in chapters 5, 6, and 7. In addition, look at the ten-minute exercises in those chapters, which may serve as a reference point for customizing your own practice. Generally, experts recommend practicing all three core meditations. However, if your intention is to relax and reduce stress, the Concentration Meditation will suffice. To improve memory and unravel bad habits and habitual patterns of behavior, use concentration in conjunction with mindfulness. To expand your consciousness, start with concentration, continue to mindfulness, and finish with lovingkindness.

Once you know which core meditations you plan to practice, it is time to consider several important factors that may affect a daily routine. Those factors include:

1. Choosing the best time to mediate
2. Deciding how many times a day to meditate
3. Choosing what to wear
4. Choosing what kind of atmosphere to create
5. Choosing what type of accessories may enhance the experience

Choosing the Best Time to Meditate

There is no perfect time of day that works best for meditation because it varies from one person to the next. What matters is creating a routine that accommodates your daily schedule and provides enough flexibility to move your session to a later or earlier time if your daily schedule at work or home suddenly changes. Making this determination is vital to making medita-

tion a daily practice that never diminishes. Some people prefer to meditate at dawn, others prefer the afternoon, and others still prefer to meditate at night. People with little time to spare may not have the option of choosing a time of day or night, so they have to meditate when time affords. The good news for these people is that meditation is a mobile practice, performed any time — and, as advanced practitioners will testify — in any place. For example, you can start a session in a car, on a train, on a plane, or while walking somewhere. For busy people always on the go, it might be possible to squeeze a session in during a lunch hour or even a coffee break at work, as long as there is an opportunity to create a suitable space at the office. It also might be fruitful to build a routine in right after work while waiting for the kids to come home from school or another chunk of time in the day where downtime is available. Those who start mobile meditative sessions are typically the type of people constantly "on-the-go" and use opportunities while in transit to get away from things for ten minutes to clear their minds and recharge the flow of energy in their body.

On the other hand, meditative exercises do not require a great deal of activity. In fact, most of the principles involve being still in mind, body, and spirit. However, developing different thought patterns does require a considerable amount of concentration, especially early on in the process; therefore, you should not begin certain meditative techniques while driving or performing another task that requires your attention (more on that later). Moreover, meditating to achieve a high-energy state should correspond to techniques that produce more energy, while meditating to achieve a relaxed trance state should correspond to techniques that produce relaxation. An ideal meditative practice combines both states to achieve a balance of relaxation and energy. To explore which energy state fits your schedule, goals, and intentions, begin the evaluation process by considering the benefits of meditating at different times.

Morning Meditation vs. Night Meditation

Advanced meditators in Eastern cultures who practice body and mind exercises usually fit their sessions into the early hours of the morning between 5:00 a.m. and 5:30 a.m. Morning meditation works for early risers who like to get a head start on their day. It also works for people who feel groggy in the morning and need an influx of energy to wake up and face the day that lies ahead. Most adults need roughly eight hours of sleep to function well throughout the day. As a rule, the best time to meditate in the morning is one hour after you wake up. Meditating within this time from can serve to heighten the meditative experience by drawing from the energy collected after a full night of sleep. The mind also tends to be quieter since it has just come out of an eight-hour resting state, in which case it will take less time to reach the internalization stage of meditation. Meditators who prefer to practice at sunrise typically feel a heightened sense of peacefulness and self-awareness. That incentive alone makes the idea of altering your sleeping patterns something to consider. The best way to alter any routine sleep pattern is to shift the hours of sleep back enough for a proper waking at sunrise. Decide how much sleep is necessary to function the next day and count backward. If time does not allow you to make this type of shift, set the alarm clock an hour back from your normal walking hour and count backward to determine what time you will need to fall asleep in order to meditate in the morning.

Conversely, some people prefer night meditation. The same principle for night meditation applies: it is best to do so one hour before bedtime. Using the right techniques can usher the body into a deep, relaxing sleep.

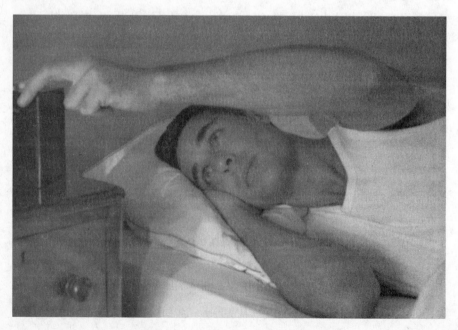

The reason that meditators use certain techniques to induce greater drowsiness or greater wakefulness has to do with the effect that meditation has on brain waves. Explored further in Chapter 5, the four types of brain waves measured by EEG are *beta, theta, alpha,* and *delta*. Sleep occurs in four stages: transition to sleep, light sleep, deep sleep, and dream sleep. Meditation can cure insomnia by helping your body transition to a sleeping state. At night, your mind is most likely to be in a beta. In beta, your mind is agitated and constantly thinking about what happened over the course of the day. A nocturnal meditative practice assists the mind's transition from beta to alpha. An alpha state is a deepening state of relaxation in which the brain's electrical activity becomes more settled and the brain wave amplitudes grow bigger, slower, and more rhythmic. As brain waves slow down further, the body enters a theta state of light sleep. Theta lasts from 10 to 25 minutes, during which all eye movement, heart rate, and body temperature decreases. After 25 minutes, the body enters a delta state of deep sleep. About 70 to 90 minutes after falling asleep, the body enters Rapid Eye Movement (REM) sleep, where dreaming occurs. Keep in mind that the quality of hours spent sleeping is more important than the number hours of sleeping.

The stages of REM and non-REM sleep form a complete sleep cycle. Each cycle lasts about 90 minutes and repeats four to six times during the night. Most adults spend about half their sleep hours in a non-REM state, about 20 percent in REM state, and 30 percent in the remaining stages, including deep sleep. Deep sleep repairs the body and builds up energy. It plays a major role in stimulating growth, repairing muscles and tissues, and boosting the body's immune system. Getting enough deep sleep is an essential part of renewing the body's ability to reenergize. Walking up in the middle of the night decreases the body's ability to obtain the cycles of sleep necessary to repair and energize itself. If you have trouble falling asleep or frequently wake up in the middle of the night, you increase the chances that your body is not spending enough time in the different stages of sleep. Thus, night meditation would be more essential than morning meditation.

Creating a Flexible Schedule

Although the vast majority of people have a 9-to-5 workday schedule, an increasing number of people have more varied professional work hours. Thanks to the advent of remote technology, more employees communicate across vast distances than ever before, and the number of people working from home continues to increase. To create a flexible schedule, some beginning meditators with more than one or two time options will keep a journal and record the times of day they feel most relaxed and open to meditation. Try this for three to five days and find as many periods during each day where you feel relaxed and have free time, then write them as options in descending order. That way, if something interrupts your daily routine, you can look down your list and choose the next best option. A journal is also a good way to reflect on meditation and track improvements in your thoughts, outlook, or energy level. It is also effective for recording meditative experiences that help you become more conscious of habitual patterns as you develop Mindfulness Meditation . Experts recommend that beginning meditators practice at the same time each day once they decide upon an optimal time, since it helps establish a practice that evolves from a routine to a ritual. Home meditators should practice their sessions when relatives are not home, as this keeps distractions to a minimum. Ideally, this free stretch of time should occur while the body feels at peak energy.

Meditation takes time to evolve from a routine into a ritual. A routine often feels forced and takes effort return to every day. A ritual, however, feels more like a necessity. Meditators who commit to a schedule, and leave enough flexibility in their day to make meditation a regular practice eventually come to see their practice as a ritual they cannot live without; otherwise, something in their day feels incomplete. Many beginners succumb to the pitfall of negatively judging their initial practice. It is important to remember that some practices are going to flow better than other times and that spending some time practicing meditation is better than not doing it at all. It is crucial to remain committed to that time and refrain, whenever possible, from planning other activities within that block of time. This is especially crucial during the early stages of creating a routine, as consistency is vital in forming a strong, regular habit that feels like a natural part of a daily regimen.

Eating habits are another consideration for creating a flexible schedule. When the body processes food, digestion draws energy away from other areas. Bigger meals, especially meals high in carbohydrates, require greater digestion which requires larger withdrawals of energy, causing drowsiness. Meditating is a difficult task to perform on a full stomach. Because it requires so much mental focus and energy, digestion often will get in the way of the process. This is also another reason that meditation experts recommend practicing in the morning before breakfast. You can either wait at least one hour before starting a session, create an alkaline diet (discussed later in this chapter), or eat smaller portions. You also should refrain from imbibing alcohol or other substances that raise the body's acidity levels. This includes tobacco, marijuana, recreational drugs, coffee, cappuccino, and any other caffeine-based beverages.

Creating a Meditative Environment

Ambiance is a specific environment defined by mood, character, quality, tone, and atmosphere. It is a space designed to evoke a specific feeling. Meditation does not require ambiance. However, some people feel that ambiance allows faster entry into meditative states; others believe it adds something to their practice. Because more distractions and gadgets now compete for people's attention, serious meditators have turned to creating an ambient environment for their practice. Meditation should occur in a calm environment that promotes a sense of peace and tranquility, therefore eliminating the possibility for any jarring sounds to occur is the first step toward creating an ambient environment. This means shutting off mobile devices or removing them entirely from your space. If you want to monitor the time without having it hang over you as a distraction, buy a meditation timer at an online or retail store.

Removing Distractions

Practicing during the daylight hours might mean blocking out excessive sunlight with heavy curtains or some other fabric. Softer lighting generally elicits relaxation, while luminous light creates intensity. Light as it relates to creating mental states of relaxation and intensity explains why romantic dinners are candlelit and operating tables have lamps with piercing lights. A room devoted solely to daily meditative sessions should be free of distractions, but as you progress further into practice and gain concentration and insight, external stimuli will lose their disruptive capacity. For now, it is best to aim for a dark space with only a small amount of incoming light unless you plan to practice Open Eye Meditation. Open Eye Meditation allows for greater amounts of light within a meditative space, but too much light can prevent the eyes from relaxing and cause them to squint. Most beginning meditators find it more productive to close their eyes to block out light. Keep in mind that some light will enter through the eyelids during closed eye meditation. You want to keep your eyes closed but also relaxed, which means that some light will penetrate into your experience.

Therefore, a small amount of incoming light is acceptable for meditative purposes. If too much light distracts your focus or works at cross-purposes with your intention, choose a very small space with no windows or openings, such as a garage or closet. Complete darkness works well depending on the type of meditation. For example, third eye meditation (discussed further in Chapter 8) activates the pineal gland located in your midbrain. The pineal gland is a bioluminescent organ that projects light into your mind's eye and thrives better in complete darkness. Even a small space such as a walk-in closet, pantry, or nook is enough room for a daily practice.

Ambient Music and Sound

When it comes to selecting a room with a dual purpose, such as a home office, den or bedroom, make sure the room has a minimalist quality where nothing noisy or visually "loud" can create a distraction. However, some advanced meditators purposely choose rooms where these distractions exist as a way of cultivating a core meditation. For example, if you live in an urban area where traffic is always part of the background noise, you might use the background noise as an object of focus in your concentration technique. If you do live in an urban area and want to block out these background noises, it might be better to substitute one noise for another. In other words, use earphones and ambient music to override the sounds of

traffic. Ambient music might include anything from binaural beats (discussed further in Chapter 5), to white noise, nature recordings, instrumentals, or some other digitized sound that draws your focus.

Even if you prefer meditating in complete silence, using certain techniques may require stepping out of an empty void and connecting to something that develops concentration or mi*ndfulness. In his book,* Teach

Yourself to Meditate in Ten Simple Lessons, Eric Harrison writes, "One advantage of ambient music is that when your mind wanders, it tends to fall into the music rather than back into thoughts. The music acts as a safety net. Another advantage is that the sensual and rhythmic qualities of music augment the sensory component of your meditation." However, any music played in conjunction with breathing techniques should be monotone or bland since interesting music can create a distraction. Do not choose music with lyrics, because the words may provoke thinking, and do not choose anything jarring, like rock or rap music. A monotone sound will not dominate your consciousness or jolt you with auditory peaks and valleys. The volume, likewise, should not be so loud that it takes up your entire focus. As a rule, keep an ambient noise to a background level in your consciousness by turning the volume no more than halfway up the dial. Some of the most popular ambient recording artists include Biosphere, The Orb, Tim Hecker, Darshan Ambient, and Gandalf. If you have a cable television package that includes music channels, television rooms can make for ambient meditation spaces. For a list of the top 25 ambient music albums of the last 20 years, go to the resource section at the end of this book.

Although it is important to give some thought to creating the right environment for each meditation session, it is more important to maintain an open mind. Sometimes distractions and interruptions will occur despite your careful planning. That is all right; let the distractions come and go without becoming angry or judgmental. Just do not allow distractions to distract you. Simply notice what is happening, and then gently return your attention to the meditation object (e.g. your breath, a mantra, or a sacred passage).

Using Candles, Crystals, and Incense

Candles emit just the right amount of light for meditation. They not only create a peaceful ambiance, but also can serve as a focal point during Concentration Meditations. Scents work as powerful mind-centering agents that help form memories and elicit behavioral cues. Aromatherapy, for example, uses potent oils to relieve stress, anxiety, and depression. If you decide to light candles and burn incense as part of a ritual, use candleholders and position the incense them in place where nothing can spill. Additional fragrances, such as freshly cut fresh flowers, could be set out to aid in meditation. Avoid using heavy perfumes or other overpowering fragrances that might sting the nostrils or create olfactory distractions. If you want to decorate your meditative space with objects that inspire focus, look for earthy objects that naturally strengthen your energy chi such as pyramid crystals and orgonites. You might also consider creating an indoor Zen garden. To brainstorm decorative ideas for a meditation space, consult the online stores listed at the end of this book. If you follow a religious faith, consider creating an altar dedicated to a famous spirit guide, such as Jesus, Buddha, or Mohammed.

Regardless of how you decorate, make sure the space is clutter free with a minimal amount of wall paintings, framed photos and posters. Focusing on these items can cause the mind to wander away from centered, present moment awareness. For rooms that serve a dual purpose, remove or cover anything that presents a potential distraction. Cover bare hardwood, linoleum, or cement floors with throw rugs. Accent couches and chairs with new, comfortable pillows. Short of using the television or radio to play ambient music, it is best to unplug or turn off these appliances. If you have any pets, find something to keep them safely occupied for at least ten minutes.

Keeping a Tidy Meditation Space

Every meditation space should be free of clutter. Meditating in a messy room filled with dirty clothes scattered about offer the mind an opportunity to start mentally organizing the room. Cleanliness symbolizes order, discipline, and a commitment to adopting a healthy regimen. However, picking the clutter up off the floors might not be enough. In some cases, it might be prudent to vacuum and steam clean rugs, wipe down dusty areas, eliminate cobwebs, open the windows, and buy an air filter to free the room of airborne allergens. A fresh, clean room will be one where you look forward to spending quiet time. The more you come back to your practice, the more your meditation space will generate and store positive energies.

Choosing Comfortable Clothes

Wearing the proper cloth-ing is just as important as choosing the proper am-bience and carving out a regular time pattern each day. Anything tight or con-stricting will prevent the body from reaching its re-laxation state. If you incor-
porate yogic poses into meditative practice, you may wind up ripping your clothes or possibly limiting your own movement while attempting to move into position. The right clothing should be breathable clothes designed for absorbing sweat, and they should either fit loosely or feel expandable. Binding, heavy, or uncomfortable threads will get in the way of meditating since these garments will make breathing challenging. Loose, comfortable clothes will make concentration far more likely during a session and ensures proper circulation.

Clothes made with natural fabrics such as cotton and silk are optimal during meditative sessions. If you ever wondered why pajamas are made of these materials, it is because these threads feel smooth against skin. Be advised that not all fabrics and clothing accessories are the same, so choose what is more comfortable over what looks better. Beginning meditators often make the mistake of being more concerned with the latest fashion trends and less on wearing clothes that feel comfortable and support the meditative inten-tion. Most meditators wear sweatpants and other related types of drawstring pants during a session, as this type of clothing accommodates movement and flexibility in a seated position. A variety of different drawstring pants and other types of flexible, athletic clothing articles are available in an assortment of styles from retailers. Making a small investment and adding this type of clothing into your regular wardrobe might be well worth it.

Room temperature is another consideration to make as it relates to personal comfort. Some people react differently to temperature than others, so be sure to adjust and regulate the thermostat to a level that feels unnoticeable. If you cannot control the temperature of the room, always keep handy an article of clothing that meets the conditions described above. Some meditative states can cause a drop in body temperature and blood pressure, so even if you begin a practice feeling comfortable, you might begin to feel chillier than usual. For a list of meditative clothing accessories, go to: **www.lululemon.com**. Additional store supplies include meditation mats, instructional videos, scented candles, meditation music, meditation timers, Yoga bolsters, incense, and altar paraphernalia. For a list of stores that carry additional supplies and accessories, consult the resource section at the end of this book.

Body Support Accessories

Choosing the proper meditation cushion depends on several factors, including how your body responds to certain postures, what postures and alignments you plan to use, what area of the body the cushion provides supports, and how comfortable the cushion feels. Each person's spine is neither flat nor curved the same way as another person's spine. Without proper support, you risk injuring your body on an unsupportive surface. Improper body support can misalign the body, create discomfort, or promote injury. If you require constant body support, you may need more than one type of cushion. Meditation in any sitting or kneeling postures requires strength and flexibility of the ankles, knees, and hips. If you have aches and pains, or a previous medical history involving any of these areas of the body, contemplate getting a cushion that offers direct support there.

Cushions come in a variety of shapes, heights, sizes, colors, and materials. Depending on personal belief, the color of the cushion may not be too important, though most people look for a color that matches the color scheme of their meditation space. Some cultures believe that colors promote harmonization with the surrounding environment. The Chinese call it *feng shui*. For example, red relates to fire energy, which they believe elevates energy. Violet restores balance, yellow elevates mood, blue calms the body, black induces deep inward focus, orange promotes healing, and green encourages slow, deep breathing. If you buy a cushion online or in a store, try to find out of the material is made of either kapok or buckwheat hull. Kapok is a cotton-like material that does not compress like other cushion products. It is also lightweight and conforms to the shape of the body in a supportive manner. Buckwheat hulls weigh more than a kapok cushion, but they also conform well to the shape of the body and create a grounded feeling. Generally, more people prefer buckwheat hull cushions because they feel more stable than the kapok cushions. So what is the best body support accessory to choose? The most common body support accessories include:

1.   Cotton Yoga mats
2.   Zabutons
3.   Zafus
4.   Gomdens
5.   Meditation benches

Cotton Yoga mats work well for lying postures. However, if you plan to sit for long periods, *zafus* are the most commonly used apparatus among Zen and Buddhist meditators. Zafus look like plump round cushions, sometimes accompanied with a soft square base called a *zabuton*. Depending on what posture you need or want to achieve, try interchanging the *zafu* and the *zabuton* to see which feels best. *Zafus* may also come with a padded bench for beginning meditators who expect to do a lot of kneeling. The figure shown on the left on the next page, illustrates the look of a typical *zafu* with its *zabuton* underneath.

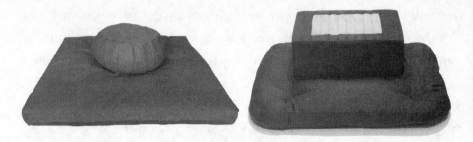

The *Gomdens* are also meditation cushions that come with *zabutons*, except they are square. Most meditators use *gomdens* for cross-legged postures that require the knees to be up off the *zabuton*. The foam block interior will keep its height in sitting. Gomdens consist of a quilted fabric with a removable and washable covers. The figure above, on the right illustrates the look of a typical *gomden* with its *zabuton* underneath.

Lifestyle Tips for Mental Well-Being and Physical Health

Finding balance between work and play is critical to achieving a successful lifestyle. Work is important, but not the sole point of living. People who bring their stress home and allow it to affect their home life have no balance in their lifestyle. People who master meditation and present moment awareness know how to reduce stress so that the responsibilities and agitations of work never come home with them. In short, they have balance. Their spouses never feel neglected or complain about a lack of interest in home life. Being truly in the moment with someone you care about is one of the great joys of life. Meditation teaches people how to push distractions away so they can deepen relationships and enjoy the social interactions that make life worth living. Try doing something new and unfamiliar if you have time left over from balancing your life and work. Think back to our Chapter 2 discussion of sacred geometry and how the male generating principal in sacred geometry creates life. Courage is a male characteristic because it gives us the power to animate our lives, but you do not have to be a male to develop courage. As you progress through your practice, you will begin to feel more open to new experiences. If you want to bring positive energy to your lifestyle, think about starting a home improvement project or volunteering with a charity organization, such as a nursing home or animal shelter. If you have not taken a vacation in years, find a place you have never visited and go there. Make a "bucket list" of things you have put off doing in life. Keep in mind that whichever new experience you choose to pursue, none may be more important than changing unhealthy eating habits, especially if stress is causing you to choose comfort foods over foods that supply the energy needed to balance your body and mind.

Healthy Eating

Returning to an earlier discussion about foods that cost the body large amounts of energy, it makes sense to consider changing your dietary lifestyle if you want to promote wellness and bring more energy to the practice of meditation. To reiterate, bigger meals, especially meals high in carbohydrates, require greater digestion, which requires larger withdrawals of energy, causing drowsiness. For this reason, starting an organic-based alkaline diet has become one of the more popular trends espoused by nutritionists, meditators, and people who need more energy to function in their daily lives. With so many scientific studies now emerging about the health risks of genetically modified foods, pesticides, and antibiotics, you should begin your personal transformation by adopting better eating habits that support your body's wellness. The process starts with avoiding foods produced and distributed by large food producers. Over the last century, industrial agro-farms have replaced local farms as a major source of agricultural production. Since industrial agro-farms distribute much greater amounts of food to much longer distances, it has become a common practice to inject livestock with eight times the required level of antibiotics and to grow genetically modified foods.

Using antibiotics on livestock prevents animals from getting infectious diseases while penned up in filthy living conditions. Using genetically modified seeds make crops both virus and pesticide resistant. Though these profitable methods of farming keep crops and animals hardy for mass distribution, many studies have linked the consumption of these foods to increased cancer rates and other biological problems. In addition to biological problems associated with large food production, *The Journal of the American Medical Association* estimates that more than 125,000 Americans die each year from side effects of drugs approved by the Food and Drug Administration (FDA). If you want to avoid getting sick from genetically modified foods and having to take FDA approved meditations, you have to change your diet for the long term. To avoid eating food produced by an industrial agro-farm, find a local farm or a supermarket that stocks food from local farms. If you cannot buy from a local farm, you can drastically reduce the odds of consuming genetically modified foods by eliminating meat, dairy, cookies, pasta, white rice, soybeans, corn, prepared or processed foods, and white bread from your diet. Given the widespread, unnatural growth methods used in today's food industry, it should come as no surprise that these genetically modified foods are also highly acidic.

Acid Foods vs. Alkaline Foods

One of the most important balances the human body strives to maintain is the need to maintain a proper acid-alkaline state called pH level. The term "pH" is an abbreviation for "power of hydrogen." What pH measures is the level of hydrogen ion concentration in a water-based solution. Since the human body qualifies as a water-based solution, the kidneys serve to monitor the pH levels by filtration and reabsorption processes. This filtration process helps the body balance blood pressure, salt, and water levels. Thanks to the kidneys, the pH level of the blood does not change. However, in a highly acid state, the pH level of the cells *can* change. Your cells have energy cycles, so when the pH level of cells become more acid, chemical reactions happen too fast and the body cannot receive the proper nutrients. When the pH level of cells become too alkaline their chemical reactions become too slow and the body does not absorb minerals. To measure the body's level of pH, scientists constructed a pH scale ranging from 0 to 14. Illustrated in the chart below, the number "0" indicates a purely acidic state, the number "7" indicates a neutral state (equal parts acid and alkaline), and the number "14" indicates a purely alkaline state. Different areas of the body require different pH levels. For example, the stomach should be very acidic (between 1 and 3), as should urine and the inside of the adrenal gland. Sweat should be slightly acid while fluid outside the cell should be slightly alkaline. Brain fluid should be slightly alkaline (roughly 7.5), and bile and pancreas should be very alkaline to neutralize stomach acid. At the cellular level, Australian author and nutritionist Barbara O'Neil recommends a slightly acid state of 6.5 because it facilitates the speedy uptake of chemical reactions. Other nutritionists believe the ideal pH level for a person is 7.3—or very mildly alkaline.

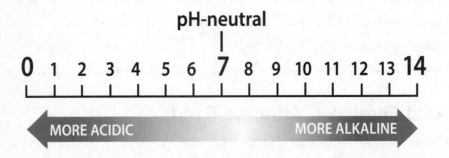

To maintain a balanced acid-alkaline balance, the total pH of food consumption should be roughly 80 percent alkaline foods and 20 percent acidic foods. However, since most Western meals consist of meats, sugars, and carbohydrates, the average person's diet is more like 80 percent acidic foods and 20 percent alkaline foods. As an example of how poisonous Western diets have become, Barbara O'Neil notes that sugary beverages like soda and root beer have a pH level of 2.7 (highly acidic). So how does a highly acidic state affect the body? When the lungs and kidneys come under intense pressure to filter high levels of acid, they begin to pull calcium phosphate (an alkaline compound stored in your bones) out of the bones and into the blood to combat the "acid crisis." The calcium phosphate restores the pH balance, but at a high cost. If the body draws much calcium out of the bones, the blood becomes too alkaline, which creates calcium deposits and bone spurs. Bone spurs can settle in the joint as gout, arthritis, and gallstones. It can build up on the arterial walls, causing even more problems. If you factor in constant emotional states like stress, worry, and anxiety, the body is fighting a two-front war to combat a rising acid-alkaline imbalance. Other behaviors, such as lack of sleep, lack of sunshine, and lack of exercise (contributing to lactic acid buildup) creates acid conditions. This is why adopting a healthy lifestyle will promote the very things you are trying to accomplish through meditation. To this end, Barbara O'Neil notes, "There is nothing wrong with stress; it is *distress* that creates an acid condition." The result of an extended acid-alkaline imbalance includes:

1. Loss of energy
2. Inflammation
3. Mucus congestion
4. Hardening of arteries and soft tissue
5. Ulceration
6. Degenerative diseases such as cancer, heart disease, stroke, ALS, and diabetes

Depending on your level of stress, you may not notice these symptoms until they have had time to evolve and cause serious damage. The higher the body's acid-alkaline imbalance, the more the body becomes at risk for developing cancer. According to Dr. Robert Young, author of *The pH Miracle*, cancer cells thrive at a pH level of 5.5. Most doctors and nutritionists accept 7.3 as the ideal pH level because that is the level at which cancer cells become dormant. Along with cancer cells, bacterial microforms can be one of the nastiest consequences of an acid-alkaline imbalance. Bacteria and funguses thrive when the body lives in an acid-alkaline imbalance. When they become overgrown, they poison the body further with their own acid waste products called *mycotoxins* and *exotoxins*. The chart below lists the physical symptoms that appear when a body is too acid or too alkaline.

Too acid	Too Alkaline
Excessive coughing	Eyelid Twitching
Irregular heartbeat	Hyperventilating
Feeling weak	Arthritis
Feeling nauseous	Allergies
Feeling sleepy but wired	Bone spurs
Frequent sighing	Low thyroid
Feeling anxious	Calcium deposits

The best way to support your meditative practice is to eat right, exercise daily, sleep 7.5-9 hours a night, consult a nutritionist, and get your pH level tested the next time you visit the doctor. Since time constraints prevent many people from exercising or sleeping enough, changing your eating habits can be the most manageable way of adopting a lifestyle that supports meditative practice. It is no secret that most people today eat highly processed foods with very low nutritional value when they should be incorporating more raw foods with higher nutrition levels into their diet. To restore or maintain your body's energy level, consider adopting an acid-alkaline diet that consists of foods that balance the acid-alkaline levels and energize the chemical reactions of cells. For a list of acid and alkaline producing foods, consult Appendices G and H.

The Calcifying Effects of Fluoride

Since the 1940s, the United States has been adding fluoride to its population's water supply, reasoning that fluoride contains preservative chemicals that prevent tooth decay. According to the Centers for Disease Control and Prevention, 61.5 percent of the American population receives fluoridated water. Because it prevents tooth decay, most brands of toothpaste also use fluoride as an ingredient. While fluoride seems like a harmless chemical, people who consume fluoride through tap water or toothpaste should be concerned about what they are doing to their body. In an August 2013 article published by Livestrong.com, Karen Eisenbraun reported that the *Journal of Applied Clinical Pediatrics* found that "high fluoride intake has a damaging effect on intellectual ability." For most people, fluoride exposure occurs on a daily basis. If your tap water contains fluoride, your body absorbs almost all of the fluoride that enters through your skin pores when you take a shower. Drinking fluoride retains about 50 percent of the fluoride since your body is able to filtrate some of it.

If consumed over the long term, studies show that drinking fluoridated water out of your tap also can produce such adverse effects as depression, weight gain, and heart disease. The U.S. National Research Council also recently discovered that fluoride lowers endocrine function, which may contribute to hypothyroidism. Given these effects, it is easy to see why fluoride can impair not only your health but also your meditative practice. Yet the effects of fluoride consumption range even further than that. In the 1990s, a British scientist named Jennifer Luke discovered that fluoride accumulates at high levels in the pineal gland, causing a hardening effect known as calcification. In fact, Luke found that because the pineal gland is a calcifying tissue with high exposure to blood flow, its hydroxyapatite crystals contain the highest fluoride concentrations in the human body (up to 21,000 ppm F), higher than either bone or teeth.

Following Luke's discovery, Japanese researchers published *Ultrastructure and X-ray Microanalytical Study of Human Pineal Concretions*, which studied pineal glands using high-resolution electron microscopy. In their report, high concentrations of calcium and phosphorous were detected at the center of each gland. So how does a calcified pineal gland affect your meditative practice? For starters, a calcified pineal will limit your ability to successfully practice third eye meditation. Activated by the pineal gland, your third eye, otherwise known as the seat of the soul, can connect to spiritual frequencies and enable you to have a sense of the euphoric oneness around you. Awakening the pineal gland enhances our learning and memory abilities. It also enhances wisdom and creativity, and can trigger our psychic healing abilities. With help of meditation, a pineal gland tuned into higher frequencies enables a person to experience dimensionality and astral projection. Any hardening or calcifying of this gland can dramatically hamper this practice. Due to constant exposure to fluoride, the pineal gland calcifies by age 12. By the time a person reaches adulthood, it lays dormant and atrophied from lack of use. You can revitalize your pineal gland by reducing consumption of fluoride and processed foods, exercising more, and eating less sugar. The graphic illustration below shows the position and size of the pineal gland in the brain, accentuated by the red dot.

To remove the level of fluoride in your drinking water, high quality water filter and reverse osmosis systems are available at many appliance stores. These systems are much more expensive than Brita filters, but they are extremely effective at removing fluoride, arsenic, chlorine, and other chemicals. For water filters, go to **www.filterwater.com**. For shower filters, go to **www.bestfilters.com/Shower-Filters_c_9.html**. Water filtration systems include countertop or under-the-counter systems. If you cannot afford a shower filter, consider talking quicker showers. If that does not sound appealing, taking dietary supplements such as calcium magnesium, liquid iodine, and boron can help remove the amount of fluoride absorbed in the body. Unfortunately, toothpaste also contains fluoride because it helps prevent tooth decay. If you want to avoid using fluoride in your toothpaste, brands such as Toms of Maine, Burt's Bees, or Dr. Ken's offer safe and fluoride-free formulas. Brushing your teeth with baking soda and glycerin or baking soda with hydrogen peroxide also can serve as safe alternatives to brushing with fluoride toothpaste. However, if you decide to use baking soda with either glycerin or hydrogen peroxide, it is important to understand that fluoride will no longer seal your teeth from tooth decay. The bacteria in your mouth are living organisms that live within dental plaque and consume sugars such as sucrose (table sugar), glucose, fructose, lactose, and cooked starches. When you consume sugary foods, your mouth bacteria digests these sugars, breaks them down, and ultimately excretes them on the surface of your teeth as very acid waste compounds (a pH of 4 and lower), which then cause cavities and tooth demineralization.

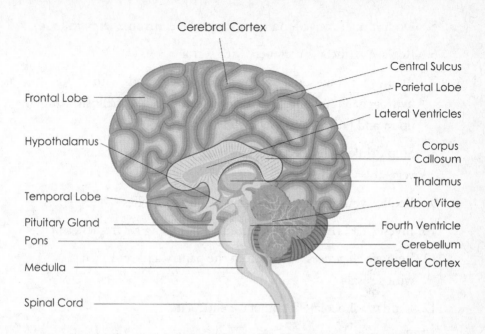

If you add to the fact that an acid-alkaline imbalance in your diet can result in the body drawing calcium out of your bones and teeth, you could be creating a very serious dental problem that not even fluoride toothpastes can solve. Keep in mind that within minutes of receiving a sugary meal, oral bacteria start to produce the acids. If you want to brush without fluoride, you must be vigilant about cleaning your teeth immediately after a meal and brush lightly, since baking soda can be abrasive to teeth. Consider buying alkaline water at a local health store if you still want to eat sugary food. Alkaline water can balance a body existing in an acid state. As a third option, you always can compromise and reduce your fluoride intake by brushing with fluoride toothpaste in the morning and baking soda at night.

Additional lifestyle tips to consider:

1. Buy local, organic produce and avoid big brand names

2. If you have metal filings in your dental work, ask the dentist to replace them with something non-toxic

3. Quit smoking cigarettes

4. Stop eating fast food (it is processed with unnatural chemicals)

5. Do not microwave food (it destroys the electron energy in food)

6. Replace artificial sweeteners with stevia

7. Avoid soda, diet soda, homogenized foods, foods with hydrogenated oil and fructose corn syrup, pork, shellfish, white flour, and fat free and low carb labels

8. Stop drinking bottled juice; instead, juice your fruits and vegetables in a blender

9. Reduce your contact with toxic cleaning supplies

10. Invest in a HEPA air purifier instead of using air fresheners

11. Remove all processed salt from the pantry and replace it with sea salt

12. Eat dark chocolate if you crave chocolate

13. Reduce the amount of time watching television (especially programs that make you feel negative)

14. Listen to uplifting music early in the morning

15. Make time for friends and loved ones

16. Practice random acts of kindness

17. Eliminate and stay out of bank debt

18. Get a gym membership

19. Buy an inversion table to decompress your spine and increase oxygen flow

20. Try acupuncture

21. Buy an alarm clock with natural earth tones (available at Sharper Image®)

22. Place an important goal for yourself in the future

23. Rescue a dog or cat from an animal shelter

Detoxing Herbs

Detoxification happens naturally when meditation becomes a regular practice. The body's chi energy starts pushing poisons out of the body so it can flow without obstructions. A purified body can direct the mind to higher states of consciousness. However, the chi only purifies when the body purifies. You can accelerate the body's purification process by detoxing with natural herbs. The areas of the body that need purification are the arteries, kidneys, liver, connective tissue, and blood. For non-herbal dietary supplements, go to the resource section at the end of this book. For herbal supplements, Detoxsafely.org lists the following remedies and their cleansing effects, which include:

1. **Alfalfa:** Breaks down poisonous carbon dioxide

2. **Black cohosh:** Loosens and expels bronchial tube mucous

3. **Black walnut:** Oxygenates the blood, balances sugar levels, burns excessive toxins

4. **Burdock root:** Reduces joint swelling, calcification deposits, clears blood of acids

5. **Cayenne pepper:** Used as antioxidant, antiseptic, and circulatory stimulant

6. **Chlorella:** Reduces body odors; can be used as a mouthwash

7. **Cascara sagrada:** Increases stomach, liver, and pancreas excretions; helps gallstones and hemorrhoids

8. **Chickweed:** Helps heal stomach ulcers

9. **Cranberry:** Treats bacterial bladder infections

10. **Dandelion:** Detoxifies the liver and promotes healthy circulation

11. **Echinacea:** Stimulates production of white blood cells; removes blood toxins

12. **Fennel seed:** Improves digestion as a diuretic

13. **Fenugreek:** Softens and dissolves accumulated mucous, phlegm, and infections from the lungs

14. **Gentian root:** Helps in the breakdown of protein and fats

15. **Ginger root:** Cleanses the bowels, kidneys, and skin

16. **Guar gum:** Used therapeutically to lower cholesterol and curb appetite

17. **Hawthorn berries:** Strengthens the heart muscles

18. **Hibiscus flower:** Used as antibacterial, mild diuretic, and anti-parasitic

19. **Horsetail:** Used in urinary tract disorders

20. **Irish Moss:** Soothes an irritated gastrointestinal tract

21. **Licorice root:** Soothes irritated mucus membranes and nourishes the adrenal glands

22. **Marshmallow:** Removes hardened phlegm in the intestinal tract

23. **Milk thistle:** Prevents liver destruction and enhances liver function by inhibiting free radicals and leukotriene

24. **Mullein leaf:** Soothes irritated tissues

25. **Oat straw:** Helps provide minerals to nourish bones, skin, hair, and nails

26. **Papaya:** Aids digestion

27. **Passionflower leaf:** helps to calm stress and slows the breakdown of neurotransmitters

28. **Peppermint:** Brings oxygen into the bloodstream

29. **Psyllium husk:** Used for all intestinal troubles

30. **Psyllium seed:** Used as a laxative agent and sweeping the gastrointestinal tract of toxins (Drink lots of water with psyllium.)

31. **Pumpkin seed:** Helps the body expel parasites

32. **Red clover:** Used as a tonic for the nerves and as a sedative for nervous exhaustion

33. **Slippery elm:** Neutralizes stomach acidity and absorbs foul gases and toxins

34. **Yarrow:** Acts as a blood cleanser, helps to regulate liver function, and heals the glandular system

35. **Violet leaf:** Used as an antifungal, demulcent, diuretic, and laxative

36. **Witch hazel bark, twigs, and leaves:** Helps heal damaged blood vessels

37. **Yellow dock:** Used as a blood builders and stimulates waste elimination

38. **Yucca root:** Helps break down organic waste in the body and relieves inflammation associated with arthritis

CASE STUDY: CREATING YOUR MEDITATION ROUTINE

Travis May
The St. Petersburg Shambhala Center
travismay108@gmail.com
www.travismay108.wordpress.com

I think the best time to meditate varies from person to person. I have no strong preference for any particular time of day, so I often practice at very different times. I do, however, like practicing in the morning because it is a good way to set the tone for the day. If I have to be somewhere early in the morning, I will shift my practice schedule to the middle of the day because that is when I need the most energy. At the Shambhala Center, we have classes in the early evenings. If my schedule prevents me from meditating in the morning and at noon, I will go there for a session. Early evening is a good time because I feel relaxed and ready to practice without it being late enough where I might feel too tired .

I will sit late at night as a fourth option if I have not meditated in the morning, noon, or early evening at the center. I may feel more tired, but knowing that meditation creates the right conditions for a deep sleep is what motivates me to practice right before bed.

If you want to create a flexible schedule to fit your lifestyle, I recommended setting a time every day. If it becomes a normal part of your routine — like taking a shower, exercising, and brushing your teeth — you will be more likely to do it. If your goal is to sit for 15 minutes a day, start getting up 15 minutes earlier than you normally do and add the sitting session to your morning routine. Perhaps it is better for you to sit when you get home from work, or during your lunch period. We each have to find what works best for us. The key is that we actually do it.

Some people prefer an elaborate ambiance. I recommend that you find a nice, comfortable, safe, quiet spot. It is good to have a space in your house dedicated for meditation practice. How you set that up will likely depend on your available space, connection to the practice, and budget. I have a setup at home similar to what we have at the meditation center. I use candles and incense to emulate the practice environment at the center. Everything in our shrine is symbolic, and I think it is good to understand the meaning of your shrines rather just doing it as a gimmick or because you think it might magically make you meditate better.

I would recommend just wearing light, loose fitting, comfortable clothing. In other words, what you would normally wear for any physical exercise. Wearing tight jeans can cut off your circulation and cause your leg to go to sleep, or it can restrict you to an uncomfortable sitting position. Many meditation centers recommend wearing layers so you can adjust to different temperatures, too. Ultimately, it is not necessary to go out and purchase a new wardrobe to meditate, but if it gets you focused on maintaining a schedule, then go ahead and do so.

I would not say that any support accessory works best because they are highly individualized. Our size, flexibility, and health can affect which cushions or chairs we might use to practice meditation. When working with posture, people often try different heights by stacking cushions on top of each other, or using a cushion plus a smaller support cushion. To figure out which accessory works best for your body type, visit a meditation center. They will probably have several kinds of body support cushions that you can try out with the help of a qualified instructor who can give you advice.

Chapter 4

Preparing the Body for Core Meditation

In addition to ambiance and environment, preparing the body for core meditation involves assessing the current state of your current physical health. While much of meditation involves sitting, *how* you sit can often determine the effectiveness of your practice. Using a *zafu* or *zabuton* as a body support will encourage proper body alignment, but if you become lazy in your posture, you will begin to strain your back, hips, and joints. Beginning meditators who strain these areas long enough will begin to risk injury if the physical core of the body's midsection (not to be confused with core meditation) is not strong enough to support a long-held posture. Therefore, having strong core muscles in your body's midsection will prevent or reduce the possibility of straining areas not designed for sustained pressure.

Having a strong core midsection instills beginning meditators with confidence that they can sit in basic or more advanced positions. Having confidence in posture means not having to think about posture during mind quieting or concentration exercises. Having a weak core midsection means worrying about sustaining injures while trying to meditate. Out of this fear of being injured, your inner dialogue will try to begin talking you out of your practice. It might replay an old injury that had nothing to do with sitting. It might recall the pain your body experienced when this injury occurred. The more you think about past hurts, the more you may begin to associate pain with your meditative practice until you become altogether discouraged from returning to your practice. It is for these reasons that the different forms of Yoga practice all incorporate poses called *asanas* with their meditative disciplines. Your body's core midsection consists of:

1. The transversus abdominis (the muscle layer of the abdominal wall)
2. The pelvic floor (the muscle fibers underneath the pelvis)
3. The diaphragm (the sheet of muscle extending along the bottom of the rib cage)
4. The multifidus (the muscle protecting the spinal column)

To strengthen the core midsection, consider buying an adjustable slant board or medicine ball and follow the exercise instructions that typically come with them, such as calf stretches, inversion stretches, ab crunches, and reverse back crunches. During these exercises, remember to exhale coming up (keeping your midsection tight) and inhale on the way down. The range of motion in the exercises performed on a slant board or medicine ball can really build the necessary midsection strength for supporting meditative postures and maintaining balance.

The Importance of Proper Body Alignment

Proper body alignment is important because meditation is about achieving balance and staying centered in the body and the mind. Meditation starts with achieving balance in the core midsection through proper posture and alignment. When the midsection loses balance, other areas of the body not meant to support posture begin to compensate for its misalignment. When other areas of the body become strained, joints and muscles eventually fatigue and begin to disintegrate from improper use. Good body alignment harmonizes the relationship between mind, body, and spirit. Since the goal of meditation is to create a connection between all three, your body's alignment is the first step in building this bridge. Correct body alignment also increases circulation to vital organs, which help bring balance to your emotional and physical state. Proper body alignment also increases the efficiency of your meditative exercises. If you become physically frustrated with meditation, examine your preparation. It may be that improper alignment of your body is causing you to work harder with less benefit. Proper alignment means working the body less and maximizing results.

The best way to assess the strength of your body's core midsection is to attend a Yoga class for beginners. Taking a Yoga class can give you a feel for your body's flexibility, which postures come easy, and which postures your midsection struggles to maintain. Whether you settle easily into each posture or not, pay attention to the instructor's directions about maintaining posture so you can apply these tips to your regular sitting practice. Another way to strengthen your core muscles is through breath work. Train your abdominal muscles, lie on your back with both knees bent and

place your palms at the bottom of your rib cage. Take a breath in through your nose and breathe deeply, allowing your diaphragm to expand your stomach while keeping your chest still. After your stomach rises to its highest point, exhale through your mouth and repeat the process.

Sitting Postures for Meditation

Sitting in a meditative posture is the most common type of stationary practice because it creates a stable position that roots deeply into the heaven and earth. Meditative stances whereby you stand while meditating may serve different but equally effective purposes. Some meditators us the horse stance, for example, to prevent or ease panic attacks. Lying down positions, such as the corpse pose, work best at the end of a Yoga practice for allowing the body to release its tension and settle into an even deeper state of relaxation. For the purpose of most beginner meditations, however, sitting postures may create the best experience. When you sit upright, keep each part of the vertebrae stocked evenly on top of each other. If it helps to visualize your spine (from the base to the top) as a skyscraper in order to keep it upright, then do so. The point of rooting yourself firmly between heaven and earth is to create a link between the physical and spiritual dimension of existence.

The seven basic points of correct meditative posture include: crossing the legs, placing both hands in the lap, keeping the back and neck straight, maintaining shoulder balance, relaxing the tongue and mouth, and keeping the eyes relaxed and either closed or semi-closed. If you wish to stand during meditation, consider using the sun salutation exercise in chapter five, putting both feet together with both hands at the side. Variations of standing meditation also include the horse stance (a common standing meditation used in Tai Chi), or the empty stance (a common standing meditation in Qigong to relieve back pain). Using the horse stance, stand with both feet shoulder width apart, keeping the back straight and feet pointed straight ahead. Bend the knees and hips as if you are about to sit down, raise both hands, and maintain that position for the duration of your practice. The horse stance is commonly used when you want to combine meditation with a physical workout that gets the blood flowing. To use the empty stance, stand with the knees slightly bent, keeping the legs six inches apart, and move one foot ahead of the other. Next, shift most of your weight to the foot closer to you, then lift the other foot and let it barely touch the ground. Raise your arms in front and begin meditation.

As an advanced alternative to standing or sitting, the bow position is an inverted pose that offers a great way to reverse stress and relax the mind before practicing meditation. To complete the bow position, lie face down on the floor with your hands at your side, and bend your knees. Using your arms, reach behind you and cuff your ankles with both hands. Once you have the right hand cuffing the right ankle and the left hand cuffing the left ankle, lift the upper half of your body by pulling on the ankles to form a "U" with your body. If you prefer to sit, the most common types of stationary sitting postures are:

1. The seated position (in a chair) — helps prevent slouching
2. The kneeling position (on a stool or *seiza* bench) — difficult without support
3. The lotus positions (half, full, Burmese) — most stable posture for beginners

Using Yoga to Improve Body Alignment and Posture

Stretching the body before each meditative practice also can help the muscles in the body to become more limber. When you start a car engine in the middle of winter, you want to warm up the engine to prevent the engine from breaking down. The same concept applies to muscles before meditation. If you attend a Yoga class, look around at other meditators to see how they stretch the muscles in their body before class begins, or simply ask the instructor for stretching tips after class. Stretching before a Yoga class is not always necessary since a good instructor always starts the practice slow to prepare the muscles for deeper stretches and postures. Good instructors also take notice of their student's posture problems and work to correct misalignment as they occur. In addition to stretching, Yoga helps build core muscles through breathing and resistance. Yoga poses useful to strengthening the body's core muscles include:

1. The child pose
2. The cobra
3. The plank pose
4. The downward dog
5. The spine rotation
6. The bridge pose
7. The boat pose with variation

The Child Pose

The child pose is a yogic position that stretches the core muscles by extending the hips and spine. To assume this position, sit on your knees and let your toes point backward, then spread both knees a little wider than your shoulders, and lean forward with your forehead on the floor. Two variations of the child's pose exist with respect to arm placement. In the first variation, place the back of your hands on the floor just outside your feet and hold this position for ten deep breaths. In the second variation (illustrated below), you would extend your arms in front of your head rather than behind you to get a diaphragm stretch. With your arms extended, both palms should lay flat on the floor. Hold this position for ten deep breaths. Repeating this stretching and breathing exercise over time will improve the overall strength of the core muscles and make your body more capable of handling meditative poses in proper alignment.

The Cobra

The cobra (illustrated below) is a yogic position that stretches the muscles that flex your spine. To assume this position, lie on your stomach, palms on the floor, elbows crooked, and fingers pointing straight ahead. Using your arms, push up the top half of your torso and hold this pose for 15 to 20 seconds, making sure your forearms hug your sides. Keep your toes point backward, and lift your head up, keeping the spine arched until you feel the abdomen begin to stretch. After 15 to 20 seconds, lower the top half of your torso back down until it is flush with the floor again.

The Plank

The plank (illustrated below) is a yogic position and form of resistance training that builds strength in the lower lumbar of the back and in the abdominals. A weak lower lumbar will strain and eventually collapse during long sitting periods, causing the body to misalign and shift weight into areas that cannot support the position. Building strength in the lower

lumbar means the body is more likely to stay properly aligned. Thus, it is less likely to slouch into a strain during long sitting periods. To assume this position, you can either use the cobra position to come into the plank pose by slowly lowering the top half of the body's torso to face the floor again, and pushing the body up off the ground, keeping the elbows bent, and the back completely straight. Having achieved this position, hold the plank pose for 30 seconds. To maintain proper positioning, make sure the lumbar stays straight and does not begin to drop toward the ground. To keep the lumbar from dropping, tighten the stomach's abdominal muscles to create underneath support. The longer the body remains fixed in this position, the stronger the abdominal muscles become.

The Downward Dog

The downward dog (illustrated below) is a yogic position that helps the body maintain a neutral spine alignment, which is important for creating balance in your meditative position. To assume this position, you can come into downward dog from the plank pose by walking the hands back to the feet and raising your hips upward until your body forms a triangle. To come into this position first, get on your knees and lean forward on your hands, then shift the bottom half of your weight back onto your feet and walk your hands backward until your body forms a triangle shape. The illustration below shows how the body should align when it arrives at the downward dog position.

The Spine Rotation

The spine rotation (illustrated below) is a yogic position that stretches the abdomen and lower back muscles that twist the torso left and right. If you have stiffness in the lower back before or after assuming a sitting position in meditative practice, using the spine rotation can help realign the spine and reduce stiffness and discomfort. To assume this position, sit on the floor and place your right hand flat and behind you, fingers pointing away from the body. With the right hand stabilized and the arm remaining straight, fold the left leg into the groin area with the left arm and cross the right leg over the folded left leg. Next, bend the elbow of the left arm, rotate your torso, and place the bent elbow flush against the right knee. Tense your core muscles for about ten seconds, then release the tension by rotating back to the original position. Repeat this position several times, then position yourself for a spinal rotation in opposite direction, and rotate and tense the torso muscles to the left.

The Bridge Pose

The Bridge Pose (illustrated below) is a yogic position and breathing exercise that can relax tension felt in the spine, breathing structures, and pelvic floor as well as activate the energy openings in these areas. The bridge pose is especially useful if energy blockages in the pelvic area create strain through long sitting periods. It also lowers pressure in the thoracic cavity (area around the lungs). To assume this position and practice the breathing movements, lie on your back, and slide your feet closer to the buttocks until your knees are bent and in the air. On the next inhale, keeping your arms flush to the floor, raise your buttocks and pelvic region to the air. On the exhale, bring the buttocks and pelvic region back to the ground. Repeat this breathing exercise for 20 or 30 seconds.

The Boat Pose

The Boat Pose (illustrated below) is a yogic position and form of resistance training that strengthens the spinal muscles against the pull of gravity. It also protects the lumbar from the kind of hyperextension that results from straining and losing support during long sitting periods. To assume this position, lie down on your back with your legs slightly apart and slowly raise

your upper and lower torso at the same time until you are balancing on your buttocks. As you balance, keep the abdominals tight and both arms pointed straight ahead and locked at the elbows. The boat pose creates a resistance similar to sit-ups. If you decide to do sit-ups as a form of resistance training, consider placing a light weight on your upper abdomen as you gain more strength in the routine. For reverse sit-ups, use a slant board to build core strength in the muscles around the spine. The boat pose is ideal for meditators looking to build core strength because it builds core strength in both the abdominals and around the spine at the same time whereas sit-ups and reverse sit-ups require two different exercises.

Gravity is a challenge in this position, but your balance will improve as core muscles become stronger. Physical balance is an important aspect of any meditation because it will keep the body in proper alignment and reduce the amount of stress that can often break concentration. Keeping the back straight is the most important part of this pose, so if you begin to slouch, straighten the back. The boat pose is a more advanced pose, so to avoid risking injury, consider building core strength through the other exercises before attempting to balance in boat pose.

Building core strength is important for reasons that go beyond meditation. Millions of people in America and throughout the world spend a bulk of their time at work sitting at a desk or in front of a computer screen. Without strengthening the aforementioned areas of the body, a significant number of these people will probably experience a gradual weakening of the spine. The answer to averting these physical problems at some point is building strength through breathing exercises, resistance training, or stretching. By implementing all three techniques, you will not only prepare your body for meditation, but activities in everyday life that require support from these areas. *Yoga Anatomy* by Leslie Kaminoff and Amy Matthews offers a greater examination of Yoga's strengthening effect on the physical anatomy as well as a number of useful illustrations.

The Most Common Forms of Yoga

The word Yoga means "union," which denotes a union between the body, breath, mind, and spirit. Practicing Yoga over time fosters an understanding that we are not separate beings, but rather one within ourselves and with all that exists. Many people in the world today practice different kinds of Yoga for different reasons. The most common forms of Yoga differ to some degree in their practice, their intention, and their results. Before committing to Yoga as a meditative practice, you should learn their differences and think about which might best fit your meditative intentions. Although each form of Yoga differs in many respects, they all use *asanas* (poses) in their disciplines. The original intent of Yoga, as written in the *Yoga Sutras,* was to reach a higher state of consciousness known as *Samadhi,* or oneness with God. The use of *asanas* is one of seven paths taken before reaching the eighth path of *Samadhi* (charted in Appendix E).

The best form of Yoga is whichever form suits each individual person. Once a person finds his or her style of Yoga, the benefits are virtually limitless. Some benefits include becoming more peaceful with oneself and with others, as well as achieving internal and external purity, contentment, austerity, and attainment of Samadhi. Improvements involve posture, mental attitude, concentration, strength, flexibility, balance, lung volume, spirituality, well-being, and a healthier immune system. Following the path of Yoga as originally intended through all eight *paths* (otherwise known as *sutras*), purification of the mind and body will occur over time. Practicing *asanas* may help detoxify the body, but many Yoga masters believe that practicing one path of Yoga is not really practicing Yoga. The eight paths of Yoga are:

1. *Yamas* — non-violence, truthfulness, moderation in all things, and non-covetousness
2. *Niyamas* — keeping the body and mind free of impurities, being austere, and studying the sacred texts
3. *Asanas* — postures for internal discipline
4. *Pranayama* — regulation and control of the breath
5. *Pratyahara* — withdrawal of the senses in order to still the mind
6. *Dharana* — concentration
7. *Dhyana* — meditation
8. *Samadhi* — achieving unity of self with all things

The first two paths of Yoga involve making a determination to set oneself on the yogic path, which begins with a commitment to positive living and being. Although practicing asana only constitute the third path, they are very useful to everyday meditators when combined with the breath (referred to as *prana*) and a focused mind. Moving through a series of poses is called a *vinyasa*. Where breath goes, energy will follow. In Yoga, energy is referred to as *shakti*, and the meditator's body is called *sushuma*. Being able to direct or control energy through the body by using the breath is what constitutes the fourth path, *pranayama*. The healing power of shakti can be very powerful once a yogi has perfected *pranayama* because the yogi can direct healing to any part of the body. This is why Yoga masters do not believe that a yogic pose by itself is Yoga, but rather, a combination of various paths that heals the body. Yoga is more effective if you have more than ten minutes a day to meditate, so if you do not have more than ten minutes a day, consider learning some yogic poses to aid your meditation and combine the third path (*asanas*) with the fourth path (*pranayama*), as this will help you eventually learn to direct energy throughout the body. This will prepare your body and mind for the fourth and fifth stages of the yogic path — quieting the mind (*pratyahara*) and concentration (*dharana*). Some of the more common forms of Yoga in the U.S. today are:

1. **Hatha Yoga** combines poses with pranayama (lengthening of the breath) and relaxation techniques. The most common reason people use Hatha Yoga is to reduce stress and achieve mental peace. Certain types of Yoga, such Kripalu Yoga and Lyengar Yoga are derivations of Hatha Yoga.

2. **Kundalini Yoga** helps open the energetic blockages that cause tension and other physical and emotional maladies. Kundalini Yoga involves meditation for the chakras, which combines a combination of poses, chanting, and *pranyama*.

3. **Ashtanga Vinyasa Yoga** helps build strength and power. Its exercises are useful for strengthening core muscles to prepare the body for longer meditative periods. Certain types of hot Yoga practices are derivations of Vinyasa Yoga.

4. **Bikram Yoga** considered the original form of hot Yoga, which involves a series of postures and breathing exercises in a room with a temperature set to 105 degrees Fahrenheit. Setting the

room to 105 degrees opens the pores and helps flush out toxins, increases oxygen flow to the cells, and improves blood flow in the body. To avoid confusion about hot Yoga, the general rule is that all Bikram is hot Yoga, but not all forms of hot Yoga qualify as Bikram Yoga. Be advised that dehydration is a potential danger that exists with Bikram or any other form of hot Yoga.

Setting Up the Energetic Openings

Negative thoughts, feelings, emotions, and behaviors diminish the body's natural energy and cause disease. Positive thoughts, feelings, emotions, and behaviors expand and generate the body's natural energy for healing. To reiterate, where breath goes, energy will follow. The more you breathe, stretch, exercise, and meditate, the more energy will begin to accumulate in your body. As energy begins to accumulate, the closer you come to tapping into a seemingly limitless energy source. The concept of healing the body through the accumulation and redirection of energy is what some meditation experts call *energy medicine*. Energy medicine unifies the rational, masculine, left-brain knowledge with intuitive, feminine, right-brain understanding. By balancing the masculine and feminine energies, the meditator comes to a deeper understanding of his or her life and creates healing.

Balancing these energy centers in the body requires treating energetic blockages wherever they exist. Old hurts and negative emotions create energetic blockages that imbalance the body intellectually, physically, emotionally, and spiritually. Therefore, one goal in your meditative practice should involve unblocking these energetic openings so that energy can flow free to do its healing work. For instance, kundalini Yoga involves the practice of awakening the divine feminine energy called the *kundalini*, which resides at the bottom of the spine. Once activated, the *kundalini* rises up through the spine and unblocks the energetic openings. The seven energetic openings along the spinal channel are called *chakras*. Each chakra, located at a different nodal point along the spinal column, vibrates at a different frequency. Meditators who awaken the kundalini typically describe it as a wellspring of energy that rises up the spine and bursts through the crown of the head, producing a feeling of ecstasy.

The Seven Chakras

Each of the seven chakras that exist along the spinal column influences the glands and organs surrounding it. They also possess the ability to transform the frequency of energy from emotional to spiritual or vice versa. The *chakras* are called energetic openings because they draw their energy from the universe. The word *chakra* means "wheel" in Sanskrit because the mystics believed the energy in them revolve as spinning energies or vortexes. An energetic blockage in one chakra can lead to blockages in the other chakras and interrupt their functioning and as well. The following diagram illustrates the seven chakras, along with their name, location, and purpose.

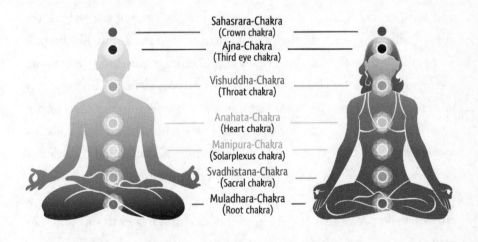

Sahasrara-Chakra
(Crown chakra)

Ajna-Chakra
(Third eye chakra)

Vishuddha-Chakra
(Throat chakra)

Anahata-Chakra
(Heart chakra)

Manipura-Chakra
(Solarplexus chakra)

Svadhistana-Chakra
(Sacral chakra)

Muladhara-Chakra
(Root chakra)

MAN MEDITATION
Padmasana/Lotus

WOMAN MEDITATION
Siddha Yoni Asana

Some meditators report being able to open the higher chakras, while the lower chakras remain closed. The lower chakras represent issues related to lower intentions, such as personal safety and well-being, while the higher chakras relate to higher intentions such as spiritual oneness and unconditional love. Lower chakras actually may be more difficult to open because of the personal issues associated with them. The first (or root) chakra is located between the anus and genitals, and it concerns personal safety. If the body is in a low vibratory state of fear, this chakra will not open until the mind-state of fear subsides. The second (sacral or splenic) chakra is located at the base of the spine (called the sacrum) and concerns creativity and emotional attachment. If the body is in a low vibratory state of clinging to either someone, something, or past regrets, then this chakra will not open until the person becomes present and releases from negative emotional attachments. The third (or solar plexus) chakra is located at the solar plexus and concerns feelings of empowerment. A body in a low vibratory state of disempowerment cannot find a way to release emotions that make the person feel small and insignificant. The fourth (or heart) chakra is located at the center of the chest near the heart. It is associated with love and self-esteem. If the body is in a low vibratory state of self-hatred, this chakra will not open until the person learns to stop punishing him/herself. The fifth (or throat) chakra is located at the center of the throat. It is associated with communication, self-expression, and confidence. A body in a low vibratory state of inexpressiveness cannot find a way to understand or deal with feelings such as mistrust or anger. The sixth (or third eye) chakra is located between the two eyes and relates to mental clarity and intuition. A body in a low vibratory state of mental cloudiness cannot make plans, solve problems, or get past preconceived and long-held beliefs. The seventh (or crown) chakra is located at the top of the head and relates to spiritual transcendence. A body in a low vibratory state of disconnection to spirit sees no God, no spirit, no meaning in anything, and no connection to anything but him/herself. Opening the seven corresponding chakras raises the vibratory levels of each energy body. Over time, or perhaps immediately, blockages fade and the meditator begins to experience an increased sense of security, creativity, detachment to emotional hurts, self-empowerment, self-esteem, confidence, mental and psychic clarity, and connection to spirit.

Because chakras govern certain parts of the anatomy, certain illnesses correspond with energetic blockages of certain chakras. If you have a particular illness and your doctor has identified where the problem is, consult the chart above to see which chakra might need unblocking. To set up the energetic openings for optimal functioning, the meditator needs to rebalance the chakras. For advice on awakening the *kundalini* to unblock the energetic openings, see the case study at the end of this chapter. Otherwise, try opening the chakras by using the following steps:

Step 1 — Opening the root chakra: Sit down in a chair or in a lotus position. Keep your back straight, your spinal column stacked upright, and avoid slouching. Bring your thumb and index finger on your right hand together until you feel a pulsation, and do the same for the left hand. To

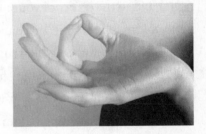

stimulate the root chakra, begin flexing the muscles located between the genitals and anus. With your mind, visualize the first chakra opening within this part of your body and repeatedly chant the sound "LAM."

Step 2 — Opening the abdomen: Sitting in kneeling position, place both hands on your lap while sitting in a chair or in a lotus position. Face both

palms upward, with one hand underneath the other and the tips of both thumbs touching each other. With your palms up and your hands near the abdominal or sacral area of your body, begin chanting the sound "VAM" and visualize the sacral chakra opening within your abdomen. Also, with the help of a Yoga instructor, try several hip opening postures, as these stretching techniques directly connect to the second chakra. The full lotus position is one such hip opening posture. Other hip opening exercises include the reclining butterfly, wide-legged forward bend, and warrior II (for a description of these hip exercises, see Appendix G).

Step 3 — Opening the solar plexus chakra: Raise both hands in front of your stomach. With fingers remaining straight, touch both hands together at the fingertips to form a triangle, and cross one thumb over the other thumb. Now close your eyes and visualize the third chakra opening within your solar plexus while repeatedly chanting the sound "RAM."

Step 4 — Opening the heart chakra: Sit with your legs crossed in a lotus position. Let the tips of the index finger and thumb on your right hand touch; then do the same for the left hand. With the index finger and thumb on both hands forming circles, place the right hand to the center of your breastbone. Next, place your left hand on your left knee, fingers still touching and the palm facing up or facing down. Close your eyes, smile, visualize the fourth chakra opening within your heart, and chant the sound "YAM." If you want to add a variation to this technique, obtain a piece of rose quartz (considered to hold a love energy) and hold it to your heart chakra as you say the words, "I accept and deserve love." Chant the mantra "Hu" repeatedly, bring the quartz to your lips, inhale, exhale, and say, "Thank you."

Step 5 — Opening the throat chakra: Sitting in kneeling position, let the tip of your left thumb touch the tip of your right thumb; then let the fingers of your right interlock with the fingers of your left hand. Close your eyes and visualize the chakra opening within your throat while chanting the sound "HAM."

Step 6 — Opening the third eye chakra: This chakra tends to close more than the other chakras due to pineal gland calcification. If you have taken the steps discussed in Chapter 3 to decalcify this gland, begin practicing the following technique for opening the third eye chakra. First, sit in a lotus position and let the tips of both middle fingers touch each other to form a triangle; let the thumbs touch each other as well. Then fold both index fingers down, allowing them to touch. Bring this hand formation to the lower part of your chest (roughly the same spot you brought your hand in the heart chakra opening). Close your eyes and visualize the third eye chakra opening between your eyes while chanting the sound "OM." As an additional technique, consider using binaural beats instead of chanting. Binaural beats (explored further in Chapter 5) are useful for chakra tuning, especially for third eye meditation.

Step 7 — Opening the crown chakra: The seventh chakra is the most spiritual. You need a strong foundation to open this chakra, so do not attempt to open it unless you have already opened the root. In fact, you should not attempt to release the kundalini through *kundalini* meditation unless you have tuned the root chakra. Many Yoga masters warn of dangers associated with following short cuts to third eye opening and improper *kundalini* release, so follow these instructions and consult with your teachers. Once you are ready to open the crown chakra, remain seated in a lotus position, place your hands at stomach level, clasp the fingers of your right and left hand together, and let the tips of your ring fingers touch to form a triangle. Close your eyes, chant the sound "NG," and visualize the seventh chakra opening at the top of your head.

CASE STUDY:
CHAKRAS AND THE
KUNDALINI PHENOMENON

Neil Crenshaw
Certified Meditation & Yoga Instructor
McIntosh, Florida
neilwc68@gmail.com
www.pureawareness.info
www.gobeyondmind-body.com

My favorite meditative posture is sitting with my legs crossed and wearing gloves, a blindfold, and earplugs to isolate myself from outside stimuli. I believe it is best to sit in an upright position and be as comfortable as possible. If this requires cushions, pillows, bolsters, etc., that is fine. It is best not to sit in a bothersome position that distracts from the meditative process. Sitting in a comfortable position reduces any possibility of injury to the spine. When the spine is stacked in vertical position, energy flows more freely. I begin every meditation with chakra breathing. This practice begins with the first chakra at the base of the spine. I visualize the chakra as a wheel with the axel of the wheel lying horizontal, from left to right, and the chakra looking much like a water wheel. The breath flows in at the bottom of the chakra and out at the top. Each breath turns the chakra and opens it further as I continue breathing.

The first chakra is very important because it lays the groundwork for the remaining chakras. It may take ten or 20 minutes of slow, rhythmic breathing at the first chakra before the breath moves up to the second chakra. For me, moving up the chakra system becomes automatic once the first chakra opens. Once I reach the seventh chakra, energy expands out the head into universal consciousness. I do not use a timer because I feel it would disturb the natural flow of energy. It may take 30 or 40 minutes to open all the chakras and about an hour or so remaining time in universal consciousness. Afterward, I usually come back into my body and go about my daily activities while attempting to stay in pure awareness as much as possible.

The first time I experienced the kundalini phenomenon was about ten years ago. I was meditating in a chair when a sudden a surge of energy rushed up my spine and out the top of my head. I have not had such a dramatic experience since that time, but I do experience smaller and varying degrees of kudalini almost every night. Typically, I will stand, press an acupuncture spot with my fingernail, and take short inhalations through the nose. After about 25 to 30 breaths, the kundalini moves up my body and finally out the top of the head. It is a very relaxing and energizing experience.

Beginning Core Meditation with Concentration

nce you have created an ambient environment, hammered out a flexible schedule, and prepared your body for meditation, it is time to begin your core meditation with concentration. In Chapter 2, we identified Concentration Meditation as the art of eliminating internal distractions so the mind can quiet the inner dialogue that clouds insight into the meaning of things. The ten-minute meditation format available at the end of this chapter is a good starting point for your meditative journey. However, the purpose of this book is not to confine you to a rigid practice, but to provide enough techniques to mix and match according to their individual benefits and your personal needs.

Chapters 5, 6, and 7 will cover the three core meditations (concentration, mindfulness, and lovingkindness) respectively. For now, practice the ten-minute format provided in these chapters before you begin to mix and match with your own ten-minute meditative recipe. For example, when you finish this chapter (or book depending on your preference), try practicing one core meditation per week over a period of three weeks. In week one, practice Concentration Meditation using the techniques you learned in this chapter. In week two, practice Mindfulness Meditation using the techniques you will learn in Chapter 6. In week three practice Lovingkindness Meditation, using those techniques will learn in Chapter 7. However, before beginning this exploration into the core meditations, it is important to understand the states of consciousness you will find yourself entering as you meditatively awaken.

The Four States of Consciousness

While Chapter 3 briefly covered the four types of brain waves measured by EEG (*beta, theta, alpha,* and *delta*), this chapter will define these states of consciousness further. To recap, beta is the state of consciousness where the mind is agitated and constantly thinking about what happened over the course of the day. An alpha state is a deepening state of relaxation in which the brain's electrical activity becomes more settled and the brain wave amplitudes grow bigger, slower, and more rhythmic. Theta is the point at which brain waves slow to the point where the body enters a state of light sleep. Delta is the point at which the body enters a state of deep sleep and the mind eventually begins dreaming. The table below illustrates the frequency and mental state of each EEG type.

EEG type	Occupied frequency bandwidth	Mental states & conditions
Delta	0.1Hz ~ 3Hz	deep, dreamless sleep, non-REM sleep, unconscious
Theta	4Hz ~ 7Hz	intuitive, creative, recall, fantasy, imagery, creative, dreamlike, switching thoughts, drowsy
Alpha	8Hz ~ 12Hz	eyes closed, relaxed, not agitated, but not drowsy, tranquil conscious
Low Beta	12Hz ~ 15Hz	formerly SMR, relaxed yet focused, integrated
Midrange Beta	16Hz ~ 20Hz	thinking, aware of self & surrounding
High Beta	21Hz ~ 30Hz	alertness, agitation

A person who has mastered meditation will typically fall within the theta category. With enough routine practice, these meditators can easily fall into theta states within ten minutes whereas beginning meditators might need more time to focus and clear the mind. This is why focusing on one practice at a time—concentration in the first week, mindfulness in the second week, and lovingkindness in the third week—makes more sense than trying to do different things in one session. Without practicing concentration, beginners also tend to fall asleep in the middle of meditating. However, this can happen for a number of reasons that may nothing to do with depth of practice. For example, a meditator might be dealing with sleep apnea, jumpy legs syndrome, or physical exhaustion. All things being equal, meditation will relax the mind because of its slowing effect on brain waves.

Beta Consciousness

The purpose of understanding brainwave consciousness is to be able to identify the moments when your consciousness has shifted into a new pattern during meditation. This will become especially useful during Mindfulness Meditation . Brainwaves are also important to Concentration Meditation because noticing a shift in consciousness can often be your signal to begin a new technique. It can also serve as a signal to shift from Concentration Meditation to either mindfulness or lovingkindness. When you begin a meditation, you will most likely always begin in beta consciousness. The purpose of Concentration Meditation is to quiet the mind and move your brainwaves out of beta. Beta consciousness equals left-brained consciousness because the left hemisphere of the brain controls linear, analytical thinking. Beta waves emit between 14 and 30 cycles per second, the amplitudes are faster, and the mind is in an alert state of thinking. While thinking is an important part of life and problem solving, its consequences come in the forms of distractions and emotional turbulence. Beta consciousness is the mind-state that the average person experiences shortly after waking until just after bedtime. It is also characterized by high energy consumption whereby the body must divert resources to many different places. At the same time, it is a low vibratory energy because it often inspires fear, anger, and ego drive. This, of course, is not an ideal state for meditation. By default, most people spend most of their lives in beta consciousness. That translates into a majority of the day exposed to the consequences of thinking in beta consciousness.

Not everyone, however, spends most of their time in beta consciousness. Depending on how stressful your life is, you may actually alternate between beta and alpha. For example, people who experience periods of stress throughout the day marked by short periods of relaxation typically shift from beta (alert and active) to alpha (relaxed and tranquil), back to beta, and so forth. During the day, it is important to try to set aside moments of relaxation, even if you have a high stress life or job. The reason for this necessity is simple. The body naturally experiences 90-minute cycles of high and low energy during the day. If the body does not rest during the low ebbs, mental, and physical fatigue will set in more quickly. Consider the fact that beta creates low vibratory energies like fear and anger and combine that with high-energy consumption. If you are someone who values productivity, you could wind up being more productive and less exhausted by simply recognizing when you have hit low energy and taking five minutes to complete a breathing exercise.

Alpha Consciousness

You may recall an earlier an earlier discussion about how the body, when engaged in the stress response, is always striving to return to the relaxation response. The same concept holds true for the body's brain waves. When the mind is in delta, it is always striving to return to alpha. Alpha consciousness is the point at which the mind begins to relax and burn less energy. Just as beta consciousness equals left brained, linear analytical consciousness, alpha consciousness, equals right-brained intuitive, emotion sensing consciousness. The mind wants to descend back into alpha consciousness because that is the mind-state whereby it can become so inactive that it rejuvenates itself. Even if your only goal in meditation is to serve a lower intention (such as recharging for mental clarity), meditating for ten minutes will accomplish just that.

The shift into alpha consciousness can happen very rapidly by slowly inhaling and exhaling a few deep breaths. Because alpha consciousness equals right-brained, intuitive, emotion-sensing consciousness, you will know you have reached this mind-state when you begin to feel an emotion rather than attempt to define it. Difficulties that come with trying to fall into beta usually occur when the mind is trying to focus on two different things. For example, if you attempt to have a conversation with another meditator while listening to ambient music, your mind will remain in beta because you are keeping the mind's beta components active. Alpha is a state of "being" rather than a state of "doing." Because alpha consciousness protects the mind from returning to linear thought, time is removed from the equation. In a state of "being," the mind has no concern of the past or the future, where the ego creates worry and inner dialogue as a form of defense. This is why Concentration Meditation comes first in meditative practice. Alpha consciousness is the gateway into the meditative state. If you cannot concentrate and keep the mind focused on a mentally simplified state, you cannot enter alpha consciousness. If you cannot enter alpha consciousness, every technique you attempt will fail in its purpose. Upon reaching a deep alpha consciousness, the meditator begins to experience "watching thoughts, emotions, and sensations with detachment."

This is not to say that awareness in alpha consciousness is nonexistent. In actuality, awareness develops in several stages as you move through different states of consciousness. One familiar characteristic of alpha is the way thoughts begin to enter the mind in more random fashion. While random thoughts may differ from the object you have chosen to cultivate concentration from (e.g. your breath), it is important to be aware of these random thoughts in an equally detached manner. Even in deeper states of beta consciousness that begin to border alpha, the mind is still aware of its own thoughts as being distractions. For example, you might say to yourself, "I can't forget to pay that bill tomorrow." In beta, you can choose to continue thinking about that bill you have to pay, or you can choose to let the thought go. As we will see in our exploration of Concentration Meditation, naming a distraction during beta consciousness is an effective technique for letting go and returning to focus. Another way to extract yourself from thoughts during beta is to return your focus to your breath. Focusing back to the breath means turning away from beta thoughts and returning to the beginnings of alpha consciousness sensations. However, one pitfall of slipping into alpha consciousness occurs when the focus on breath becomes so intense that awareness actually begins to wane. As we explore Concentration Meditation further, you will begin to see how to avoid this potential pitfall.

Theta Consciousness

In beta consciousness, the mind is unable to focus on two different things without triggering ego and inner dialogue. In alpha consciousness, the mind can focus on multiple thoughts and sensations without feeling taken away from true focus. Passing thoughts now become just that, passing thoughts free of the emotional baggage that comes with them. As the mind enters deeper states of quiet focus, it eventually reaches the initial stages of theta consciousness. In theta, the mind becomes more expansive. As the mind becomes disengaged from the body, internal and external stimuli cease to become distractions. Having distanced itself from the ego, the mind gains new perspectives about life from its newly acquired vantage point outside the prison of the mind. In the wake of this liberation, what begins to emerge is curiosity and pleasure. Meditators in theta consciousness often report lucid dream imagery, the rise of deeply buried emotions and memories, timelessness, and self-revelations. Concentration Meditation is crucial to leaving late frequency range beta and entering early frequency range alpha. It remains crucial during the mid-frequency ranges of alpha but less so as you enter the late stages of alpha into the initial frequency range of theta. You will know you have entered into the initial stages of theta when focus becomes effortless and nothing takes you away from it. However, it is during mid-range theta frequency that the body and mind is at most risk of falling asleep. For this reason, the focus of meditation should shift from concentration to awareness. As we explore Mindfulness Meditation in the next chapter, you will begin to see how to avoid the pitfall of falling asleep during this dream-like stage.

Delta Consciousness

Delta consciousness exhibits the lowest frequency of the four brainwaves. This is the point at which astral project, divine vibration, and third eye meditation are all possible. Buddhists describe divine vibration as the true state of being, third eye meditation as the spiritual channel of the inner mind's eye, and astral projection as an out-of-body experience whereby your spirit encounters and communes with other spirit entities. During astral projection you might float through walls, penetrate other dimensions, or instantly teleport to other parts of the universe. During dream sleep, Buddhists believe that this is what our spirits are doing anyway. As the mind leaves theta and enters the early-range delta frequency, not falling asleep becomes even more challenging, and requires maintaining awareness and mindfulness. In delta consciousness, the most deeply transcending experiences of universal love may occur. This is where meditators who managed reach the mid-range theta frequency often begin their Lovingkindness Meditation. Not only can the practice of lovingkindness help maintain awareness as the mind enters early-range delta frequency, it also can deepen the practice of sending and receiving love. You can practice lovingkindness in alpha as well, but the effect of Lovingkindness Meditation is more likely to amplify in a mind-state where you encounter a divine vibration.

Using Binaural Beats to Alter Consciousness

Another way to move your consciousness into altered states is by using headphones and listening to binaural beats. Binaural beats are auditory tones used to facilitate brainwave entrainment by creating two slightly different audio waves in each ear. Listening to both tones together generates a specific unified brain wave pattern, which correlates to each of the four states of consciousness (beta, alpha, delta, and theta). Discovered by Heinrich Wilhelm Dove in 1839, binaural beats became the subject of scientific experimentation in the early 1970s when physicist Thomas Warren Campbell used them to alter subjects' mental states. During this time, Dr. Gerald Oster presented a paper in *the Scientific American* with findings that showed binaural beats improved medical conditions such as Parkinson's disease. The use of binaural beats became a mainstream phenomenon when double-blind, controlled research in the 90s linked the use of binaural beats to:

1. Weight loss
2. Smoking cessation
3. Sleepiness
4. Detached awareness
5. Reduction in depression and stress
6. Changes in consciousness
7. Increased energy flow,
8. Heightened focus and memory
9. Heightened creativity
10. Heightened intuition

Binaural beats can help you achieve a deeper state of consciousness or a more alert consciousness if you so choose. How can you tell which binaural beats create beta, alpha, theta, and delta mind-states? While most online stores that sell binaural beats will provide the information, the best way to tell is to find out, if possible, the frequency of both tones and divide the difference. For example, if one audio wave registers at 240 hertz and one at 244 hertz, the brain synchronizes the difference between the waves at 4 hertz. To determine which state of consciousness this beats produces, you would refer back to the frequency table provided earlier in this chapter. In this case, 4 hertz is a late-range theta wave bordering on delta consciousness. Therefore, a mental state of intuition and creativity bordering on a feeling of universal love is the effect produced by the beats. If your intention is to become extremely alert and awake for performance reasons, you might look for binaural beats producing beta consciousness. If your intention is to practice Concentration Meditation in an alpha state, you might look for binaural beats that produce alpha consciousness. For Mindfulness Meditation , binaural beats that produce theta might be most effective. For Lovingkindness Meditation, you might look for beats that produce delta waves. Keep in mind that binaural beats only form when two tones are less than 26 hertz apart. Some binaural beats specifically work for the purpose of opening and balancing the seven chakras. Using binaural beats in this regard is a great way to prepare the body for core meditation by cleansing the energetic openings of any blockages. Binaural beats designed for opening and balancing the seven chakras will contain a different frequency for each chakra, starting with the root and working up toward the crown. If you listen to beats for chakra cleansing, direct your concentration on both the sound of the beat and the corresponding chakra region. As you do so, feel the circular, pulsing energy of the chakra growing at the center of the region.

There are no negative effects of using binaural beats; however, inappropriate use of beats in conjunction with certain activities can be very dangerous. For example, using binaural beats to create a mind-state that causes sleepiness right before getting behind the wheel of a car endangers the driver and other people on the road. This is why it is important to make sure that the beats creating certain mind-states correspond to the activity and intention. In addition, overusing binaural beats can lead a meditator to burn out on brainwave entrainment to the point where the beats are no longer effective. For this reason, meditation experts recommend using binaural beats no longer than one hour a day. The best way to use binaural beats depends on when and how you want to alter consciousness. For someone just starting out, listening 15 minutes a day might produce enough benefits. For advanced meditators looking to increase the length and depth of meditative practice, 60 minutes a day might work better. Binaural beats are available on Youtube channels (www.youtube.com) courtesy of uploaders who also use them. If you want to download binaural beats as an mp3 file or buy as CDs, several online stores include:

1. The Unexplainable Store® **www.unexplainablestore.com**
2. MindSync **www.worldofalternatives.com**
3. Meditation Power **www.meditation-power.com**
4. HoloThink **http://holothink.com**
5. EquiSync® **http://eocinstitute.org/meditation**
6. BrainSync **www.brainsync.com**
7. Immrama Institute **www.immrama.org/order.html**

Beginning Core Meditation with Concentration

As a beginning meditator, you should practice meditating for concentration for at least one week before moving on to other forms of meditation. Getting started is very easy. After you assume the meditative position of your choice (lotus, sitting, kneeling, etc.), soften and close your eyes, relax your face and jaw, and begin the techniques for opening the seven chakras. Since this practice involves focusing on each individual chakra, you have already begun to use a form of Concentration Meditation. Doing so will help slow the mind into mid-stage beta consciousness where you become relaxed and the mind's inner dialogue begins to slow down. Concentration Meditation involves singular, focused concentration on a thought, sensation, object, or idea. What should be the focus of your attention?

1. **Thought:** You might focus on a mantra that calms the mind. Mantras are affirmations based on energy and create thought waves. Examples of mantras include the sacred word *Om*—the spoken essence of the universe pronounced in three sounds (a), (u), and (m)—or any positive affirmation that resonates with you, such as *I am free from anger,* or *I am happy and safe.*

2. **Sensation:** You might focus on the rising and falling of your chest or abdomen as you breathe in and out. You also can focus on the sensation your breath creates as it passes in and out of your body.

For example, simply notice the feeling of your breath as it passes through your nostrils or brushes your upper lip.

3. **Object:** This may involve open-eye meditation on an object in front of you or visualizing an object in the mind. Your meditation object might be a point on your body, the flame of a candle, a flower, or some other object in your meditative space that you find pleasing.

4. **Idea:** You might focus on a particular passage from the Bible or Qur'an, a poem or other inspirational quote or text. Just be sure to keep the idea or passage short.

Regardless of which you choose, the goal is to deliberately direct your entire focus on one thing. The idea of sitting still and thinking about one single thing might seem easy at first glance, but it can be difficult to do in beta

consciousness. First, you must get past that part of your social conditioning that believes "just sitting" means being lazy. Meditation requires giving yourself permission to exercise your mind. You are not wasting time with meditation or taking time away from another "more important" activity.

Ten-Minute Concentration Exercise No. 1: Using the Mind Quieting Technique as Your First Sitting Meditation

1. **Choose a space that is tidy and free of distractions.** A meditation room is nice but not necessary. You can choose a quiet, tidy corner of any room or even a corner of your yard.

2. **Set a timer for at least ten minutes. Use an alarm clock, cell phone, or a kitchen timer.** Setting a timer is especially helpful in the beginning when one minute can seem longer than it usually feels. Eliminate the worry about how time is passing by attending to this detail before you sit. If no timer is available, the Insight Meditation Center (**www.insight meditationcenter.org**) offers several meditation timers for online purchase. Sharper Image also sells alarm clocks with earth tones that slowly grow louder in cadence.

3. **Sit comfortably.** Remove or loosen any restrictive clothing, shoes, or jewelry. Give special attention to your posture, eyes, mouth, hands, and feet. The following list offers a guide to positioning your body during meditation. Remember that the following only offers a guide, so adjust as needed. Ultimately, what matters is how comfortable you are in your body as you sit

4. **Posture:** Posture is the foundation for effective breathing, which will be the foundation of your meditation practice. As you sit, you should be comfortably erect with the chin tucked in, with your spine lined up straight from the base to the crown of your head.

5. **Eyes:** You might choose to meditate with your eyes open or closed. With open eyes, adopt a soft, unfocused gaze. Simply fix your eyes on a point about four to six feet in front of you. If you choose to close your eyes, be aware that this choice often leads to feelings of sleepiness. Posture will be particularly important for supporting alertness if you meditate with your eyes closed.

6. **Mouth:** You can hold your mouth slightly open or closed. What is most important is that your jaw is relaxed. Place your tongue comfortably behind your teeth.

7. **Hands:** If you are sitting in a chair, rest your hands comfortably on your thighs. On the floor, cross your legs and rest your arms and hands on your thighs.

8. **Feet:** If sitting in a chair, place your feet firmly on the floor. Do not cross your legs or ankles. If sitting, consult the illustrations in Chapter 3 to make sure your sitting position is correct.

9. **Breathe normally.** As you sit, begin with one or two deep exhalations to calm and settle yourself into this time. With each breath, you might even want to inhale through the nose and exhale through the mouth. Loud exhales through the mouth affirm feelings of relief and can help you settle into a more relaxed state. After the deep breaths, you have nothing to do but breathe normally; no special breathing is required.

10. **Focus attention on your breath.** Your mind will wander; that is all right. Each time your focus moves beyond your breath, gently bring it back to an awareness of each breath as it moves in and out of your body. Sometimes, it can be helpful to label or count the breaths. For example, as you inhale you might hear the word rising in your head, or you might say inwardly, "exhale," "falling," or "out" as the breath moves out of your body. You might also count each in and out breath cycle to keep your mind focused only on your breathing. It does not matter if you need to do this 200 times. Each time your mind wanders, resist the urge to judge or scold yourself. Instead, simply refocus your attention on your breath. It does not matter if your mind wanders as you begin; expect that it will. It only matters that you start sitting.

Advanced Breathing for Concentration

As you can see from the exercise above, breathing for concentration requires more than just regular, anaerobic breathing. Exercise No. 1, however, is a very rudimentary breathing technique. There are a number of different breathing exercises that can enhance concentration by relaxing the body. By concentrating on breathing, the mind slows down and begins to match the other rhythms of the body. In other words, the breath begins to synchronize everything. The counting technique is another preliminary exercise that you should use as you spend the first week on Concentration Meditation.

Ten-Minute Concentration Exercise No. 2: The Counting Technique

1. **Experiment with the meditation positions and try holding them for ten minutes.** If you can hold one of the lotus positions comfortably, use it for this exercise. If not, sitting in a chair or kneel with a seiza bench to support your knees.

2. **Set a timer for at least ten minutes.**

3. **Close your eyes, take a few deep breaths, and exhale slowly.** Do not try to control your breath; it is better to let your breath find its own rhythm.

4. **Once your breathing has found its natural rhythm, begin counting each inhale and exhale.** Count each breath until you reach ten. You can do this in two ways. The first way, count "1" on the inhale, "2" on the exhale, "3" on the inhale, "4" on the exhale, and so forth. The second way, disregard counting the exhales and count "1" on the first inhale, "2" on the second inhale, "3" on the third inhale, and so forth.

5. **Extend the numbers as you whisper them in your mind.** Obviously, it is impossible to whisper numbers aloud while breathing, and if you tried, it would become distracting. By mentally counting the numbers and extending them for the length of the inhale and exhale, you can synchronize the counting with the breath. For example, as you begin the inhale, you would think "onennnnn." On the exhale, you would "twoooooo," and on the next inhale, "threeeeee..."

6. **If you lose track while counting, simply start again.** It does not matter how many times you lose track; each time you lose track the mind is learning about concentration.

During these two breathing exercises, thoughts occasionally will arise and claim your attention. When a pleasing thought arises, the temptation is to stay with it because the beginning meditator assumes that this is the point of meditation. Good feelings are important, but they are not the main goal of Concentration Meditation. Any thought, emotion, or sensation that arises during meditation will inevitably fade and give way to a new thought, emotion, or sensation. The point is not to hold on to them, but to notice them, and let them pass. Meditators who dwell in pleasing thoughts, emotions, or sensation during beta consciousness try hard to hold on to them. What ultimately occurs is frustration when they eventually pass, which gives way to anger if the next thought, emotion, or sensation is troubling. Do not examine any of these things while in beta consciousness. If you do, the inner dialogue will grow louder to the point where it has consumed your attention and it becomes harder to return to focus. Simply let these thoughts, emotions, or sensations go without judging or examining them, and return to the in-and-out breath.

Ten-Minute Concentration Exercise No. 3: The Breath Wave

1. **Set a timer for at least ten minutes.**

2. **Lie down in a corpse pose.** You cannot perform this exercise in a sitting position because it requires expansion of the belly, which sitting can limit or impair. To execute the corpse pose, lay down a tatami matt or lie in bed.

3. **Close your eyes, take a deep breath by breathing through the nose and expanding the stomach like a balloon on the inhale.** The emphasis of the inhale should be breathing into and oxygenating the pelvic area.

4. **Let the chest rise slightly just before the end of the inhale.** Do not let the chest rise too much at the end of the inhale. Keep the movement of breath in the high chest shallow, remembering that most of the movement should be in the stomach, not the diaphragm. In many ways, your focus is the lower half your body, in concert with your breath.

5. **Exhale through the nose.** Keep the respiratory and stomach muscles relaxed on the exhale. Do not worry about expelling all the air out of the lungs. Before you lie down in corpse pose, try this breathing technique standing up or sitting and watch how the front of your body creates an undulating "wave" that rises and falls.

The breath wave is more than just a technique for concentrating. It opens the respiratory system which allows the body to deliver oxygen to areas that normally receive little amounts due to restricted breathing patterns. Yoga uses a variation of this technique whereby the meditator expands the stomach like a balloon on one inhale, and then, without exhaling, contracts the stomach muscles inward to force oxygen up the spinal column and into the chest. Expanding oxygen into the pelvic area and sending it up to the diaphragm in this manner cleanses the body from the root chakra to the crown chakra. This is why a Yoga instructor might instruct you to use the respiratory muscles to "send the breath" into an area of the body that may feel tension during a long-held yogic pose. Oxygen has a healing quality that eliminates pain. The flow of breath in this way raises the vibrational frequency of the body, clearing away thoughts, emotions, and sensations caused from being in a low vibratory state of being.

If you wish to cleanse the body further, use the yogic variation to exhale through the mouth instead of the nose at the end of each breath. Continue exhaling through the mouth, contracting the diaphragm as much as you can, thus pushing the air forcefully out of the lungs. When there appears to be no more air left to exhale, push a little harder until you achieve a wheezing sound. Take a moment to inhale regularly to recover, and then repeat this process again. The effect achieved by this exercise is expelling the lungs of any stale air that has accumulated from limited breathing and oxygen distribution over long periods. To determine if your lungs have stale air, or if your

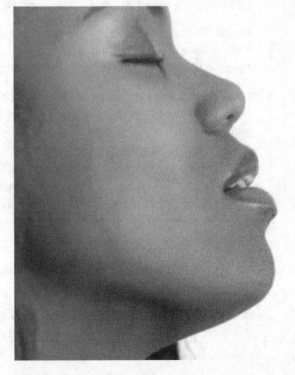

body needs more oxygen distribution, start monitoring the trends in how you normally breathe. If your breathing is too short or shallow, then you are not distributing or expelling enough oxygen throughout your body. In this case, consider adding the breath wave to your ten-minute meditation as a precursor to breathing for concentration.

Ten-Minute Concentration Exercise No. 4: Breath Motion Synchronization

1. **Set a timer for at least ten minutes.**

2. **Stand upright, feet together, hands at your side, and close your eyes.** You will remain standing throughout the duration of this exercise.

3. **Begin the breathing technique in exercise 1, this time standing instead of sitting.** Begin with a deep exhalation through the nose, but as you do so, slowly raise both arms up in a "sun salutation." A sun salutation is the motion you make with both arms whereby the arms extend away from your hips as you raise them, similar to a flapping motion. As you slowly raise both arms to the sky, gently lift your chin so your head is tilting upward by the time your hands meet above your head.

4. **Exhale through the mouth.** As you exhale, begin to bring your hands and chin downward in the same motion you brought them up. When both hands reach the side, begin the next inhale and repeat the process.

5. **Keep the focus of attention on the synchronicity between the movement of your body and your breath.** When your mind wanders, gently bring it back to an awareness of this synchronicity. Once you have tried this exercise a few times, consider adding another wrinkle by incorporating the counting technique where by you inwardly synchronize the words "inhale" and "exhale" with the movement of the sun salutation. You could also inwardly use the counting technique instead of thinking words.

Beginning meditators usually find this exercise to be one of the more powerful antidotes to mind chatter because of the results often felt within a single practice. Breath motion synchronization is about incorporating any type of motion in concert with breathing techniques. The sun salutation is just one type of motion for this exercise. It can be something as simple as moving one hand back and forth. In breath motion synchronization, the object of attention does not even have to be the breath. For instance, you might start paying attention to the breath, and then focus on sensations such as pulse rate, the sound of your breathing, or a bodily sensation that naturally arises from the practice. As an alternative, try closing both eyes and visualizing bodily motion as you breathe if this sounds like too many things to do at once.

The Role of Hypnosis in Meditation

Although psychologists have been practicing hypnotherapy in some form or another for the past 130 years, many people today still regard the term with some degree of suspicion. Despite very few abuses of the practice, people tend to doubt its efficacy or fear the idea of being under someone else's suggestion. In reality, hypnosis is markedly similar to meditation, and in some cases, may work well if practiced together. If you suffer from a severe anxiety disorder, a certified hypnotherapist can help you find ways to relax using proven methods. The purpose of hypnosis is to direct the mind toward solving a difficult problem or relieving an overwhelming emotional state. Hiring a professional to address an emotional state resulting from serious trauma is something you should consider anyway.

If you decide that you need professional help, but also want to meditate as a form of self-help, hypnotherapy might work as a reliable CAM therapy. In fact, hypnotherapists often prescribe meditation as a form of additional treatment. The reason is because using hypnotherapy can improve meditative practice, and practicing meditation can improve your sessions in hypnotherapy. Keep in mind that hypnotherapy does not involve making people do things they would normally be unwilling to do. Its methods are not a form of mind control. Rather, it is a way of exploring hidden emotions and memories or assisting the mind back to its naturally desired resting state. Those who would be determined to seek out a hypnotherapist should contact the American Council of Hypnotist Examiners (ACHE). The council, with its membership of more than 9,500 certified hypnotherapists, holds its members to strict educational, training, and licensure requirements. The ACHE is a state and federally recognized organization that holds conferences yearly. If you contact the ACHE, ask for a list of hypnotherapists with Level 5 or Level 6 certification. For further information on the American Council of Hypnotist Examiners, go to **http:// hypnotistexaminers.org/**.

Auditory Meditation

Most beginning meditators find themselves in a serious struggle with distractions when they first begin to meditate. One technique for reducing the impact of internal or external distractions is to name the distraction. The first wave of distractions for beginning meditators typically comes in the form of external stimuli. This may be something as faint as a voice on the street, the general hum of traffic, or a bird chirping outside. One effective method for eliminating external stimuli as a distraction is to make external stimuli the object of focus. This is the practice of auditory meditation. The beauty of this meditation is that it requires no specific position or space, and is a good way of turning any discomforting environment (such as a subway ride) to your benefit. Sit down, lie down, or stand. Close both eyes or keep them open, just find a spot to rest your gaze. Follow your breath for a few minutes using any of the breathing techniques that suit your situation. After focusing on the breath, turn your attention to the sounds around you. Some sounds may be close while others may be distant. You do not need to respond to these sounds, just let them continue or fade as they please. Notice the change in cadence or intensity. Notice two sounds at the same time, then switch to focusing on one of them and vice versa. Passively hearing sounds has a hypnotic effect that eventually settles the mind and moves it through beta consciousness.

Naming your Distractions

As you settle into meditation and move through beta consciousness, the external distractions are more likely to fade because you have begun the process of turning inward. Turning inward means opening up to the internal distractions that might have been just background noise in your consciousness. The sound of that bird chirping is no longer distracting, but the sound of your inner voice is louder than before. You cannot continually focus on distractions, but you cannot continue to ignore them either, especially if inner distractions carry important messages that eventually need your attention. Being able to name your distractions can reduce their power in your mind, so you can limit the time they take away from your focus. For example, if you hear the bird chirping outside, tell yourself (in your mind), "bird chirping." If an inner voice starts replaying an argument with your spouse, say (in your mind), "argument with spouse." If the naming technique does not quiet the distractions, try naming the emotions. For example, if a spousal argument becomes a distraction, ask yourself how this argument made you feel while you were having it. In your mind, name the feeling associated with the memory of this argument. Whether the feeling is anger, despair, frustration, or some other emotion, naming it satisfies the subconscious emotions trying to reach the surface in the form of conscious thought. If you allow the subconscious to express itself, the distraction is more likely to dissipate. In other cases, you may feel a distraction related to a bodily sensation. If a painful sensation related to your position becomes too great, either stick with the sensation to see if it passes or stop meditating. To see if it passes, try naming the sensation repeatedly in the mind for at ten or 15 seconds before deciding to stop.

Ten-Minute Concentration Exercise No. 5: Releasing Thoughts Meditation

1. **Set a timer for at least ten minutes.**

2. **Lie down in corpse pose and leave your eyes open or let them close.** If you leave them open, find a spot ceiling to rest your gaze.

3. **Begin breathing in a normal way, feeling the inhale and exhale.** Center your attention on breathing through the nose. Feel the sensation and (in your mind) say the word "breath" for each inhale and exhale.

4. **When a thought arises, say (in your mind) the words "not breath."** Even if the thought is pleasing, saying the words trains the mind to resist even good distractions. No matter how many positive or negative thoughts arise, the entire purpose of this exercise is to learn detachment by acknowledging thoughts as not belonging to focus.

5. **At the end of ten minutes, get up and continue your day.**

Inner Quieting with Big Mind Meditation

As we have learned, quieting the mind means going into a deeper state of consciousness. We have also learned that distractions cannot be ignored forever and, at some point, have to be dealt with. This is what makes auditory meditation an effective means of confronting and quieting external distractions. If you can directly confront the external distractions using auditory meditation, how do you confront inner voice? If you need an alternative to naming distractions as a means of quieting the inner voice, the answer is big mind meditation. Big mind meditation involves the process of provoking a conversation with your thoughts and allowing your thoughts to express whatever they please. This form of meditation requires some degree of visualization, so imagine that a central brain (or big mind) controls all the conscious and subconscious voices running through your head. The trick here is to remain respectful of the big mind and talk to it like an equal. Your goal is to convince the big mind that while you may disagree on things, you both have mutual interests. Whatever benefits you also benefits the big mind. Whatever hurts you also hurts the big mind. Once you have gained the big mind's trust, ask the big mind for permission to control the conscious and subconscious thoughts it currently controls. What you are asking the big mind is to have control over yourself. At this point, visualize the big mind giving you control. Using that control, you begin talking to the voices. They listen because you now control them. You visualize changing old dialogues, negative thought patterns, habitual behaviors, and thus undesirable things about yourself. Since you now have access to the central brain, you have access to files you can now erase. If two voices arise that present two sides of an argument, allow them a fair hearing and work as an arbitrator to reach a conclusion that both sides can live with. Working through problems this way can sometimes quiet inner voices that will not go away until you have satisfied them with a solution.

Keeping a Journal

A journal is important for several reasons. It also allows you to reflect on your previous meditation and set an intention for the next one. When reflecting on previous sessions, it is important to remember that self-judgment is not part of meditative progress. At the beginning of your meditative journal, it may be helpful to record inner dialogue that arises during meditation. When a thought comes and goes, it probably does not need much attention. However, any thoughts that continue to arise during meditation will need special attention, and it is a good idea to write them down to see if a recurring theme exists. The best time to write in a journal is when your mind feels most alert, analytical, and open to observations. In other words, the best time to write in a journal is in beta consciousness, when thoughts are moving and arising at a faster pace. Exploring inner dialogue through a journal is a good way to figure out the intention you want to set for the next session. After devoting one week of practice to each of the three core meditations, use a journal to customize your own ten-minute meditation. Based on your intentions, customize each session by mixing-and-matching the techniques learned in this chapter as well as the chapters to come.

CASE STUDY: FOCUS AND VISUALIZATION WITH TONGLEN

Will Ryken
St. Petersburg Shambhala Center
willryken@gmail.com
http://stpetersburg.shambhala.org

Beginning meditators often will find that practicing Concentration Meditation will overlap with Mindfulness Meditation and Lovingkindness Meditation. Tonglen, for example, is a meditative form of lovingkindess that I frequently practice, but it involves concentrating on people and visualizing breath. Tonglen practitioners send and receive the breath by visualizing an exhale as hot, thick darkness, and an inhale as cool, weightless, and refreshing breath. Since Tonglen is a form of Lovingkindness Meditation, the meditator will typically practice breathing in peoples' suffering and concentrating on sending fresh, healing air to the objects of the practice. In this practice, we begin with people that we love, continue by concentrating on people that we feel have neutral feelings for, and finally to people that we may not like. It is important to begin Tonglen with Concentration Meditation so that we begin with a settled mind.

Whichever meditation you set down to practice, the most important thing is to begin with Concentration Meditation so that you have a settled mind. Sometimes this involves meditating with our eyes open and having a soft gaze. That way, we are practicing to become more awake to our world. We then make a connection with our bodies by simply feeling ourselves being relaxed and present. We bring our attention to the breath by feeling the breath coming in and going out. When a strong thought or emotion breaks concentration, we gently bring ourselves back to our breathing. We are not trying to stop thinking! There are no good or bad thoughts during meditation; we are simply using the practice to strengthen the mind to be in the present moment.

At the beginning of practice, you may notice that your mind is more active and that meditation makes the chatter worse. The more you try to quiet the inner chatter the wilder the mind gets. Watching thoughts with detachment and returning to your breath focus will increase your ability to return to an object of concentration over time. I have found that most beginning meditators come to the meditation with too many immediate expectations. Buddhist master Trungpa Rinpoche once said that more people have reached enlightenment at the sound of the gong ending the sitting session than during the practice itself. The benefits of the practice show up more in our lives outside of sitting because we have strengthened the mind to be more awake to the present moment. Our senses touch us more and we begin to enjoy our lives in the simple things we do, seeing the world with new eyes. It is amazing how the world changes when we are awake at this very moment.

Continuing Core Meditation with Mindfulness

fter you have spent your first week of meditation on developing concentration, your second week will involve developing mindfulness. Mindfulness Meditation, which is the second core practice, involves conscious attention to the present experience. While Concentration Meditation involves the practice of letting go of thoughts, emotions, and sensations, mindfulness involves the practice of exploring them. In other words, whatever is happening now, whatever comes to occupy the mind, should remain the object of attention until it fades from consciousness. When Gautama Buddha first introduced Mindfulness Meditation to his students, he instructed them to develop four types of awareness:

1. Awareness of the body and sensations
2. Awareness of thoughts
3. Awareness of emotions
4. Awareness of the relationship between things

By developing awareness in four ways, Buddha reasoned, the meditator could unlock answers as to why the mind creates suffering. By directing attention to difficult emotions, the meditator eventually develops a penetrating insight, which he or she uses to correct the pattern. In the first few centuries after Christ, Indian culture developed this practice into a form of meditation called *tantra*. Tantra is a meditative practice that uses the sensory experience to gain spiritual realization. In fact, some tantric practices deliberately awaken the *kundalini* as part of this process. Whether you choose to awaken the *kundalini* or not, you will use mindfulness to take an important evolutionary step in your practice. It is the point in meditation where the mind truly begins to dwell inward after quieting down and becoming focused. So the question is, at which point do you stop practicing concentration and begin practicing mindfulness? As the case study in the previous chapter noted, some degree of overlap exists between concentration, mindfulness, and Lovingkindness Meditation. To some extent, welcoming thoughts and letting them pass without judgment during periods of concentration is mindfulness. It may not constitute a full-fledged attempt to explore inward, but you are still using awareness to bring your attention back to concentration. In short, the answer really depends on you.

When the mind stops judging and begins concentrating with ease, and when you recognize (with mindfulness) your descent into deep alpha and theta consciousness, you can begin Mindfulness Meditation . At that point, be ready to begin exploring the inner experience by shifting your focus from concentration to awareness of content. Remember that meditation is not about shunning negative feelings that build up within. Until you confront buried emotions, no amount of avoidance behavior is going to make your problems disappear. Most people who repress painful memories and emotions pay a price

mentally, physically, and socially over time. Until they learn to release the negative energy accumulated by the chakras and expose the source of their suffering, they continue to move through life without a compass, bumping into one another without understanding why.

How to Explore the Inner Experience

After concentration becomes effortless, the following meditative guidelines will help you turn your attention inward in a way that promotes mindfulness. First, it is important to forget about trying to decipher the meaning of thoughts and emotions at the outset. To do this, consider expanding awareness to bodily sensations. Instead of looking for meaning, simply acknowledge to yourself that this is a thought you are experiencing. If an unpleasant thought arises, and you begin to feel anger or anxiety, shift away from the emotional resonance and notice the bodily sensations created by the anger or anxiety. In other words, instead of asking what the fear or anxiety means, notice the increase in pulse rate, how the stomach tightens, or the way your throat seems to swell up as part of the body's stress response. Second, it is important to shift gradually from concentration to mindfulness rather than all at once. This means balancing the inner and outer experience the way you might balance a tray with a martini glass on it.

Third, be aware of how the mind distorts thoughts about the past. Because the mind is always striving to return to a relaxed state, it may try to suppress memories. When the mind filters the negative into the subconscious, the past may appear rosier in the conscious mind. When this happens, your mind leaves you with distorted memories. Distorted memories are the result of secondhand experience, whereby the mind aims to escape the present and live in a distorted memory of a more comforting past. Contrary to secondhand experience is direct experience. Beginning meditators most frequently encounter the distortions of secondhand experience where the mind wants to keep returning to the past or future. Direct experience, on the other hand, is the experience of the present moment.

This is why experts recommend expanding to sensations during Mindfulness Meditation. Sensations are part of direct experience, while thoughts and emotions tend to be rooted in secondhand experiences that distort the truth. If you find yourself slipping into the distorted memories and emotions generated by secondhand experience, shift away and expand to the bodily sensations of direct experience. The final guideline of exploring the inner experience is to remember that the most important part of this exploration is being rather than doing. When we talk about shifting from one mind-state to another, what we are really talking about is shifting from a state of doing to a state of being. When you are in a state of simply being, you are meditating.

Expanding to Sensations

After you have used the concentration exercises in the previous chapter to stabilize breathing, expand your awareness to any of the five olfactory senses: taste, feel, sight, smell, and hearing. If you meditate with your eyes closed, you can still focus on what you see with both eyes closed (floaters, pinpricks of light, pulses of electrical energy emitting from the ocular nerves, etc.). Do not actively look for sensations; just sit and practice being until a sensation arises. Pain is the most likely first sensation to arise first. Sitting in the same position for ten minutes is bound to bother beginning meditators, especially meditators with weak core muscles. During Concentration Meditation, try to ride out a painful sensation by redirecting attention back to the breath. If the sensation continues to break your concentration or it has not dissipated after a minute or so, consider stopping and try to meditate in a different position. If a painful sensation arises after you have shifted to Mindfulness Meditation , turn your attention to the pain instead of redirecting attention back to breath. By exploring the painful sensation during Mindfulness Meditation , you may find that the pain eventually subsides until it no longer holds your awareness. Mindfulness still involves the focus required during Concentration Meditation, but in this practice, you are adding receptivity. By training the quiet mind to become receptive, you begin to absorb things without judgment as a means of gaining clarity.

To reiterate, awareness develops in stages as the mind enters deeper states of consciousness. If you are still trying to turn indirect experience (*i.e.* past thoughts and emotions) into direct experience (*i.e.* sensations), trying a concentration technique such as naming your distractions can help you get there. This is where meditation becomes an organic process. You can mix-and-match techniques from different core practices in order to meet meditative challenges and achieve balance. Expanding to sensations is a perfect way to go into a deeper state of consciousness because sensations constitute peripheral awareness. However, as you edge closer to delta consciousness, the challenge is creating a balance between maintaining awareness and guarding against falling asleep.

One way to balance this challenge is by alternating between peripheral sensations rather than focusing on just one. Focusing on one sensation can become monotonous, and monotony can cause the mind to relax into oblivion. To keep the mind quiet but active during theta consciousness, try shifting attention to different sensations. For example, if a sensation arises in your toes, put your focus there for a bit, and then shift to another sensation, such as the hum of an air conditioner, or a heartbeat felt as a pulse at your lips. By expanding awareness to sensations, thoughts and sensations are no longer distractions, and you are ready to examine the content embedded within your conscious and subconscious mind. At this point, your receptivity enhances to the point where you see everything in more detail, and from a new perspective. This is the point at which you can take awareness a step further; you pick something out of your thoughts and emotions and begin to explore it in full. This is why Mindfulness Meditation typically begins with exploring sensations.

Ten-Minute Mindfulness Exercise No. 1: Body Scan Meditation

1. **Set a timer for at least ten minutes.**

2. **Lie down in corpse pose and stretch.** Relax every muscle for a few moments. Once settled, raise your arms all the way over your head, lift your feet and point your toes away from your body. To get a full body stretch, clasp your hands and reach above you as if being pulled in the opposite direction of your toes. Pointing your toes, use them to push in the opposite direction of your head.

3. **Continue stretching for 20 seconds, then bring both arms to your side, feet down, and relax the entire body, including the toes.** Take a minute to sense your body as a whole. Feel the effect of the stretch. Let go of any tension.

4. **Start a body scan.** Begin by bringing awareness to individual parts of your body and imagine each muscle group softening as you bring awareness. Start with the toes, then to the lower legs and hips, and continue to the abdomen, the chest, the neck, the throat, the shoulders, the arms, the hands, the head, the face, and finish with the eyes.

5. **Think of your body as a whole again and imagine a red line acting as a bio-scanner.** After bringing awareness to individual parts of the body, the red line moves up and down your body, detecting any remaining areas of tension.

6. **Stop scanning and remain motionless in corpse pose until the timer sounds.** During this time, keep the awareness on your entire body as a whole and allow it to settle into deep relaxation.

7. **At the end of ten minutes, either get up and continue your day, or start Mindfulness Meditation.** If you want to include Mindfulness Meditation into the ten-minute practice, simply shorten the body scan technique down to a couple of minutes and begin Mindfulness Meditation using the remaining minutes on the timer.

Body scan meditation is a way of training the body to become more aware of sensations. It is especially important to stay with direct experience when pain arises. If the mind falls into the trap of dwelling on the past or future, the meditator may begin to compare the current experience of pain with pain from the past or future. If this happens, the present moment may dissolve into reenactment of a distorted memory or the anticipation of pain in the future. For example, if a sudden physical pain arises, the mind starts to wonder how many minutes the pain is going to last. Anxiety sets in, the inner dialogue begins, and the overwhelmed mind, using habitual patterns, distorts the immediate future by making the pain seem intolerable. Another minute of mind chatter goes by, and next thing you know, you are projecting a more generalized pain years into the future by drawing from pain in the past. Being stuck in a pattern of habitual responses to pain clouds us from understanding the difference between actual experience and distorted experiences that we add without merit. Not reacting to physical pain teaches us not to react to emotional pain. We do not run from it, but rather return to present non-judging awareness and not become overwhelmed. In her book, *Real Happiness*, meditation expert Sharon Salzberg writes, "Meditation helps us see what we're adding to our experiences, not only during meditation sessions, but elsewhere. These add-ons may take the form of projecting into the

future (*my neck hurts, so I'll be miserable forever*), forgone conclusions (*there's no point in asking for a raise*), rigid concepts (*you're either with me or against me*), unexamined habits (eating comfort food), and associative thinking (yelling at your daughter and revisiting your own childhood problems)." In essence, seeing what we are adding to our experience allows us to realize that pain is not permanent, and there is no need to feel overwhelmed by it.

Muscle Relaxing Techniques

A variation of the body scan is the muscle tensing technique, which is a very relaxing way to expand to sensations. To implement this technique, sit in corpse pose (as you would to prepare for a body scan). Lying down, the muscle tensing technique starts the same way; you begin focus on each muscle group in sequential anatomical order. The difference here is that instead of starting with a full body stretch, you tense and relax each muscle group as you move through them. Starting with the toes, tighten the muscles as hard as possible by curling them. Hold the tension for about 15 seconds and release. Enjoy the sensation of releasing stress for a few moments, the move focus up toward the calves. Flex the calf muscles as hard as possible, hold for 15 seconds, release, and enjoy the sensation for a few moments and move further up toward the thigh muscles. Repeat the tension/release/relax method for the stomach muscles chest muscles, shoulder blades, biceps and triceps, hands, larynx, and facial muscles. To flex your neck muscles, press the chin down to the collarbone and apply pressure. To flex the hands, curl them into fists and squeeze as hard as possible. To flex the larynx, contract the muscles used to swallow.

Some Yoga instructors use the muscle tensing technique at the beginning of Yoga practice to release muscle tension. In similar fashion, these sessions typically end with meditators laying in corpse pose while meditating on the relaxing physical sensations produced by tension release. One hour of physically rigorous Yoga exercise is likely to amplify the effect of the muscle tensing technique, so it may not be necessary to implement this technique in an individualized Yoga practice unless you just want to squeeze out tension at the beginning. If you are not practicing Yoga and only have ten minutes to spare, try this exercise at the beginning of practice. It is a great way to release not only physical stress, but also mental and emotional stress pent up over time. The technique works best in the morning because it increases blood flow and produces a feeling of relaxed alertness.

Visualization exercises also work well as muscle relaxing techniques. The purpose of visualization, as defined by Buddhist monks, is to use the imagination to transform negative energy into spiritual realization. When you lie down in corpse pose, visualize taking a warm shower and the feeling of warmth that slowly rolls down your body as the water cascades to your feet. Imagine the warmth of the water taking the muscle tension with it as the water flows down your body and into the drain. To create your own visualization exercise, find a physical sensation that you find deeply relaxing and mentally create a scenario where the physical sensation heals the tension.

Ten-Minute Mindfulness Exercise No. 2: Body Sensation Meditation

1. **Set a timer for at least ten minutes.**

2. **Sit down in one of the lotus positions, eyes open or closed.** Take a few deep breaths to calm the mind, and then begin to focus on sound. Let any sound that enters your awareness come and go as it pleases.

3. **Shift attention to the sound of breathing.** Focus on how the air sounds going in and out through your nose, then your mouth, and then your chest. Continue listening to the sound of the breath until another physical sensation becomes a distraction.

4. **Shift focus to distracting physical sensation and name the distraction.** For example, if you develop an itch, think the word, "itch." If you experience a chill, think the word "chill."

5. **Continue to welcome and sit with physical sensations until ten minutes are over.** The important part here is to practice present moment awareness so that the mind does not begin to wonder how much time is left.

6. **At the end of ten minutes, sit up and either go about your day or extend your practice with more Mindfulness Meditation.**

Slowing Down Daily Activities to Encourage Mindfulness

While you may not feel improvements in your meditative practice during the first few weeks, you may begin to notice improvements in your everyday life. Improvements may take the form of feeling centered or having a heightened sense of awareness and appreciation of things in the surrounding environment that you never noticed. This type of dual awareness is what colors life and makes it more interesting. Even so, the rigorous schedules that come with having a busy lifestyle have a way of jolting people out of present moment awareness and back into constant anxiety and anticipation of the future. If you begin losing the centeredness created from daily meditative practice, several mindfulness techniques can help return the mind to this desired state. The goal of each practice is to slow things down to the point where you are back to experiencing things directly (i.e. sensations) rather than experiencing things indirectly (i.e. distorted memories/future dread). The best way to do this is to apply this concept to everyday activities that are part of your normal routine. Normal activities where you can apply Mindfulness Meditation to might include:

1. Eating a meal
2. Exercising at the gym
3. Drinking coffee or tea
4. Walking
5. Cleaning the house/apartment
6. Driving
7. Having sex
8. Having a conversation with someone
9. Watching television

Slowing down time in normal activities with Mindfulness Meditation is about slowing down the actual activity itself. Rather than rushing through something, you want to take time to notice the smaller details that encapsulate the experience. For example, if you apply Mindfulness Meditation to an activity such as washing the dishes, the point is not to think about cleaning the dishes. The point is to experience everything that involves such a seemingly mundane routine that you would ordinarily rush through without thinking about. In this case, set the faucet to medium, begin making slow, circular motions with the sponge, and notice how the lukewarm water feels against your skin as you clean each dish. Expand your awareness to multiple sensations (the sponge, the sound of the water, the smell of the food, etc.) until your mind has returned itself to the type of dual awareness that made everyday experience more interesting after meditative practice. The key to maintaining that centered feeling with you into high stress situations (such as a job) is to set the tone for the day by meditating, staying mindful as you go through the day, notice how your mind unnecessarily adds indirect experiences to direct experiences, and practice breathing exercises and mini-meditations throughout the day. Practicing everyday meditations is a great way to deepen the enjoyment of simple pleasures. When choosing an everyday activity to transform into a meditative practice, the best choice is an activity you have performed a thousand times on automatic pilot.

Ten-Minute Mindfulness Exercise No. 3: Walking Meditation

1. **Find a time during the weekend to visit a park or nature preserve.** You may think a walking meditation depends on the weather and time of year since the ideal time for a walk in nature is during warm months. The natural habitat may provide more sensations during warmer months, but even winter months in cold regions offer sights and smells that can cultivate mindfulness. This may include fresher air, seeing breath, or the feeling of snow and cold.

2. **Use a mobile device as a ten-minute timer and pick a starting point along a walking path.** Very slowly, place one foot in front of the other and feel the distribution of weight as you take the first step.

3. **Begin walking at normal speed. Instead of starting with focus on breath, shift attention to the legs and the sensation of your feet as you lift them and bring them down.** To keep the focus at your feet, visualize seeing things from the perspective of your feet. Continue this way for at least a few minutes.

4. **Shift your focus to the sensations caused by the constant redistribution in weight.** To do so, slow your pace and see if it is possible to feel the full range of sensations as the heel lifts, then the foot, then the leg, and the foot again as it comes back down. Here is where you can implement a walking version of the counting technique. Instead of counting each breath, or mentally thinking "inhale/exhale," try thinking, "lift/land" or "up/down" every time your foot comes up and down off the ground.

5. **Expand your awareness.** This can be the way leaves or snow crunch underneath your feet. It also can be sensations outside the feet, such as birds chirping or the feeling of sunlight through the trees.

6. **Consider walking for longer than ten minutes if time provides.** In this exercise, longer walks mean more opportunities to expand the sensory experience. Being in the quietude of nature for longer periods also offers a peaceful way of reconnecting to spirituality.

If you want to meditate in nature, but are not sure how what constitutes a good place for this activity, take into account the following considerations. First, avoid a public park or nature preserve that has too many people. Finding a place where people are constantly jogging back and forth is a potential distraction for the mind. Second, if you go into the wilderness, make sure the area is safe and free of wild animals. Third, for this type of meditation, the time of day does matter. Any place too dark may not bring enough visual sensations to focus on, and you do not want to run the risk of getting hurt if you cannot see where you are walking. You do not want to be alone at night in an empty public place or park either, since these can be opportunities for crimes to occur. At the same time, any place in broad daylight or with too much light can hurt the eyes and make the mind too active. If you live in a city, public parks can be surprisingly quiet respites from the congestive sounds of traffic.

If you cannot make accommodations to walk in nature, consider a drinking tea meditation. Drinking tea meditation is a popular practice that originated in Japanese teahouses as a form of Zen. Tea became an integral part of Japanese culture and meditation in the eighth century when two Japanese monks named Kukai and Saicho returned from China after spending years studying Buddhism in China. When they returned to Japan, they introduced tea seeds to the home country. After tea became infused into everyday life, tea master Murata Juko built the first teahouse in a secluded area with the intention of using it as a place where one could drink tea and engage in spiritual contemplation. In today's modern Japan, teahouses are as common as Buddhist temples. In Western life, it is a perfect everyday meditation for anyone who enjoys tea in the morning or uses rituals to get the day going. Be advised that drinking coffee is not part of this meditation due to the nature of caffeine and its acidic effect on the body. When it comes to tea, choose green over black, as black tea contains too

much acidity. Morning is an ideal time to double up on Mindfulness Meditation because of the habitual routines most often practiced while getting ready for work or starting each day. For example, instead of visualizing a shower as an everyday meditation, mindfulness might start with the actual act of talking a shower and slowing it down to experience deeper sensations. Drinking tea meditation might follow, or perhaps using breakfast as a form of meditation, feeling the sensations of taste and texture in your mouth as you slowly chew the food.

Ten-Minute Mindfulness Exercise No. 4: Drinking Tea Meditation

1. **Brew a pot of tea.** Slow down all the actions involved. Feel the weight of the pot as you place it on the stove; smell the tea packet before you dip it into the water.

2. **Stand in front of the stove.** Note the changes in water as the temperature in the pot rises and watch the bubbles form and gain movement. Close your eyes and listen to the sound of the steam. Inhale the fragrance of the vapor.

3. **Pour a cup of tea.** Listen to the sound of the tea is it pours into the glass. Cup the glass with both hands and focus on the heat coming from the tea.

4. **Lift the tea to your mouth and place the cup to your lips.** Feel the vapor in your nostrils. Drink slowly, noting the first taste of the tea as it hits your tongue. Let the tea linger in your mouth for a moment before swallowing.

5. **Explore the different flavors as you drink the rest of the cup.** You do not have to be right about which flavors exist. Simply contemplate what the flavors could be. Slow down the entire process of drinking the cup. Do not focus on how much tea is left. Instead, focus on each individual sip.

Working with Difficult Emotions during Mindfulness Meditation

It is almost inevitable that meditation will stir up buried emotions that may be difficult to confront. The further you explore the inner experience the more likely and frequent this becomes. For this reason, mindfulness is a process of recognizing difficult emotions, accepting them as part of what cannot change, understanding that they do not define you, and then investigating their true meaning. This process cannot be undermined. Any attempt to avoid or circumvent negative thoughts will only serve to keep the chakras blocked and keep the positive energy you want from flowing. Negative thoughts may be subjective or they may be definitively vile; either way, putting them in one category or another defeats the intention and purpose of meditation, so do not bother.

Instead, welcome the difficult emotions that arise during Mindfulness Meditation and develop a penetrating insight into their existence. In Tibetan tradition, the story of a master named Milarepa chronicles one man's meditative retreat into the Himalayas where he encountered demons that attempted to take him from his path. First, he tried to subdue them by his own will. When that failed, he decided to give them love and compassion. The fear controlling the demons could not understand the concept of love and compassion, and so they fled. Your communion with difficult emotions is much the same. They are demons governed by fear, and the antidote is acceptance, love, and understanding. It is also the point at which Mindfulness Meditation and Lovingkindness Meditation may overlap. The same is true for people. When you combined mindfulness with lovingkindness, particularly disagreeable individuals no longer appear as ogres, but lost souls in need of healing. To heal an emotion, that emotion first needs your understanding and patience.

Difficult Emotion #1: Anger

Due to expectations about what constitutes civil behavior, anger is one of the most suppressed emotions in modern society. When children learn that anger is not an appropriate reaction in any situation, feelings that arouse anger become internalized and emotions stay buried deep in the subconscious. Over time, suppressing anger becomes a habitual pattern that children eventually to carry into their adult life. By the time they reach adulthood, years of suppressed emotions have created an individual with an unexamined inner life. People who live unexamined inner lives do not know themselves well enough to understand why they do what they do, which in turn, leads to more suppressed anger and confusion. Questions of fairness and misfortune play thematically into the lives of people who feel angry. When the expectation of life does not match the result, people feel wronged, even surprised when they feel they did everything society told them to do. The tragic fact of life is that bad things happen to good people, and people who deserve better may not always get what they want. However, if you open your eyes to true wisdom, if you see that the things others convinced you want is not what you really need, you will see that you already have everything you need. Failure is a common if not necessary process in spiritual evolution. There is no shame in falling; what matters is whether you continue to get back up, as many times as required.

The key to dealing with anger during Mindfulness Meditation is to first unblock the emotions with chakra healing or allow them to rise and flow without suppressing them. At that point, expand to sensations by focusing on how the stress response triggers physical reactions within the body. For example, the stress response may come in the form of stomach butterflies, a rise in blood pressure, or perhaps jittering. Focusing on sensations caused by anger allows the meditator to observe with detachment. Being able to observe through detachment enables the process of recognizing difficult emotions, accepting them as part of what cannot change, understanding that they do not define you, and being able to investigate their true meaning. Most people who explore their anger eventually discover that the true suppressed emotion behind the anger is hurt or fear.

Difficult Emotion #2: Anxiety and Fear

Self-image is one of the most closely guarded aspects of individualism in modern society because for most people, it directly reinforces one's self-esteem. Self-image can manifest through one's own perception or through the opinions and perceptions of others. However, the opinions and perceptions of others only matter when artificial means of identification and belonging have replaced true internal wisdom. "Know thyself," as the Ancient Greek aphorism goes. Are you the product of divine creation or the product of your individual environment? To understand the pettiness of social conformity, think about how many people make "fitting in" an all-consuming goal during adolescence. If you were like most kids, you probably worried about how your teachers, parents, or friends perceived you, and this caused you some degree of existential anxiety. The concept of fitting in, however, does not end with adolescence. Instead, it carries on well into adulthood. Because social conformity requires that people submit to the system, many people find themselves making choices they would never make if liberated from the opinions of themselves and others. They deny their true self because they fear the system may consider it unacceptable.

In short, people are constantly auditioning to meet the established standards of approval and, in the process, attain ego gratification. If you have ever had a job you hated, a relationship you found damaging, or a habit you found destructive, meditation may reveal that fear and anxiety was part of the problem. It is no surprise that the struggle to belong triggers these emotions when you consider the Buddhists belief that an individual's false sense of separateness is the source of all suffering. When you feel like you do not belong because some institution, group, or clique has not welcomed you into their group, you feel like an outsider, separate, unvalued, and unwanted. Suddenly the opinion of others matters more than what you may feel to be true about yourself. You have allowed their ignorance or lack of intimate knowledge to define your existence. In many respects, the emotions of anxiety and fear are what sow the seeds of repressed anger when the very thing you fear manifests into reality.

The key to dealing with fear and anxiety during Mindfulness Meditation is the same for dealing with anger. After unblocking the chakras, use mindfulness to recognize an emotion as anxiety or fear (perhaps using the naming technique). After that, redirect your focus to the physical sensations created by the fear or anxiety. Doing so will have the effect of being able to explore and observe the true causes of fear and anxiety with detachment and a fresh perspective. As new insights come, any fear and anxiety generated by a false sense of separateness will begin to diminish, and the perceived barriers will begin to fall.

Difficult Emotion #3: Sadness and Depression

Sadness and depression is one of the most paralyzing emotions because the underlying causes may attribute themselves to feelings of emptiness and despair. Quiet desperation eventually turns to resignation when people see their lives as hopeless. Depression can be the final destination for a person with unresolved conflicts and repressed emotions. It physically manifests into lack of focus, lack of interest, lack of confidence, and lack of energy. At the same time, the individual perpetually relives negative memories and emotions that further erode the spirit, while completely removing them from the present. More than any other emotion, the destructive effects of this manifestation are far reaching. The key to dealing with sadness and depression during Mindfulness Meditation is to begin by focusing on any chest constrictions in the heart (commonly known as a heavy heart). After that, focus on opening the heart chakra (explored further in Chapter 7), and begin to meditate on the thoughts and emotions that cause the sadness or depression. To begin a thinking meditation, assume any meditative position, close both eyes, and feel the support coming from the ground beneath you. Next, settle down the mind with any choice of breathing technique. As thoughts arise, pleasant or otherwise, to take you away from the breath, implement a version of the naming technique by naming the thoughts as "thinking." As you progress, name thoughts more specifically, such as "planning" or "remembering." When difficult emotions arise, name them accordingly as "hating," "worrying," "stressing," and so forth. The point of thinking meditation is to recognize what arises as nothing more than a thought, having no association with identity. Practicing thinking meditation during mindfulness can pave the way to unraveling habitual patterns until they no longer control the mental and behavioral aspects of self-image.

Working with habitual patterns is also a point where Mindfulness Meditation overlaps Lovingkindness Meditation. In order to unravel habitual patterns, it is necessary to disarm difficult emotions by respecting them, or as the Milarepa allegory demonstrated, to heal your demons by loving them. As the Hawkins scale in Chapter 1 indicates, love is the highest vibration of consciousness. If we ascend to the highest vibration of consciousness, life reveals the more deeply rooted issues, and we achieve true understanding, clarity, acceptance, and peace. When illusions become apparent, we begin to see pessimism, self-criticism, and criticism of others in their real form. The more these patterns unravel, the more we begin to release long-held negative energy. Our capacity to absorb positive energy increases as negative energy dissipates. For this reason, it makes even more sense to dissipate negative energy by habitually infusing the body with positive energy during meditation. Infusing positive energy into thoughts promotes the karmic law of cause and effect—whatever you express into the universe comes back to you.

Ten-Minute Mindfulness Exercise No. 5:
Positive Thinking Meditation

1. **Set a timer for at least ten minutes.**

2. **Sit, stand, or lie down in one of the meditative positions.** Close both eyes or keep them open.

3. **Think of a positive memory or recent experience.** This memory or experience should be something that evokes a positive emotion whenever you have previously thought about it, such as happiness, contentment, gratitude, joy, and so forth.

4. **Capture one image from this memory or experience in your mind as a video recording.** Explore what it feels like to sit with this memory in a state of deep meditation and mental stillness. Allow yourself to smile if the impulse arises, and focus on the sensation of the smile (e.g. the pulsing sensation at the lips, the crease of the mouth, etc.).

5. **Maintain mindful, dual awareness of body sensations created by the recollection of this memory.** For example, if you feel a sudden rush of excitement, notice how it manifests as a sensation, but allow the sensation and the image to pass. Trying to hold on to a pleasurable sensation or thought may invite anxiety or a sense of loss; both are negative thoughts and emotions.

6. **Notice what thoughts arise when you evoke positive memories.** Do you start thinking about how wonderful it feels to be free, to feel part of something? Do you start thinking about how you wish it could always be like this? Does that thought begin to spiral into worries or negative thoughts about being stuck? If you start to tread into negative thinking, practice mindfulness by reminding yourself that the negative thoughts are add-ons from the distorted mindset created by your ego. If the negative thought persists, bring your attention back to breath. When the thought disperses, go back to dwelling in the positive memory and experience.

7. **End the meditation by taking a few moments to focus back on breathing.**

Mindfulness-Based Stress Reduction (MBSR)

If you feel more comfortable working with people in the medical profession than people in the new age movement, Dr. Jon Kabat-Zinn created Mindfulness Based Stress Reduction (otherwise known as MBSR), which combines medical research with traditional forms of meditation. MSBR is a behavioral medicine offered in more than 200 integrated medical centers, hospitals, and clinics around the world. The majority of students who enroll in the MSBR program suffer from either severe stress or chronic diseases. Studies on MBSR show the program improves conditions such as rheumatoid arthritis, lower back, and side effects from HIV and cancer treatment. MBSR is essentially meditation without the spiritual aspects of meditation. Because it is secular in nature, the program is most appropriate for those who are just looking to use meditation for physical healing. To learn more about Mindful Based Stress Reduction, go to www.mindfulexperience.org. If you have a smartphone, consider downloading the Mindfulness Meditation™ app available at www.mentalworkout.com.

CASE STUDY:
BECOMING MORE
CONSCIOUSLY AWARE

Djuna Roberts
Asheville NC 28805
droberts0001@live.com

I started using positive visualization exercises when I was a kid participating in high school sports. During these exercises, I would visualize how I wanted to play and would often experience a mental state called "being in the zone." Getting into the zone is about finding an inner peacefulness. As my practice evolved, I decided to attend the NC School for Natural Healing where I discovered a practice called "energy healing." This practice helped me learn more techniques for meditating and "getting into the zone."

My favorite technique involves the simple but profound use of various breathing techniques, as well as emotional cleansing, which involves breathing to go into deeper states of consciousness and relaxation in order to clear repressed emotions. I have found that following the breath is the best form of connecting with inner quietness.

Meditation has helped me become more consciously aware of my emotions, thoughts, and general energy during my normal daily activities. It has also helped me become present with the emotional energy, not from a "thinking" mind, but from a place of feeling the currents of various emotions. Emotions during regular meditation do not feel as turbulent when I am looking at them from the inner/higher self and being an observer. In this detached, observing state, I can allow the energy of emotions to exist as energy that moves through me. I practice Mindfulness Meditation each day to stay aware of tension that I need to address. It also helps me stay in a meditative state while walking about in my daily activities. It always will be my challenge to remember to check in with my breath at various times during in day. If my breath feels too shallow, I just take a moment to breathe deep. This expands my awareness immediately and helps me return to centeredness.

I also think Mindfulness Meditation has helped me become more aware of certain emotional patterns. It is only when I become aware of certain patterns of thoughts or behaviors that I am able to make a more conscious choice to try to change the pattern. Meditation helps people become an observer of mental thoughts from a detached place of loving kindness and acceptance. Many patterns are contained in the subconscious, and I feel meditation helps bring that material to conscious awareness. When the mind becomes conscious of a problem, the meditator becomes more equipped to deal with and eventually break any pattern that might be harmful to everyday living and wellness.

Chapter 7

Finishing Core Meditation with Lovingkindness

After you have spent your second week of meditation on developing mindfulness, your third week of meditation will involve developing lovingkindness. Lovingkindness Meditation, which is the third core practice, focuses bringing love, compassion, sympathy, and joy into your life. To review, Concentration Meditation involves the practice of quieting the mind, and letting go of thoughts and emotions, while mindfulness involves the practice of exploring them once the mind becomes quiet. Lovingkindess meditation is the meditative practice whereby you extend caring to yourself and others to bring universal harmony. Once you have quieted the mind and explored the meaning of thoughts and emotions, you will use Lovingkindness Meditation, the meditative practice whereby you extend caring to love, compassion, sympathy, and joy to all things. Lovingkindess is the meditative practice that elevates the individual into higher realms of consciousness vibration.

The Benefits of Practicing Lovingkindness Meditation

Learning how to love yourself and others sounds simple, yet so many people behave in unloving ways toward themselves and others on a daily basis without examination. If we apply the ancient Greek aphorism ("Know thyself.") to the practice of lovingkindess, we begin to realize that part of knowing oneself means loving oneself. To truly love oneself means never needing to search for love anywhere else. Many people look for the approval of others as a form of love to compensate for what feels lacking within. Therefore, we can identify the benefits of practicing lovingkindness through several outcomes. When we practice lovingkindness, we experience peace and well-being without having to depend on any particular reason to make us feel this way. Life itself becomes joyful. We feel liberated from the ego drive when we feel happy independent of circumstances. When the ego drive does not define our happiness (*e.g.* getting what we want in order to be happy), the mind lives in the beautiful moment, undaunted by what may or may not

come to us in the future. Likewise, the past does not hold us in fear of repeating old hurts, and we live forward with courage and optimism.

Love energy is Tao energy that gives us vitality and raises our vibratory communication with the universe. If we wish to will something into existence, the universe is listening. This vitality and vibration heals us physically. We feel more awake and renewed when we previously may have felt tired and worn down. The love energy we draw from lovingkindness keeps us in good health, nourishes our body, and extends our lifespan. Many people who prematurely die suffer from physical symptoms that love energy can heal. Dr. Dean Ornish, author of *Program for Reversing Heart Disease*, conducted a well-known series of lovingkindess meditation studies that linked physical healing to patients that made changes in their psychological, emotional, and spiritual lifestyle. Notable improvements in patients included discontinuation of medications, diminished chest pain, higher energy levels, increased calmness, significant weight loss, and reduced blockages in coronary arteries. From these studies, Dr. Ornish developed the Opening Your Heart Program which includes meditation, breathing exercises, and guided imagery to treat addictions, lower cholesterol, and reduce stress. When we practice lovingkindness, we expand our sense of connection to others; life feels more meaningful. It is this sense of meaning and connection that paves the way to a greater spiritual awakening.

Directing the Flow of Love Energy

Think back to the Hawkins vibrational scale. When you begin to extend love to yourself and others, you enter an expanded state of awareness and begin to experience energy flow. During Lovingkindness Meditation, the individual encounters pure Tao consciousness by drawing in the universal energy of eternal love. Tao is a metaphysical concept in Buddhism that signifies the fundamental energy of the universe, that which is eternally formless and nameless. By directing this energy flow to yourself and others, you begin to build a connection, or rather a *reconnection*, to all things. The single greatest source of all suffering is the false sense of separation. Lovingkindness removes this illusion so that the meditator may experience the sensations of peace, love, and joy. The heart chakra is the energetic opening that assists in this process. In its most fully realized form, lovingkindness is the expression of unconditional love. No matter what others do, no matter what you do to others or to yourself, this love never diminishes. In many ways, it is the beginning of what the Christian religion terms "Christ consciousness."

It is worth noting, however, that using lovingkindness to direct the flow of positive energy as a means of fulfilling ambitions and desires only strengthens the ego drive. For example, you set an intention to love someone hoping that good things will happen for you in life. While the universe may respond to this lower intention, it may keep you from ascending into higher states of divine consciousness (explored further in chapter 8). Directing love toward yourself or others on the belief that the universe will bestow material reward is not an expression of true unconditional love. The bestowal of love when motivated by self-gratification is a purely conditional intention and therefore does not have its place in higher intention. Since the true purpose of your spiritual journey is to break free of the ego, you are encouraged to use lovingkindness for higher intentions rather than lower ones. In addition, when we talk about lovingkindness as a practice of extending love to others, we are not talking about liking people or accepting bad behaviors. We are talking about extending love as a means of understanding that our lives are spiritually connected. It is an expression of understanding that our own faults (and the faults of others) are the result of ego bondage, a disconnection from spirit, and a lack of true understanding.

Deepening the practice of lovingkindess also means using it to achieve compassion for others. Compassion is takes love a step further. When you feel compassion for others, you not only love them unconditionally but also feel their pain and suffering as you would your own. Developing compassion for others strengthens the bond with everything. The individual congruently begins to lose his or her sense of feeling separate from others. However, compassion does not mean that the individual expressing it for another person suddenly feels the same degree of sorrow, but rather relates to it enough that he or she feels compelled to act. When people avoid other people's suffering because of how thinking about it makes them feel, they cannot call themselves compassionate because this is an act of isolating oneself from another. Therefore, avoiding the pain of others is an expression of separateness. Sympathy is the result of compassion. When lovingkindess meditation reaches its fullest expression of love and compassion, the meditator experiences genuine joy and happiness for another's good fortune. No longer is the individual consumed by petty jealousies or wonders why some people perceived as less deserving experience better fortune in life. Jealousy is the ego's way of believing that good fortune has unfairly redirected away from us to someone else.

The best way to nourish lovingkindness is to look for the good in people, to want the best for them, and to understand that some people need more love and understanding than others. To prepare for Lovingkindness Meditation, begin to think about how you view other people. Some perceptions of others may be positive while others may be more negative. Either way, the important thing to realize is that despite your differences with other people, everyone wants the same things, and that some have different ways of expressing or trying to obtain it, right or wrong. All people, no matter who they are, want love, admiration, respect, and so forth. Try putting yourself in that person's place, and ask yourself how you would feel in those shoes. You also might think about the suffering of someone you do not know and imagine that person's problems belonging to a loved one. When we feel separate, we only feel suffering when it intimately touches us. When we feel connected, everyone's suffering matters in equal fashion.

Ten-Minute Lovingkindness Exercise No. 1: Extending Love to Yourself and Others

1. **Set a timer for at least ten minutes.**

2. **Sit, stand, or lie down in one of the meditative positions.** Close both eyes or keep them open.

3. **Offer lovingkindness to yourself.** To do this, silently say the words: *"May I be happy. May I be safe. May I be healthy. May I live with ease."*

4. **Keep repeating the words silently or in your mind.** As you continue, it is important keep an even pace between each declaration so that the mind can focus on each one. Breath is not important in this exercise. The main focus is the words.

5. **After a couple of minutes, or when you feel a loving sensation, choose a person you like or has been kind to you, and extend lovingkindness to that person.** If thoughts and memories associated with this person arise, just let them pass. To extend this person lovingkindness, silently say the words: *"May you be happy. May you be safe. May you be healthy. May you live with ease."* To deepen this practice, choose someone who you know may be hurting or sad, and extend the words of lovingkindness.

6. **After a couple of minutes, choose a person you feel neutral about, and extend the words of lovingkindness to that person.** This person might be someone you do not know well or a person you encountered for a brief moment in public, such as an unhappy looking grocery clerk, a nervous child, or a lonely looking woman at the bus stop.

7. **After a couple of minutes, choose a person you have negative feelings toward, and extend the words of lovingkindness to that person.** This might be a difficult person you encountered for a brief moment on the road or someone you see on a regular basis who may be making your life difficult. If you find it difficult to extend lovingkindness to someone you feel wronged you, extend the words of lovingkindness to yourself since that is an indication of suffering. Your inability to express unconditional love may also mean you still hold negative energy due to a contraction in the energetic opening of the heart chakra.

Opening the Heart Chakra

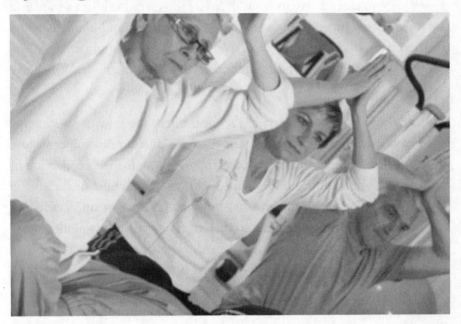

Opening the heart chakra allows the meditator to release energetic blockages in the chest accumulated by negative energy. If the heart chakra is closed, the individual cannot radiate love, compassion, joy, or peace. Freeing these openings and releasing blockages allows the meditator to receive and direct the flow of energy in lovingkindess meditation. The practice of opening this chakra works well at the beginning of a meditation, or at the end. If you open the heart chakra before you begin a meditation, follow the instructions outlined at the end of Chapter 3. If you open the heart chakra at the end of your meditation, consider using it as a dedication to someone. For example, after practicing lovingkindness, feel the sensation of peace, joy, and love accumulated in the body, and offer the energy to someone else. With both eyes closed, bring yourself into a sitting position (if you are not sitting already), and picture this person in your mind. When in sitting position, bring both hands together, and say in your mind, "May my practice be dedicated to your well-being." Having dedicated the practice, offer the energy by slowly parting your hands into a "V" as you raise them over your head. Keep in mind that to direct the flow of love energy, the heart chakra needs to be open, so before you extend love to someone else, it makes sense to extend love to yourself first. However, this is not a hard and fast rule because meditation is not about following rules. No one is going to tell you that you cannot retroactively extend lovingkindness to others as a means of opening the heart chakra. Try different methods. Whichever methods work best for you are the ones you should follow.

Another way to open the heart chakra and direct the flow of love energy is through visualization exercises. For example, instead of extending love individually to people who have been kind to you, visualize a collection of these people, and in your mind, merge them together as one. As they begin to merge, imagine seeing the love and kindness of each person as radiating light. As each individual merges into this singular entity, the singular entity becomes even brighter. When each individual has merged into a collective entity, imagine the collective entity shaping into a ball of light. With both eyes remaining closed, extend your chest as if pushing your heart chakra forward, and visualize this ball of light descending into the heart chakra. You might also consider using the Tonglen exercise discussed in the Chapter 5 case study. In this exercise, you imagine a person who may be suffering from negativity or a sense of disconnection and breathe in the negative energy they radiate. On the exhale, concentrate on sending positive, healing energy to them.

The same exercise works for sending love to an actual environment inhabited by people. For example, you might visualize an economically depressed neighborhood or a war zone. First use a technique to open the heart chakra, and imagine a white ball of light at the center of your chest. Next, visualize a place, perhaps one you have seen on television or in person, and on the inhalation, breathe in any negative energy, depression, agitation, or spiritual darkness you perceive emanating from the environment. As you draw in the negative energy, visualize it coursing down into the chest area, absorbing into the ball of light, and transforming into love energy. On the exhale, breathe out the love energy and direct the flow toward the environment. You can apply this transformation technique to yourself when you are suffering, to others who may be suffering, and to situations that create suffering.

The important thing to remember is that a healthy heart chakra is the gateway to experiencing love, compassion, sympathy, and joy. Visualization techniques have a transformative power over undesired emotions, especially if you find it difficult to extend love to someone who has caused you difficulty. To transform any difficult emotions you may have toward others, join each index finger with the thumb on the same hand, and put the right hand to your chest. Close your eyes, concentrate on the heart chakra. After a few breaths, visualize the white glow in the center again, and begin chanting the sound "YAM." As you chant, imagine the sphere increasing in size until it surrounds your entire body. Bring this difficult person into mind, and the feelings of anger or anxiety this person triggered. See them filled with the same white light and let your energy body merge with theirs to create a sphere twice as big. Continuing to chant "YAM," let all of your emotions absorb into this light and listen for the hidden message in them.

Ten-Minute Lovingkindness Exercise No. 2: Seeing the Good in Everyone

1. **Set a timer for at least ten minutes.**

2. **Sit, stand, or lie down in one of the meditative positions.** Close both eyes or keep them open.

3. **Think of one good thing you did yesterday.** Nothing is too inconsequential. It can be something as minor as a smile you gave someone on the street or something as meaningful to you as accomplishing a goal you set for yourself.

4. **Meditate on the good thing you did.** Just sit and be with the memory for a couple of minutes Do not examine it; simply meditate.

5. **Think of someone who has helped you.** Think about the center of good within that person and the qualities you admire about them.

6. **Think of someone you feel neutral about and recall something that may reflect their center of good.** For example, if you witnessed an act of kindness by a stranger in public, think about how they helped someone when they did not have to. Imagine the center of good in them as being similar to the person who helped you.

7. **Think of someone you may dislike and try to recall a time when this person demonstrated an admirable quality.** It may be difficult to view someone you perceive as unlikable in a positive light. When this happens, the mind is resisting an established pattern, so think about a choice this person made or some good thing this person accomplished. Meditate on this good thing and imagine the center of good in this person as being similar to the people you like.

Mantra Meditation

In Sanskrit, the word mantra refers to a sacred sound that caries the vibratory energy of the cosmos. The word *man*-tra means "mind-tool" or "magical spell." In the ancient tradition of Buddhism, monks used mantras to connect to higher levels of consciousness. By chanting a sacred sound, the meditator resonates in concert with higher vibrations of consciousness. It is like hearing a tune being played by a band and whistling along with the music. According to holistic healer Dr. Alka Khurana, the sound "AUM" (or "OM") "is the eternal sound of God and is the primordial vibration which created the universe." It is made up of three Sanskrit letters, "aa," "au," and "ma"...it is believed to be the basic sound which contains all other sounds." Other common mantras include:

1. HAMSA
2. OM MANI PEME HUNG
3. OM AH HUNG

There are many ways to chant a mantra. Some people chant aloud (on the exhale); others chant in their own minds. The basic key to chanting is to do it slowly, avoid thinking about meaning, and to blend the chant rhythmically with the breath. The more the meditator repeats the mantra, the louder the chant grows in the mind until the mediator's whole body resonates at the same vibratory level. Chanting aloud creates vibrations in the body. Different mantra sounds have different vibrations that trigger different effects in our bodies. For example, the mantra "HUNG" resonates in the chest and holds the vibratory energy there. When you try a new mantra, feel where the vibration appears in your body and use it to open a corresponding chakra. Third eye meditation involves mantra chanting the sacred sound "AUM." Therefore, you might also consider visualizing the white sphere of light between the eyes for this sacred chant.

Using the HAMSA chant, you might visualize the breath as a wave rolling back and forth from head to toe. This chant is useful for caressing physical aches and pains. Mantra meditation requires longer mantras chanted faster and spoken as a three-beat (for example, OM-*MA*/NI-*PE*/ME-*HUNG*). In the case of OM MANI PEME HUNG, the accent would fall on the second, fourth, and sixth syllables. Accenting these syllables, the sound would come out as "om-MA/ni-PE/me-HUNG." OM MANI PEME HUNG is a mantra that Tibetans use to extend friendliness to all living things. For this reason, OM MANI PEME HUNG is a heart opening mantra appropriate for Lovingkindness Meditation. If you do not feel comfortable chanting mantras that involve Sanskrit, consider using affirmations. In this case, an affirmation would be a phrase repeated in English, such as "peace," "joy to all," or "quiet mind." To choose an affirmation, think about your intention. If you want to change a negative behavior, choose a phrase that counters this behavior and repeat it aloud or in your mind as an affirmation.

**Ten-Minute Lovingkindness Exercise No. 3:
Lovingkindness in Nature Meditation**

1. **Find a time during the weekend to visit a park or nature preserve.** The time of year matters less for this walking meditation, because it does not involve focusing on sensations (i.e. sights, sounds, smells, etc.).

2. **Use a mobile device as a ten-minute timer and pick a starting point along a walking path.** Instead of concentrating on movement, talk a few deep breaths and begin to walk leisurely.

3. **Choose an affirmation or chant and begin repeating it.** The chant is the object of your focus. If repeating a chant or affirmation aloud makes you feel self-conscious, even in seclusion, repeat it in your mind. Since this is a Loving-kindness Meditation, choose a chant that extends love to yourself, to others, or to all living beings.

4. **Focus on the repetition.** It is all right to rest some attention on the environment, as long as you keep returning focus to the chant.

5. **Extend lovingkindness to the environment.** If someone walks by you on a nature trail, or you hear a dog bark in the distance, acknowledge their presence by extending the chant to include them. For example, if you are chanting, "May I be happy, may I be safe," etc., then include the passersby and chant, "May you be happy, may you be safe," etc. After a few moments, come back to extending the chant to yourself.

6. **If a person you have negative feelings about enters your thoughts, extend them lovingkindness.** After thoughts of this person dissipate, come back to extending the chant to yourself.

Causes of Energetic Blockages in the Heart Chakra

The trials of modern life never end, no matter how balanced meditation makes you. When society exerts its will, the pressures that come with having a job, being a parent, or living up to some other expectation begin to build if meditation ceases to remain a regular practice. When this happens, the chakras begin to contract and the body stores negative energy that causes blockages in the chakra system. If you begin to harbor anger, hurt, resentment, or some other unloving quality, this energy will clog the heart chakra the same way an artery clogs. When the heart chakra contracts, blockages occur, and the person begins to harbor agitation and anger, which eventually manifests in some physical or habitual form. This is why opening the chakras should be a routine practice in Lovingkindness Meditation. The key to detecting a blockage is to locate an area of the body feeling physical pain and determine its corresponding chakra region. As such, a closed heart chakra may take the physical form of chest or shoulder tightness, any uncomfortable sensation in the area of the heart chakra triggered by the body's stress response.

Evidence of an energetic blockage in the heart chakra caused by habitual patterns of behavior may take a more subtle and complex form. To determine whether habitual patterns of behavior have caused a blockage in the heart chakra, look for any recent behaviors rooted in fear, resentment, grief, jealousy, irrational attachment, and ego drive. Fear, for example, closes the heart when the ego fears attack or criticism from others. When fear blocks the heart chakra, a person's behavior turns confrontational. The fearful mind perceives everything as an attack, and thus the person expresses outrage and often becomes judgmental. If you find yourself expressing constant criticism of others, including yourself, look to open the heart chakra and release the negative energy causing you to act in these destructive ways. If you find yourself going back to negative memories that perpetuate your resentment of someone or something, then the object of your anger is probably life. By unblocking the heart chakra, you give yourself an opportunity to unravel the habitual pattern of dwelling in the past and laying blame for what you perceive as misfortune. Jealousy is a form of resentment directed inward. People express jealousy when they perceive something in themselves as lacking. In this instance, the object of your anger is you. In this instance, you would unblock the heart chakra by extending love to the person who is really suffering. When the heart releases jealousy, it releases you from the blame you lay at your own feet for not measuring up to some type of standard. If jealousy continues to block the heart chakra, resentment eventually becomes grief. Much like resentment, grief can hold people hostage to the past. Grief is an emotion often felt in the wake of regret. Regret comes with a sense of loss for something that used to be. Because regret perpetually returns the mind to the past, the mind dwells in the time before the moment of loss. The realization that we cannot recover what is lost causes grief. Grief keeps the heart chakra blocked when we turn away from the pain caused by our grief.

When grief festers, the pain it causes creates an ego-constructed wall in the heart that refuses to let emotions enter or leave. Over time, we incorrectly come to believe that this wall keeps us from feeling pain when in reality it keeps us from feeling love and moving on. At its most effective, the walled up heart becomes territorial and views its own space as sacred ground that must remain secure. At this point, emotional experiences stop altogether and the heart becomes dead inside. If you find yourself trapped in one of these patterns, do something selfless for someone and notice its effect on the pattern. The mere act of doing something selfless can open the heart chakra and reverse the patterns occurring in your life. The more you self-lessly do for others without any expectation of reward, the more you keep the heart chakra open. The more you keep the heart chakra open, the more life rewards you with its love.

Ten-Minute Lovingkindness Exercise No. 4: Cultivating Optimism

1. **Set a timer for ten minutes.**

2. **Choose a meditative position, close your eyes, and start a breathing exercise.**

3. **After a few deep breaths, imagine being the person you aspire to be.** When the image of your ideal future self comes, imagine having the life you always hoped to have. This might include anything to do with a job, a relationship, a social life, a hobby, a pleasurable activity, etc.

4. **After spending ten minutes visualizing this future self, open your eyes and spend a few minutes writing anything about this future self.**

5. **Go about your day and notice if you feel more positive toward life than before.** If so, consider doing this activity on a daily basis and see if your optimism builds exponentially over time.

Additional Tips for Deepening Lovingkindness

The positive effects of lovingkindess meditation usually become more noticeable outside practice, as opposed to during practice. People who continue to meditate over time begin to feel the deepening of love, joy, compassion, and sympathy. Outside of practice, there are ways to deepen the effects of lovingkindness even further through reflection. Reflecting on meditative practice might mean taking a few moments to write down observations of the past week in a journal, or it might mean thinking about them. Reflection is a way of mentally acknowledging positive changes and noting with enhanced mindfulness any changes about your practice, your behavior, or your thoughts that you would still like to make. To deepen lovingkindness, take an active role in extending love outside your practice. This may mean agreeing to becoming more flexible to change, learning to forgive people for their transgressions, finding the beauty in even the smallest things, or developing gratitude for what you have. Being more flexible to change involves accepting the fact that change is inevitable and nothing in life is static. Life moves in forward motion, and you must move with it the way a tree swaying without resistance in the direction of the wind. If

you keep a journal, note when change happens, what thoughts occurred as you learned about this change. Ask yourself if you approached this change with less resistance or the same as usual. If nothing in this area of your life has changed, take this to your practice and make developing flexibility to change part of your intention in meditation.

The same holds true for learning forgiveness. Instead of reflecting on a time when someone hurt you or betrayed your trust, reflect on a time when you hurt someone or betrayed someone's trust. This person may be someone from your recent past or long-ago past. No encounter with this person is too insignificant; it may even be someone you have not thought about in years. Begin to think, following this person in your mind, and see the effect your behavior had on them. Practicing lovingkindness is about understanding that people are the same and need the same things. If you feel their pain, dwell on it for a few moments, and think about how much you would like this person's forgiveness. When the memory of this person passes, relate your desire for their forgiveness to someone who has hurt you, and forgive that person with the understanding that they need forgiveness. Afterward, reflect on what you learned about that person you hurt and how you have grown since then.

Another way to deepen lovingkindness outside of your practice is to find the beauty in things. Finding the beauty in things can happen through reflection or in present moment awareness. If you have ever noticed a homeless person on the street and thought how ugly that reality must seem, turn it around and find the beauty. Imagine that person sitting in a warm home surrounded by loved ones or eating a home-cooked meal. Imagine that person with dreams and aspirations or enjoying something. Find the beauty in inanimate objects and organic life. Look at a piece of steel and think about the heating process that tempered it. Watch a butterfly crawl along a flower and think about the transformation process of the butterfly from a caterpillar or a seed to a colorful flower. The spiritual science of Kabbalah tells us that the purpose of existence is to allow the creation to experience delight. When the creation expresses delight, it honors the Creator. In this sense, expressing gratitude is a form of reciprocity that deepens lovingkindness. To cultivate gratitude, find the beauty in even the smallest things, and thank creation for allowing you to see it. When you have time to reflect or write in a journal, think about all the good things that happened over the previous two days. If at first you have trouble finding anything, remember that beauty exists in even the smallest things, a gesture, an offering, an experience, and so forth. Think about your positive contributions to the world in that time. Perhaps you opened a door for someone, got a report finished on time, pleased a client, or cooked someone dinner. In your thoughts, express gratitude toward life for giving you the opportunity to make the world better in some way. When you have done this, think back further in time and look for the beauty in your memory or positive contributions to the world. If time provides, reflect further back in time — a month, a year, a decade, and so forth. In your reflection, realize there is enough happiness to go around. It is not in limited supply. Joy, peace, beauty, etc., are limitless. There is enough for everyone, and it is open to you at any time.

Ten-Minute Lovingkindness Exercise No. 5: Altar Meditation

1. **Set a timer for ten minutes.**

2. **Create a meditation altar of a spiritual leader.** The altar should comprise a compilation of anything that reminds you of this spiritual leader (for example, a Bible, a picture, a cross, etc.) This this spiritual leader can be a historical figure such as Jesus, Mohammed, or Buddha. It also can be a personal figure, your own teacher or someone you feel expresses unconditional love.

3. **Sit in a meditative position, focus on the altar, and start a breathing exercise.**

4. **After a few deep breaths, imagine this leader's loving energy radiating outward and in your direction.** Imagine the radiating energy continuing to expand until it engulfs you. Imagine receiving and absorbing this energy for yourself.

5. **Repeat a lovingkindness mantra.** You might start by extending loving-kindness to yourself by saying or thinking, "May I be happy, may I be safe, may I be at peace, may I be free of suffering." After a few minutes, imagine holding this love energy from your spiritual leader and extending it through mantra to someone you care about, someone you feel neutral about, and someone for whom you harbor negative feelings.

6. **End the meditation.** Go about your day and notice if you feel more posi-tive toward life than before. If so, consider doing this activity on a daily basis and see if your love energy builds exponentially over time.

CASE STUDY: AWAKENING THE LOVE WITHIN

Jack Kornfield
Spirit Rock Meditation Center
Woodacre, California
www.spiritrock.org

Excerpt Taken From: **http://www.kripalu.org**

Article Title: **Balancing Act**

What transformations can people have when they practice meditation?

There is a glow people have, a "meditation facelift" that leaves people profoundly refreshed, their eyes open and skin clear. You do not have to become a card-carrying Buddhist. You can tend to the awakened inner beauty from meditation practice in moments, by skillful use of inten-tion, and the practice of loving-kindness. You can do this anywhere—in the airport, supermarket, or workplace. In any circumstance, even tend-ing young children, having the skills of wise intention is invaluable and makes that circumstance more alive.

Body-based practices, such as being aware of the breath, can help you embody the power of mindfulness and live fully in the present, whether you are jogging or cooking. The result is the ability to live your life in the reality of the present, rather than in the worries of the future and regrets of the past. And you have the flexibility and ability to re-spond to your circumstances with a tremendous sense of inner power.

How can someone use mindfulness and loving-kindness every day?

You can sit on a subway in New York City and begin, without looking weird at all, to direct the force of loving-kindness to those around you. You might imagine people in their original beauty as children. In a minute, your relationship to them transforms and they connect with your heart. Look into your heart, and it will show you that you are looking for ways to connect and create bridges.

What mantras do you like to use, if any?

I use a loving-kindness meditation at times, for inner recitation. When I encounter people, I use, "May you be well, may you be safe."

Sometimes, I use one from the Beatles: "Let it be." I really take it to heart in a deep way when I recite that. There is a way I'm letting the world be as it is, I know how to respond, and I don't have to be worried or rushed. I feel what response comes from silence.

What are your goals as a teacher?

My goal is for people to awaken to their fundamental dignity, nobility, and freedom of the heart regardless of their circumstances. My goal is for them to remember how to love and bring compassion to all parts of their lives. Also, to give people ancient practices and tools they can use when they return to their everyday lives so they can quiet the mind, open the heart, and develop a spirit of compassion no matter where they are. People can heal and transform themselves and learn to be their own enlightened master. My goal is for them to trust their innate wisdom.

Divine Meditation

nce you have finished three weeks of core meditation practice, you have the option to either customize your own ten-minute practice according the techniques that serve your individual needs or go further into divine meditation. While lovingkindess lifts the meditator into the higher echelons of pure Tao consciousness (love, joy, peace), divine meditation aspires to the highest point of consciousness on the Hawkins vibrational scale, divine (or ultimate) consciousness and enlightenment. Divine meditation is any meditation that seeks to contemplate, communicate, and become one with God. Divine meditation cultivates spirituality and cosmic insight, which must then translate into actions that gradually allow the spirit to infuse divine knowledge into the physical self. In letter six of *Christ Returns, Speaks His Truth*, the anonymous author writes, "Your true purpose in your spiritual journey is to break free of the bondage of the ego and make evermore pure contact with divine consciousness. It is your eventual destiny to recognize its omnipresence in both yourself and throughout your daily activities. Your highest spiritual goal is to come to that spiritually exulted moment when you finally realize that your human mind and its desires are only finite and therefore can never bring you the happiness and fulfillment you experience when you lay down your selfhood and come to divine consciousness, asking only for the higher way."

The most striking part of this statement is the notion of divine consciousness as our eventual destiny. You can put off this destiny for a while, but at some point in your worldly or otherworldly existence, you will come to know the truth. As spiritual teacher and radio host Mark Passio explains, "To experience a cosmic epiphany is to penetrate the stargate of cosmic consciousness that lies on the other side of the divide that we experience as separation. It is the idea that we are one infinite consciousness experienc-

ing itself in the physical world to come to know itself better. The physical reality is not who we are — it is the vehicle for us to have experiences. Your feeling small does not serve the world. We were born to make manifest the glory of God that is within us. It is not just within some of us; it is within *all* of us. As we let our own light shine, we unconsciously give other people permission to do the same. As we are liberated from our own fear, our presence automatically liberates others."

Entering Deeper Realms of Spirituality

To move from the divide that we experience as separation to the stargate of cosmic consciousness, we first have to recognize the levels of spiritual transcendence. In the first stage of spiritual transcendence, the meditator comes to believe in spirituality. At this stage, the mediator has not established any contact with the spiritual realm, but he or she senses a *synchro-mysticism* in about life. Synchro-mysticism is an extraordinary coincidence that occurs in a way that has extreme meaning to the observer of the event, which leads to increased insight or personal enlightenment. It supports the idea that nothing is really coincidence, even though many things appear to be so, and that everything is connected. For some, synchro-mysticism may occur as an experience that coincides with a certain thought. For example, let us suppose you are walking down the street and feeling like your boss is taking you for granted. You feel underpaid and under-appreciated at work. Five minutes later, you come across a storefront window that displays a book about how working class people get nickel and dimed. At first, you shrug off this coincidence with amusement, but then another experience coincides with another thought. For example, just before a surprising event happens, you might find yourself wondering what it would be like if this surprising event ever occurred. Synchro-mysticism may also take the form of patterns. For example, let us suppose a picture in your bedroom falls off the wall, and the next day, you receive news that a relative has passed away. A year later, the same thing happens; the picture falls off the wall, and another relative passes. Synchro-mysticism can occur in two forms, positive synchronicity or negative synchronicity, and you will experience either depending on the type of energy you carry. Practicing divine meditation may begin to trigger glimpses of spiritual dimensions, thus the spirit within you awakens. Once the spirit within you awakens, you feel transformed and have a sense that something is communicating directly to you.

As your divine meditation progresses the spirit within not only awakens; it also becomes infused into your consciousness, and you have no doubt of your transcendence. You experience life in a completely interconnected way. As you begin to transcend into deeper levels of spirituality, you will also begin to experience an increased number of synchronicities. Negative synchronicities attract negative "coincidences." Positive synchronicities attract positive ones. Thus, cleansing the chakra system of negative energy will reduce the number of negative synchronicities you experience and increase the number of positive synchronicities both experienced and observed. Once you attune yourself to synchro-mysticism, the practice of recognizing its occurrence and extrapolating meaning from it becomes an art form. Whatever meaning you take away from a synchro-mystic occurrence, it is important to understand that you are in tune with something that wants you to listen and perhaps even act upon it. Synchro-mysticism allows you to prove the phenomenon for yourself through active involvement with it. Once you have proved its presence to yourself, you can act on behalf of the spirit communicating to you through synchronicity.

Those who reach the transcendent stage of spiritual infusion, however, still maintain a distinction between the physical body and the spirit. As you progress through divine meditation, the ego drive that binds you to your sense of self begins to dissolve and you achieve a state of oneness with spirit. Dissolution of self and integration with spirit means that everything you do in life is on behalf of the spirit communicating to you. In the final transcendent stage of spirituality, every moment, person, action, or thought contains some form of divine expression, without the slightest trace of separation. No longer does anything appear as a random coincidence devoid of meaning. At this stage, it becomes possible to use synchro-mysticism as an attempt to foresee future events or decode everyday situations with greater clarity.

Common Experiences in Divine Meditation

Because we typically experience three dimensions in linear time, the concept of the spiritual dimension confounds and evades us. Where does the spiritual dimension exist? The answer is, anywhere you look. Some encounters are internal, and others occur in the external environment. When

Christ said, "The kingdom of heaven is within you, and it is all around you," He was talking about God as all encompassing, not some separate entity between the observer and God. The separation does not exist literally, as organized religions are often inclined to teach, but merely as our current perception of reality. This is why, in order to transcend into deeper levels of spirituality, you need no book, and you need no designated place of worship to connect with God.

Meditators who experience spiritual transcendence often report insights into deep truths that others might not be able to understand. For example, in 2007, an anonymous Youtube uploader named Jonathan "Adampants" posted an audio series about his spiritual transcendence that went viral called, *The Healing Begins Now*. In it, Jonathan says, "You become anything but stupid when you connect to the creator. I've had light explained to me. Why does light exist as particles and wavelengths? I know why it is, *exactly why* in my head. There is no explanation about it because scientists usually bumble around about it. So how does the creator communicate with me? It takes what I know and assembles things together to create a font that I understand. If it is information that I have had no experience

with, it still puts the knowledge in me, and then I'm directed to see something in life that I can extract a metaphor from to explain what I know. That's how it works... An artist can say what I'm saying in a picture. A musician can write a song that expresses what I know with notes. God will intervene and command the individuality of everybody with the truth, and that is the beauty of individuality." Not surprisingly, those who experience deeper levels of spiritual transcendence also report receiving their experiences more passively. Deeper levels of transcendence cultivates a deeper the sense of peace, even in the face of adversity. Meditators on this spiritual level also report a continual revelation of truth. To these observers, nothing is static and the meaning of things may change and evolve over time.

Through divine meditation, consciousness expands from the physical body into your self-image and ego. Expansion into these areas acts as a form of cleansing and rebirth. From there, consciousness expansion continues beyond the mind into your energy body. Your energy body is your surrounding vibratory energy known as the *aura*, which expands and contracts depending on the emotions and thoughts you emit. Meditators who achieve the higher levels of divine meditation may experience communication with otherworldly beings. Spiritual gurus at this level often experience astral projection and report contact with divine historical figures such as Christ, Mohammed, and other trans-dimensional entities. Because divine meditation requires a lengthy session to achieve an intense level of stillness and concentration, you are not likely to achieve astral projection within ten minutes. If you attempt astral projection, make sure you are breathing regularly, paying attention to the sounds around you, noting all sensations. Try to visualize yourself sitting in place as though being an observer to your body. As an observer, watch your body's movements as you breathe. Visualize your astral body rising up like a mist out of your physical self. As an observer, study your astral body the same way you studied your physical body. Next, visualize you the observer moving toward your astral body and merging with it. After merging with your astral body, look down at your physical body, and then begin to move across the room, visualizing yourself passing through the walls, floating outside, away from your community, into different parts of the world, and into the cosmos. The deeper you fall into the practice of astral projection, the more intense and vibrant images may become. In a sense, astral projection is both a search for God and another method to cultivate spirituality. Other ways to cultivate spirituality include:

1. Developing and living life by virtues that adhere to natural law
2. Cultivating unconditional love
3. Transcending duality

Developing and living life by the virtues that adhere to natural law requires that you know and understand the seven laws of nature. To read and put into practice the seven laws of nature, go to Appendix B. Likewise, cultivating unconditional love requires that you always extend lovingkindness to people who have wronged you. Duality is an existential state of existing in two parts, seeing yourself and God as different. Cosmic illumination creates a state of non-duality. Therefore, overcoming duality requires that you go beyond the five-sense worldly reality, work to breakdown the negative, harmful, poisonous worldviews, balance the mind equally between left and right brained consciousness, and harness the energy of the heart.

Ten-Minute Divine Meditation Exercise 1: Experimenting with Aura

1. **Close your eyes and take a few deep breaths.** Feel yourself relax further upon each exhale.

2. **Visualize yourself with someone or some place that you love.** Imagine your aura experiencing an energetic expansion in concert with the positive feelings this person or place brings. As it reaches its fullest expansion, study its appearance (color, brightness, thickness, etc.).

3. **Visualize yourself in a taxing situation, one that has caused you distress in the past.** Imagine your aura experiencing an energetic contraction in concert with the negative feelings this situation brings. Study the contraction. Note how the physical characteristics you noted earlier seem diminished.

4. **Open your eyes, stand up, and move to the center of the room.** Note the boundaries of the room, close your eyes, and visualize filling the entire room with your energy body.

5. **Retract your energy body until it forms a sphere around you.** Expand and contract it a few more times, then relax, open your eyes, and notice how you feel.

Understanding and Healing Ego Consciousness

Divine meditation goes beyond the lower intension of harnessing positive energy for human needs, desires, and ambitions, which only strengthen the ego drive. When you reach this level of spiritual understanding in your meditation, divine meditation becomes possible, and you begin to experience it in the form of spiritual infusion and synchro-mysticism. However, it is important to understand that you do not have to relinquish material possessions or make a radical lifestyle change to be spiritual. Material things simply serve as opportunities to strengthen ego drive and for this reason may inhibit how spiritually connected you become. As meditation brings the individual closer to divine consciousness (in the form of non-duality,

unconditional love, and adherence to natural law), the meditator begins to understand that there is nothing evil about the ego drive. It is, in fact, a necessary tool of creation. Without it, you would not survive, experience, or have the opportunity to transcend your physical manifestation. When destructive events occur in the world, the *individual* is responsible for giving the ego drive full control. Those who achieve the spiritual infusion of unconditional love understand that the mind possessed by the ego drive should not receive scorn because the individual knows nothing about self-control. *In Christ Returns, Speaks His Truth*, the anonymous author writes, "You take on living form and exist in two dimensions. One dimension is unseen—the divine consciousness—and the other dimension is everything the living human can sense or comprehend until spiritual development lifts its human consciousness into the spiritual plane. As this process of gradual enlightenment proceeds, the uplifted human consciousness then works *consciously* with both the unseen and the visible dimension. The higher the frequency of vibration in individualized consciousness, the higher and more perfect are the forms created in the mind. The lower the frequency of vibration, the more divorced from universal perfection of love are the forms created in the mind possessed by the ego drive."

From the moment of conception, the ego takes control of your fetus so that by the time of your birth, the imprinted instincts of survival prompt you to become aware of an emotional and physical emptiness, as well as a need for physical nourishment. When your needs were met, you could slip back into peaceful sleep. When you woke, the returning emptiness began to create a mental and emotional awareness. You remembered that your mother created fulfillment, so again you cried and she fulfilled your needs. This process continued with variation until you eventually became aware that needs were sometimes unfulfilled and you would have to adapt. Depending on the creative factors imprinted in your consciousness to ensure individuality, you reacted with acceptance or anger. During childhood, your ego developed likes and dislikes through personal experience, along with habits that corresponded to these feelings. When bad habits formed out of negative, ego-driven experience, they hid in the subconscious mind and erupted whenever the memories that formed them came to mind. The ego drive's only purpose is to bring the individual happiness. Therefore, until you learn to break the patterns created by nascent and post-nascent experience, the pain and suffering created out of the ego drive will persist. Again, this means using divine meditation to work *consciously* with both the unseen and the visible dimension.

Third Eye Activation and Meditation

The third eye is the sixth chakra, the energetic opening where the stream of prana feeds into human form. Located between the eyes, mystics call this chakra "the seat of intuition" because it connects us to higher dimensional consciousness, namely the fourth dimension. Every chakra is involved in some form of extrasensory perception, but the sixth chakra fosters extrasensory perceptions that include:

1. Intuition
2. Clairvoyance
3. Precognition
4. Astral projection
5. Seeing people's aura
6. Lucid dreaming

Everything we see with our physical eyes narrows our perception to three-dimensional reality. We are born into this world with enhanced third eye perceptions that gradually close the more we see with the physical eye. By activating the third eye, you can reverse this process and experience higher, multidimensional aspects of consciousness. Quantum physics tells us that reality has ten different dimensions. In his book, *Hyperspace: A Scientific Odyssey Through Parallel Universes, Time Warps, and the Tenth Dimension*, renowned quantum physicist Michio Kaku states that the tenth dimension is the dimension at which all the laws of the universe become unified. Since we experience life in the third dimension, much of what exists remains hidden from us. Because the third dimension experience keeps so much hidden from our five-sense perception, we experience extreme contradictions to universal truth, which creates confusion and a belief that no certain answer exists. However, the laws that apply to one dimension do not apply to other dimensions, so when you are dealing with the full truth of the universe, you will deal with contradictory information. For example, fear on a lower dimensional level is an illusion created for the purpose of expansion. On another level, it keeps you safe and alive. Contradictory teachings and beliefs only appear contradictory among people with different vibrational set points in this universe. If at any point you receive what seems like contradictory spiritual teaching, remember that in a multidi-

mensional universe, contradictions can co-exist and be equally truthful at the same time. As Teal Scott, spiritual guru and author of Askteal.com explains, "The objective truth is that this is an interdependent universe and so there really is no separation between us and other people. We are made of the same energy, so there is no [individuality]. The relative truth is that in the third dimension, we experience our individual perspectives and beings. We live our lives through our eyes only. There is [individuality]... and there isn't."

You might be asking yourself, what might third eye meditation in a higher dimension look like? The answer is not limited to one thing. For example, you might command an affirmation that tells fourth dimensional reality to organize itself in a way that is understandable to you. Remember that you are interacting with fourth dimensional reality, where time does not exist linearly, so you only need to think something in order to manifest it. In the

fourth dimension, you can get creative in your exploration, and you do not necessarily have to experience things through sight alone. You might ask the universe a question and have it explained to you. To gain insight, you might ask for an experience from a different perspective. As Teal Scott elaborates, "Let's take a given event. Let's say you wanted to go back and experience Hiroshima. You could experience what it was

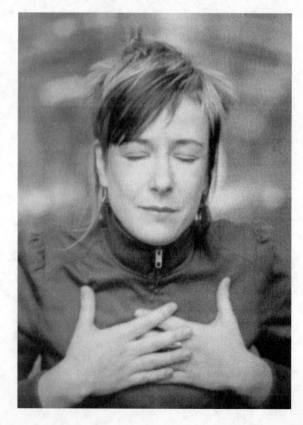

like to be a small boy being bombed, or what it was like to be a soldier dropping bombs. You could experience the universal conscious mind and experience its perspective about that event. There is no perspective that is off limits to you."

Before you activate your third eye, it is important to have already explored your inner self through your core meditation. Doing so helps you understand your fears, which have the potential to cloud your perceptions, interpretations, and projections during third eye meditation. For third eye meditation, it is especially important to open sacral chakra, which controls fear and releases negative energy. You need to be aware that certain dangers exist if you implement incorrect procedures for third eye activation, which mainly involves activating and opening the third eye without opening the prior chakras. For example, activating the third eye requires that you open the root chakra beforehand to release excess energies that might overwhelm you during third eye meditation. If you fail to open the sacral chakra, and you encounter frightful images during third eye meditation, you may not be able to distinguish your projections from what is real. If you fail to open the heart chakra, you may leave yourself vulnerable to a psychic attack by a demon or inter-dimensional entity. A demonic entity is a creation of Man's disconnected consciousness, a thought that vibrates at a vastly different frequency than love energy. It is light source resistance, both a figment of imagination and a real thing. What that means is that if you choose not to make them the focus or object of your attention, you work your way into a vibration that exists apart from demons, and they cannot be a part of your subjective reality.

If you continue your practice over a lengthy period, the third eye will eventually stay activated and you constantly channel for extra-dimensional information in between meditative sessions. Some of the symptoms you might experience include the extrasensory perceptions bulleted above. Additional symptoms might also include food and noise sensitivities, increased creativity, changing perception of time, experiencing life changing events, random encounters with spiritual teachers, manifested thought forms manifested, increased synchronicity, and so forth. Everyone who practices third eye meditation receives extrasensory information in different ways. The four main ways are physical, emotional, spiritual, and mental. For example, mental psychics have clairvoyance, emotional psychics feels intense empathy for other beings, spiritual psychics know things without being able to provide an explanation, and physical psychics feel extrasensory information. Most people possess at least one psychic sense that resonates stronger than the rest. However, as you further your practice in third eye meditation, your strongest psychic sense will expand to the point of exhaustion and begin to raise the resonance of your other psychic senses. A mental psychic who practices third eye meditation may then begin to experience increased physical, emotional, or mental extrasensory perceptions. Before you activate your third eye, consider using your core meditation to explore which psychic sense you believe is your primary strength. For example, you might quiet your mind and meditate on how you often hear sounds that no one else seems to hear, or moments where you experienced synchro-mysticism. Based on your experiences, go back to the four types of extrasensory perceptions and see which one, if any, matches your experiences.

Since Chapter 3 already covered how to prevent further pineal gland calcification, you already have a good idea why third eye mediation requires some preparation. While an acid-alkaline diet can be an important step toward adopting healthier lifestyle, some recipes may contain meats or other foods that in prevent third eye activation. To avoid such ingredients, consider adopting a vegan diet. Veganism is a type of vegetarian diet that completely excludes meat, eggs, refined sugar, wines, dairy products, processed foods, and all other animal-derived ingredients. To reiterate, a vegan diet essentially includes the same foods found in an acid-alkaline diet, but some acid-alkaline diets may allow for foods, such as chicken, that are not vegan. Meats such as chicken are not vegan because they are spiritually grounding.

Vegan foods such as oatmeal, vegetables, cereal, whole wheat bread, frozen fruit desserts, lentil soup, and chickpeas may not have the optimal acid-alkaline balance, but they are spiritually elevating. If you plan to activate your third eye, choose a vegan diet or an acid-alkaline diet that does not include meat. For more information about veganism, go to **http://www. vrg.org/**. To activate the third eye, go back to Chapter 4 and follow the instructions from step 6 under section that covers opening the seven chakras or practice the exercise below.

Ten-Minute Divine Meditation Exercise 2: Third Eye Activation

1. **Limit your physical vision.** Darkness is an important factor in third eye activation/meditation because it stimulates the pineal gland to produce melatonin. Melatonin plays an important role in getting the brain produce higher states of consciousness. This is why people produce melatonin when they dream. Dream sleep is a form of astral projection.

2. **Sit in lotus position and begin breathing.** On the inhale, breathe through the nose. On the exhale, breathe through the mouth. As thoughts occur, let them pass without judgment and allow them to pass. After a few breaths, focus on facial tension. Facial tension reduces your ability to open the third eye, so focus on tense areas and relax them.

3. **Take a deep breath and hold it for as long as you feel comfortable.** Part your jaw slightly, and on the exhale, and create the sound, "Thohhhhhhhhhhh" and extend it for as long as is comfortable. Specific sounds such as this will cause a vibration in the midbrain that stimulates the pineal gland. Repeat this breathing process six times in a row.

4. **Breathe deep and hold the inhale for six seconds.** On the exhale, create the sound "Maaaaaaaaaaaaaaay," and repeat this breathing process six times. You can experiment with different tones to see which tone best causes a vibration in the midbrain. For example, Step 6 in Chapter 4 stretches out the tone "OM." Use whichever tone works best to make the area between your eyes vibrate. Eventually, you should feel a vibration from the crown chakra. This vibration is the seventh chakra bringing extrasensory information to your third eye.

5. **Eyelids remaining shut, rotate your eyes upward as if looking toward the center of your head.** This may feel like a strain, but it helps activate the third eye. Some meditators can open their third eye without looking toward the center of the eyes, so try this step if you are having trouble activating the third eye.

6. **Looking toward the center, image your third eye, and imagine it slowly opening.** At this point, you may start to see patterns or colors. Observe what you see or feel without judgment. You will eventually begin to see extra-dimensionally.

7. **To end the session, shift your focus back to the breath for several moments and open your eyes.**

Using Binaural Beats for Third Eye Meditation

Using binaural beats is another way to activate your third eye. You do not necessarily have to descend into delta consciousness to open the third eye, but this state is usually optimal for divine meditation. Therefore, if your initial goal is to activate the third eye with a binaural beat, you might choose a 13 Hz low beta frequency, which contains enough stimulation to vibrate the pineal gland. For example, a binaural beat set at 13 Hz for third eye opening might utilize 70 Hz tone for the left ear, and an 83 Hz tone for the right ear. The 70 Hz frequency would stimulate mental and astral projection while the 83 Hz frequency would stimulate third eye opening. In addition to binaural beats, some meditators use (and even prefer) isochronic tones for meditation. Isochronic tones are the most powerful type of brainwave entrainment. They differ from binaural beats in that they combine two equal intensity pulses with intervals of silence while gradually increasing pulse speeds. Isochronic tones use cleaner waveforms than binaural beats, which some believe more efficiently harmonizes the brain. Headphones are necessary for binaural beats, and optional (though still recommended) for isochronic tones. To get an idea about which audio may be more suitable for your personal use, consider the following pros and cons.

Binaural Beats (Pros)

1. Greater variety of audio options
2. More effective for deep trance Delta consciousness
3. Research well established

Binaural Beats (Cons)

1. Less effective than isochronic tones outside the delta frequency range
2. Headphones more necessary than for isochronic tones which may be less convenient

Isochronic Tones (Pros)

1. More effective than binaural beats in beta, alpha, and theta frequency ranges
2. Headphones not necessary which is more convenient

Isochronic Tones (Cons)

1. Smaller variety of audio options
2. Less effective for delta consciousness
3. Research less established

Ten-Minute Divine Meditation Exercise 3: Using Binaural Beats or Isochronic Tones

1. **Find a dark room and assume a meditative position.** You can use any comfortable position, or the step 6 position from Chapter 4.

2. **Put on your headphones.** Begin playing the binaural beat or isochronic tone, and close your eyes.

3. **Use any breathing technique and focus the breath into and out of your third eye chakra.** On the inhale, feel the oxygen entering your third eye. On the exhale, feel the chakra pulsate as it receives the air.

4. **Repeat step 3 for the length of the audio.** The audio for a binaural beat or an isochronic tone is usually between 30 and 60 minutes.

5. **When the audio ends, stay with the meditation or come back to the breath to end the session.** Take a few deep breaths, and slowly open your eyes. Continue this practice daily for at least three weeks. The more you do it, the more fourth dimensional sight your third eye will gain.

After each session, rub your hands quickly together to heat them up, and bring them to your face to absorb the energy. This helps integrate your brain to the new experience. Third eye meditation can be the most interesting practice when it comes to keeping a journal. After you come out of a session, write down what you experience, continue this meditative process for at least three weeks, and examine what has changed. It is common for some third eye mediators to experience symptoms such as headaches, migraines, or dizziness after activating such a long-dormant part of the brain. Understand that this is normal, that you are still in control, and that it is not easy to awaken and open up to what the universe wants to show you.

Chanting Meditation to Evoke the Divine

If you have trouble opening the third eye, try mixing a chanting meditation into your practice as it can help stimulate the energetic openings. Chanting meditations are not for everyone, but those who practice devotion to a religion such as Christianity or Islam may be more inclined to use them. Again, this is where different forms of meditation intersect with devotional religions. Singing gospel is a form of devotional chanting much the same way that the contemplative prayers used by various religions are a form of meditation. Chanting also serves as a valuable tune up for meditation when combined with some of the other preparatory methods described in Chapter 4.

Insight vs. Devotion

Ultimately, the point of practicing divine meditation is discovering who you are in relation to everything else. Divine meditation offers two paths, insight and devotion. Devotional meditation typically practiced in religions such as Christianity or Islam use representations of divinity as an object of meditative focus. In devotional meditation, you work to achieve spiritual union with ultimate consciousness. It is the intention of having the universal creative source work through you and allowing it to pervade every aspect of your life. Insight meditation uses present moment awareness and spiritual connectivity to investigate further into the nature of things. Doing so reveals the deeper reality, achieving a divine meditation in its essence, but without the characteristics of devotional practice.

If you have an interest in gaining insight into your existence but do not have an interest in cultivating spiritual devotion, it is best to choose divine meditative practices that cultivate insight rather than devotion. Buddhism, for example, practices insight rather than devotion, and some religions, while devotional in nature, offer insight practices as an alternative. The Judeo practice of Kabbalah (explored further in Chapter 10) is one such practice that focuses on this path. Insight meditation teaches that reality has two levels, relative and absolute. The relative world is the physical reality and everything it encompasses such as your job, the bills you have to pay, the family you must care for, etc. While these things contain meaning for people, they do not contain true cosmic meaning. Absolute reality is true cosmic meaning, the divine presence that gives everything its reason for being. Accessing the points at which *relative* and *absolute* reality intersect to create enlightenment is what insight meditation aspires to achieve. Therefore, consider any meditative exercise designed to expand boundaries a path to insight.

Chapter 9

Meditation in Performance Enhancement and Living Everyday Life

Books on meditation attract different people for different reasons, but the common thread among the people drawn to the practice is the desire to see its results extended into everyday life. Meditation has become popular in western culture because mediation is a results-proven practice, and this is a results-oriented society. In short, meditation yields the kind of mental and physical results most people in modern life need to run their everyday lives. In addition to being a devotional and insightful art, it is a performance art which prepares the body for physical activity. No single better example of meditation as a performance art exists than in the mar-

tial arts. When people think about martial arts (tai-kwan-do, judo, jujitsu, and so forth), meditation is not the first thing that comes to mind. However, meditation plays a large part because it involves achieving a synthesis between the body and mind which mediation aims to achieve. Meditation as performance enhancement not only helps martial artists but also a wide variety of people in competitive sports and performing arts because it cultivates what athletes call "being in the zone." If you suffer from anger, anxiety, or depression and you try to learn a martial art, play a competitive sport, or pursue a performing art, negative mind-states are likely to hinder your training and level of performance without some form of meditation.

Meditation as Performance Enhancement in Martial Arts

Why do people learn martial arts and what are its benefits? Again, the answer is different for everyone, but performance enhancement is always a common thread. Some individuals practice martial arts to promote general

fitness, such as developing flexibility and stamina, while others use it to reduce stress. Martial arts are essentially an action form of meditation which develops the mind and what the Chinese call the semi-sleeping state. The semi-sleeping state is the meditative component of marital arts that optimizes concentration; it awakens the subconscious mind and tells the conscious mind to release control. Practicing meditation to develop the semi-sleeping state allows the martial artist to achieve a level of focus where outside distractions do not register. To reach the full potential as a martial artist, training begins with calming the mind so that it will focus and allow your body to work in harmony with it. Without meditation, the martial artist can tense up with fear. When this occurs, the mind mentally dictates things to the body rather than letting the body flow with what the Chinese call *Qi* energy. The two polarities in the body that regulate Qi energy are the brain and the abdomen region, otherwise known as the yin and yang. The brain (or yin) regulates the quality of energy. The abdomen (or yang) stores and supplies the body's energy quantity.

As Bruce Lee attested in a 1971 interview with Pierre Berton, "Martial arts have a very deep meaning in my life because everything I have learned as an actor, as a martial artist, and as a human being I have learned from martial arts. It is a combination of natural instinct and control, and you have to combine the two in harmony. In either extreme, you become unscientific or mechanical, no longer a human being. Therefore, martial art is the art of expressing the human body." Martial artists call their form of meditation "embryonic breathing." Through embryonic breathing, the yin and yang communicate through the spinal cord, which enables the two Qi energy polarities to act as one. In martial arts training, the quality of the energy supplied by the yin and the quantity of energy stored in the yang increases though a constant coordination between the mind and the semi-sleeping state. Martial artists also use meditation as a way to mentally reviewing techniques in their mind. During meditation, a martial artist will replay moves with precise changes, isolating footwork, balance, state of mind, timing, power, and so forth. They might also use it as a form of self-reflection with respect to training. For example, if performance training becomes difficult, meditation is a place where you can re-examine your motives, contemplate your weaknesses, and refocus your approach. Those who sustain injuries in combat also use meditation as a way to heal faster. As a way of gaining a competitive advantage, martial artists may also use meditation to understand the opponent. In the seminal book, *The Art of*

War, Sun Tzu writes, "If you only know yourself, but not your opponent, you may win or you may lose."

Meditation as Performance Enhancement in Competitive Sports

Athletes who play at peak performance through mental and physical harmony often describe a phenomenon they call being "in flow" or "in the zone." Athletes describe this experience as a state in which extremely difficult tasks come easier than normal, and the brain flows smoothly with acute concentration from one activity to the next. Hall of Fame basketball player Michael Jordan once described an experience where his shooting accuracy was near perfect because the basketball net seemed much bigger than normal, and it felt as if he could not miss. Joe Greene, Hall of Fame defensive end for the Pittsburgh Steelers once said, "A lot of players talk about being in the zone, but for me, it only happened one time in my career. In fact, the one time it happened, it felt like the whole team was in the zone and we were playing as one unit. We could anticipate exactly what our opponent was going to do and we executed to perfection."

Many professional athletes have trouble identifying how or why they get into the zone, but those who meditate to enhance their performance are likely to find the zone more often than those who do not. When meditation opens the zone to athletes during the biggest moments of their career, the gravity of the moment does not faze them. When athletes wilt in the big moments, anxiety and the fear of failure overwhelms them. The gravity of the moment becomes too much; thus, the body and mind falter in disharmony and they miss their opportunity to shine. Self-awareness during competition causes the very anxiety and stress that causes poor performance. Many athletes adopt the practice of mediating before a match to reduce stress and increase their focus. Other athletes meditate during resting periods in between to develop the energy and endurance necessary for later use. According to sports meditation consultant George Mumford, who was hired during Phil Jackson's tenure with the Chicago Bulls, "Meditation offers opportunity to be in the moment. In sports, what gets people's attention is this idea of being in the zone or playing in the zone. When they are playing their best, they can do no wrong, and no matter what happens they are always a step quicker, a step ahead. That happens when we are in the moment, when we are mindful of what is going on. There is a lack of self-consciousness, there is a relaxed concentration, and there is this sense of effortlessness, of being in the flow." Because meditation reduces self-awareness and heightens mindfulness, the athlete immerses more fully into the surroundings. As you transfer the focus away from yourself, you focus more on the environment. In his book, *Flow: The Psychology of the Optimal Experience*, Mihalyi Csikszentmihalyi identifies several characteristics of athletes who surpass the dimension of human experience, which include:

1. Deep concentration
2. The transformation of time
3. Letting go of control
4. Loss of self-consciousness

Because physical prowess is a third dimensional gift, some athletes are faster and stronger. However, the athlete that masters all the characteristics of flow beyond third dimensional consciousness is far more likely to outperform the physically superior athlete that does not. Bruce Lee was by no means a physically imposing person, but to this day many consider him the greatest martial artist of all time. What being in flow demonstrates is that consciousness plays an essential role in athletic training. To this end, Csikszentmihalyi writes, "Because optimal experience depends on the ability to control what happens in moment-by-moment consciousness, each person has to achieve it on the basis of his or her own individual efforts and creativity. This happens when psychic energy is invested in realistic goals, and when skills match the opportunities for action."

Csikszentmihalyi teaches athletes that having the right skills to perform requires that the activity be stimulating and enjoyable when trying to perform it. When beating the opponent takes precedence in the mind over performing as well as possible, enjoyment tends to disappear and with it the characteristics of flow. This is what some allude to when they say that sports and competition nurtures spiritually disconnected ego consciousness. Out of fear, anger, or anxiety comes the fear of being controlled out of which arises the desire to dominate or control others. Paradoxically, and as an example of how spiritual truth feels contradictory in third dimensional reality, having real control means allowing one's self to let go of control. As Csikszentmihalyi notes, "The flow experience is typically described as involving a sense of control or, more precisely, as lacking the sense of worry about losing control that is typical in many situations of normal life. What people enjoy is not the sense of *being* in control, but the sense of *exercising* control in difficult situations. However, when a person becomes dependent on the ability to control an enjoyable activity, he or she then loses the ultimate control: the freedom to determine the content of consciousness." Outstanding performances in flow are examples of transcendent, egoless consciousness. The most captivating moments in sports are the ones that speak to something greater than leisurely indulgence or competitive-minded ego consciousness. Whether the miracle underdog comes out of nowhere and surprises everyone, or the dominating favorite runs through the competition with ease, what we often witness is a theater for enacting the drama of self-transcendence or what coaches call "team concept." While competition does drive some to nurture unhealthy egoistic tendencies, the most unforgettable moments in sports do serve to remind us of our own inner potential as masters of divine power.

Meditation as Performance Enhancement in the Creative Arts

What is inspiration and where does it come from? Whether you are someone pursuing a career as a creative artist or just enjoy hobbies like painting or writing as creative outlet, people have sought the answer since the first great works of art appeared in human history. Inspiration implies the idea that some external source must create an internal spark. The truth about inspiration is that it is nothing more than clarity, the act of gaining insight by accessing a creative source that exists within each person at any given moment. One of the most common questions asked by creative artists is where ideas for great works come from. According to renowned Hollywood screenwriting teacher Robert McKee, "Stories unearth themselves inside the mind of the writer. They are not buried somewhere in the ground of life trying to come up and tell themselves. The stories worth telling already exist within you. You are responding to your own inner life, whether by something you see on the street, experience in a dream, or read in the newspaper....So it is useful to imagine that your unconscious mind has already created stories living within you." Susan K. Perry, author of *Writing in Flow*, contends that conscious, critical thinking also leads to procrastination. "Why is it that some people can spend so much time composing

email to their friends, but when it comes to their 'serious' writing, they always find something else they need to do? The answer has everything to do with allowing yourself to full reign to play with words. When you are writing to a friend, your internal critic does not usually bother rousing itself to pester you about how well you are doing....If you procrastinate over your 'real' writing, it may be because you believe on some level that your first drafts have to be excellent, perhaps even perfect. But that is not the way to get yourself to do your best work."

For creative artists, inspiration should not to be confused with craft. Craft is the learned ability to methodically shape and organize the ideas from inspiration according to proven, established principals in such a way that transforms those ideas into a profound, meaningful, and moving work of art. Just as flow demonstrates that consciousness plays an essential role in athletic training, so too does it play a role in the development of craft. Rarely does any great works of art immediately arise from the mind in its final form. The creative artists who combine mastery of craft with inspiration from within are the ones who create works of lasting importance. Claudio Naranjo, the psychiatrist responsible for introducing spiritual traditions into psychotherapy, once said about the art of composing music, "Only repetition invites spontaneous innovation." Without constant practice and development of craft, meditation cannot inspire you to organize inspiring ideas in a way that creates a masterwork. Rather than relying on meditative practice and hoping to get lucky, use meditation to learn how to work with your mind in a skillful and open way. Meditation is a very powerful way to expand creative vision, but only when practiced free of agendas. Susan Piver, *New York Times* bestselling author of books on meditative practice, notes, "Meditation teaches the skill of relaxing the mind by resting attention on breath without agenda. The moment we apply an agenda to our meditation practice, even a great artist practicing to be more creative will have their energy drained. When we practice in a way that is both free and disciplined (the discipline of not applying an agenda), our innate brilliance is unleashed, and that is when mental and emotional innovations spontaneously arise." Meditation tunes down the logical mind and allows the creative subconscious to have more influence. Relaxation then enhances the powers of creativity. Research shows that slower brainwaves introduce flashes of creative insight and intense focus. Thus, alpha waves associated with relaxation are the gateway to the creativity that exists in a state of theta consciousness. In fact, many audio entrainment manufacturers specifically design binaural beats as an aid to the meditative practice of inducing the alpha/theta states that enhance creativity.

Meditation as Performance Enhancement in a Professional Business Career

Even in today's business world, meditation has hit the mainstream. At major Fortune 500 companies, CEOs now hire meditation consultants to train their employees in meditative techniques designed to optimize their on-the-job performance. When it comes to the pressures of performing well, the corporate world places more demands upon the individual than in almost any other setting. Whether you work in a large, mid-size, or small business setting, the higher you rise, the more you probably worry about falling. What constitutes aspects that meditation can enhance work performance? For one person, performance may depend on giving crisp but relaxed presentations or public speaking; for someone else it may depend on needing the focus to produce numbers or meet quotas. Others still may depend on quick thinking to make critical business decisions or the mental balance to manage staff and other professional relationships. With any of these responsibilities comes pressure, and with pressure comes the fear of failure. While fear does drive many headlong into greater success, the destructive toll of the stress response becomes the price their bodies pay over the long term. Moreover, the sum of one's experience in the business world is not simply limited to work experiences, but also career training and unemployment. Today, the average person changes careers approximately five times over a lifetime, while changing jobs about fifteen times. Changing global dynamics drive people to seek employment opportunities in new cities where they do not know anyone. Global expansion into overseas markets takes business professionals away from their families for long periods. For the unemployed, the pressure of finding a job in a down economy means facing the challenge of performing well in an interview.

These are just a few reasons for why meditation has found its way into the business setting. Branded under the category of career management specialists, firms such as London-based Whitefield Consulting Worldwide help businesses harmonize their professional goals and aspirations through meditation seminars. Meditation consultants typically offer a diversity of services which include career consulting, personal development, MBA coaching, and so forth. Even at the academic level, meditation is now part of some curriculums. For example, the Maharishi University of Management located in Fairfield, Iowa, has introduced a consciousness-based approach to its MBA program, which includes the practice of the Transcendental Meditation® technique. Schools like the Maharishi University of Management understand that, just as consciousness plays an essential role in athletic training and creative artistry, so too does it play a role in career management. For business professionals, success sometimes calls for a transformation in attitude.

The research on the effects of mediation in business are now so extensive that writers and business strategists like Peter Bregman of the *Harvard Business Review* publicly support data that shows meditation's impact on people's capacity to focus and resist distractions in the workplace. In one such study published in *Frontiers in Human Neuroscience*, Researchers at UCLA used MRI scans to compare the brains of experienced meditators versus those who had almost never meditated. Experienced meditators showed higher levels of cerebral cortex folding which is associated with faster information processing. The scans further revealed that more years meditating equaled greater cerebral cortex folding. To test this data, researchers at the University of Arizona recruited 45 human resources managers for an eight-week training course in mindfulness-based meditation, and compared a control group with no training at all. At the end of eight-weeks, both groups took a multitasking test, and the results showed that the mindful-mediation group reported less stress than the non-meditation group. If you are like so many people who experience fear, anxiety, or depression about their job performance, you can begin to understand why meditation has become such a valuable tool for everyday life.

Gamma Consciousness

Due to the contrasting nature of tasks required among martial arts, competitive sports, creative arts, and professional careers, some states of consciousness necessary for optimal performance may differ, or they may be the same. For creative artists, optimal performance comes from entering deep states of alpha and theta consciousness. By contrast, a business manager may have no use for intuitive cognition, just as a creative artist may have no use for critical cognition. In the business world, theta consciousness will not provide the kind alertness necessary to perform certain tasks. Therefore, some business professionals who work well into the night may only find binaural beats useful if they produce high beta states of alertness. Business professionals who need to be at high alert might then consider a binaural frequency not yet mentioned in this book, *gamma waves*.

If you are the type of business professional, such as a security agent, private detective, soldier, who works at night and relies on being in a constant high state of alert, gamma waves offer the fastest brainwave entrainment on the frequency spectrum. Ranging from 40 - 70 Hz, gamma waves can enhance peak performance for tasks that require intense states of cognition. First championed by Nobel Prize winning scientist Sir Francis Crick, gamma waves correlate to increased memory as well as en-hanced mental learning and pro-cessing. The irony about meditat-ing with gamma waves is that they *enhance* perception of reality through the five senses, whereas most meditative practices covered

in this book relate to *transcending* them. To this end, gamma waves can enhance any task that requires improved sight, acute hearing, a heightened sense of smell, or elevated taste sensitivity. In the business world, some people rely heavily one or more of the five senses to do their job. Take taste, for example. Let us suppose you are a food critic who runs a blog. Would your heightened sense of taste help you experience the subtle flavors of food better so you can write more descriptively about them? Would an el-evated taste sensitive enhance your performance as a food critic? Though some meditators aspire to only the higher intension, meditation is strictly yours to practice how you choose, for the benefits you intend. To find high quality and effective binaural audios for Gamma brain waves, refer to the online audio stores listed in Chapter 5.

How to Create Flow State

Learning how to enter flow state will increase both your productivity and happiness, but the key is developing the right habits and executing them on a regular basis. According to Dr. Csikszentmihalyi, a person enters flow state when he or she has sufficient interest, enjoyment, and skill to complete a challenging task. At some point, the individual in flow begins to feel an energetic rush and fluidly performs the task without having to think about it. At some point, without even recognizing it, the activity becomes so pleasurable that the individual keeps going without wanting to stop. In a presentation given at the 2004 Technology, Entertainment, and Design Conference (TED), Csikszentmihalyi explained that the nervous system is incapable of processing more than 110 bits of information per second, and that accurate processing occurs at roughly 60 bits per second. This means that in order to enter flow state, the mind requires full engagement, a state of deep concentration on the task, and mindfulness of fear and other self-defeating behaviors. Therefore, to enter flow state, consider using any of the meditation techniques from your core concentration and Mindfulness Meditations.

Furthering his point at the 2004 TED Conference, Csikszentmihalyi presented a Flow Chart diagram (illustrated below) which measures the point at which the skill of the individual and the challenge of the task begin to create flow.

As the diagram shows, anxiety, worry, and apathy (all coincidentally the same low vibratory states listed on the Hawkins scale) are typical emotions of individuals who have negative perceptions toward the task and therefore low skill level. However, these negative emotions differ when it comes to the individual's *perception* of the task. Those

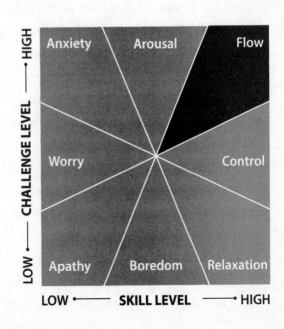

who demonstrate apathy may not care about completing the challenge and therefore have less skill to complete it. Since these individuals do not worry about completing the task, it makes no difference whether they succeed or fail. Those with an interest in completing the task demonstrate worry and anxiety about their ability to do so. Since these individuals have little experience or skill, they focus on their own fear of failure rather than on the task itself. Individuals with mid-level skill experience apathy more often than boredom. For these individuals, the goal is to simply complete the task rather than excel at it. Once able to complete the minimum requirements, they quickly become bored. However, those with mid-level skills who demonstrate extreme interest in the task have an aroused desire to excel further. This is the point at which optimal preconditions for flow state exist.

Therefore, to elicit flow, the perception of the task as enjoyable, interesting, and challenging must combine with having attained at least a mid-level skill. Even with without these preconditions, meditation can still allow the skilled individual to relax while completing the challenge. However, if the task does not create enough enjoyment at this stage, flow is not possible. As a mild interest, the skilled individual may use meditation to exhibit greater control but still not flow. As the individual's perception of the challenge as interesting and enjoyable begins to rise in concert with skill level, meditation can take the individual into higher levels of consciousness that create flow. Many people who experience unhappiness in their careers often report a sense of boredom or anxiety associating with the tasks they perform, and thus experience varied forms of depression. When people choose unsatisfying careers, external factors like money or lack of available options may play a role, and, as a result, they wind up pursuing careers that feel either meaningless or overwhelming. If you have options in life, remember that no amount of money is ever worth the price of well-being. Whether you are in the middle of a career change or just starting out, use Csikszentmihalyi Flow Chart to find out where your true passionate lies. The greater the match between your skills and interests, the greater the chance of choosing a career that fosters your flow. As the old saying goes,

"If you love what you do, you will never work a day in your life." In other words, everything will feel timeless and effortless, the very characteristics of flow. In order to use meditation as a means of inducing your flow state, the preconditions necessary before you meditate include:

1. Finding a challenge, something you enjoy doing
2. Developing enough skill to meet the minimum requirements of the challenge
3. Having set clear goals that make the task challenging enough
4. Eliminating other distractions before attempting the challenge
5. Making sure there is enough time set aside time to get in flow state (roughly 10-15 minutes) and to complete the challenge
6. Developing mindfulness of what emotions typically arise when attempting this challenge

Using Guided Visual Imagery

The Buddhist practice of using visual imagery in meditation incorporates the use of the imagination to invoke spiritual forces that fuel spiritual realization. Any meditation that requires you to visualize or imagine something constitutes a guided visual meditation. This includes some of the previous mediations discussed earlier, such as Big Mind meditation or experimenting with aura. Instead of invoking spirituality, some meditations using guided visual imagery can work specifically for getting in flow. According to Belleruth Naparstek, author of *Staying Well with Guided Imagery*, visualized meditation consists of three basic principles.

Principle #1: The body and mind cannot tell the difference between a current sensory experience and a past sensory experience. In other words, once you immerse the mind and body with a visualization of a past or imaginary experience, the body interprets the experience as real and happening now. If you have ever recalled an embarrassing experience, you probably noticed that your body reacted as if the experience was happening all over again. The same is true when recalling a pleasurable experience.

Exercise: To employ this principle to a meditation, take ten minutes to close your eyes and visualize yourself immersed in your task or challenge as if it is happening right now. Note the physical or emotional sensations and become mindful of how your body reacts.

Principle #2: Altered states induced by meditation have a healing effect that can cause the individual to grow and change. Altered states allow you to explore new behaviors and change existing ones. When dealing with performance enhancement techniques, the best way to excel is to learn how to do something better. Meditation gives you the clarity to contemplate mistakes and see what you can improve for next time.

Exercise: To employ this principle to a meditation, take ten minutes to close your eyes and visualize a time in the past when you attempted your task or challenge. Become mindful of the mistakes you made and meditate on what you need to change about your approach.

Principle #3: Imagery makes mastering a challenge seem more possible. Some guided meditations call for visualizing a near impossible task, so that when you take on the actual task, it seems that much easier. As the saying goes, "Shoot for the stars so that you land on the moon." For example, some guided meditations ask professional swimmers to visualize swimming through molasses so that when they prepare to swim through water, it seems much easier than what they mentally prepared for.

Exercise: To employ this principle to a meditation, take ten minutes to close your eyes and visualize a similar but much harder version of your task or challenge. Notice how your body and mind reacts to this near impossible task. When you come out of the meditation, notice how much easier the task feels compared to your visualization. This exercise is one of the most common meditations used among martial artists, athletes, creative artists, and career-oriented people. However, this exercise, like most others, is more useful when the preconditions for flow are right. A more skilled individual using this guided meditation may enter relaxation, control, or flow, whereas a less skilled individual may evoke apathy or boredom.

Ten Minute Performance Meditation: Guided Visuals for Enhanced Creativity

1. **Close your eyes, take ten deep breaths – through the nose on the inhale, through the mouth on the exhale.** Say the world "Relax" on each out breath.

2. **Imagine standing at the top of ten steps. Imagine seeing a door at the bottom of these steps.** Imagine taking a step and feeling more relaxed, then another and feeling even more relaxed.

3. **Imagine reaching the bottom of the steps.** Imagine opening the door and seeing your ideal place of relaxation (for example, a beach, a home, a garden).

4. **Imagine stepping through the door, into your ideal place of relaxation.** Use your senses and begin to explore this place. What does it look like, sound like, smell like, and feel like?

5. **Visualize an imaginary lake appearing in the middle of this idea relaxation place.** Visualize a stone on the ground, then pick it up and throw the stone into the lake. Watch the ripples in the water created by the stone.

6. **As you watch the ripples, imagine that creative thoughts are beginning to flow to you.** Do not try to force anything. Just enjoy this place and stay relaxed while waiting for the creative mind to activate.

7. **When you feel sufficiently relaxed, open your eyes and take on your creative task.**

Will Power Concentration

Will Power Meditation is similar to the Big Mind Meditation in that you use visualization to gain cooperation with larger parts of your brain. The difference is that this meditation works well for performance enhancement. Using Will Power Concentration requires keeping a journal. Write down a list of objectives and goals for tomorrow's daily activities or meditative practice. Writing these goals the night before gives you some time to think about them and "sleep on it." As you lay down in bed, close your eyes, practice a breathing technique. If nothing about the challenge causes negative emotions that may inhibit your performance, visualize the stages of each task and begin to visualize completing each with ease and with great accuracy. It may also help to visualize challenges that arise, and overcoming these challenges with high competency. If something about the challenge causes fear or anxiety, verbalize the task aloud and ask yourself what about this task causes fear or anxiety. As discussed earlier, sometimes naming a fear serves to lessen its power in the mind. The purpose of will power concentration is to command the unconscious mind into an understanding of what you are asking it to do and gaining its compliance.

Healing Meditations

In Chapter 1, we explored how meditation correlates with mental, physical, and emotional well-being. When we meditate, the nervous system activates *the relaxation response* which lowers the body's adrenaline levels, softens the muscles, and decreases blood pressure. The same concept applies to healing meditations. Healing meditations work to eliminate injuries caused by the stress response. Since healing meditation works to maintain the body's wellness, one might also consider it a form of performance enhancement. Light is a common visual image that meditators use for healing. To experiment with light as a healing practice, assume any meditative posture, begin breathing to quiet the mind, and after a few minutes, imagine a sphere of light suspended a foot above your head. Imagine this sphere full of positive, healing energy. If you are religious, this sphere may represent your spiritual leader. Next, imagine the sphere of light growing more luminous as it draws in all the benevolent forces of the universe until the light radiates everything around you. As the light radiates, imagine it streaming its energy down into your body, replacing toxicity, pain, and stress with vitality and health. Feel the light energy soaking into your muscles and cells, leaving you energized and strong. Imagine the sphere itself descending into your heart, creating harmony and peace until you begin to radiate this energy to every other being in the world. For aches and pains, also consider using the meditative practice below.

Ten Minute Healing Meditation: The 4-4-8 Procedure

1. **Assume a meditative posture, close your eyes, and inhale deeply for four seconds.**

2. **At the end of four seconds, hold your breath for another four seconds.**

3. **At the end of four seconds, release your breath and exhale for another eight seconds.**

4. **At the end of eight seconds, inhale for four seconds and visualize that you are breathing in a cool, bluish, healthy air.** Visualize the air flowing like water into your nose, feeling it cleanse your body, and feeling its coolness soothe your lungs.

5. **At the end of four seconds, hold the healthy air on your lungs for four seconds.** As you hold the breath, envision the tension and stress gathering in your lungs, ready to expunge on the exhale.

6. **At the end of four seconds, exhale for eight seconds, and release the tension gathered in your lungs.**

7. **Repeat as many times as you want, and adjust the length of the inhale and exhale according to your needs.**

CASE STUDY: PERFORMANCE ENHANCEMENT

Brian Sheen
Florida Institute for Complementary and Alternative Medicine
Boynton Beach, FL
drbriansheen@yahoo.com
www.BrianSheen.com

Meditation is a developmental process of learning how to create attention and inner focus while expanding your awareness of the bigger picture of Life. Feeling grounded and connected to existence provides an opportunity to tune in to the deeper powers of the body and mind when you feel aligned to the flow of life energy. Instead of struggling to fulfill your desires, you learn to move with the currents and ride the waves of existence. Being in tune with the life energies can enhance the result of *any* action, as the action becomes an expression of life and existence. You become the vehicle for extending this action in whatever action that involves you.

For the last 40 years, I have practiced and taught thousands of individuals to develop their attention to enhance their task performance objectives. I have worked with presidents of Fortune 500 companies, major hospitals, politicians, actors, writers, football players, golfers, doctors, nurses, teachers, accountants, waiters, secretaries, and students. Using meditative practices, my students have developed improvements in their ability to get results in their personal and professional actions. As a part of a core practice, I have developed a Seven Keys for Attention Development Program, which has helped individuals become drug free, while helping others become calmer, focused and more effective in their job.

Most of my students attend my classes to improve upon a number of different personal or professional tasks, such as wanting to focus better at work, wanting to improve sleep patterns, wanting to increase their creativity, wanting to improve communication with co-workers or loved ones, or wanting to reduce blood pressure medications. To achieve performance results, I have found that the clear mind--open heart meditation is one of the most effective techniques. In addition to enhanced task performance, my students report drastic improvements in their emotional state of being. When the mind is calm, only then can the body function at optimal levels. This is so important to being happier, healthier, and more empowered in every area of life.

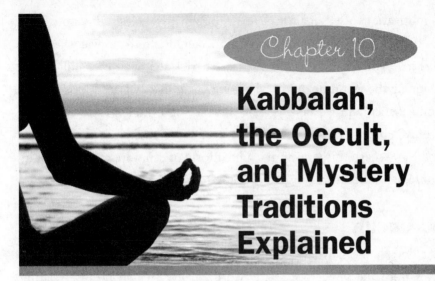

Chapter 10

Kabbalah, the Occult, and Mystery Traditions Explained

Some of the information based in this chapter and the accounts therein are claims directly experienced or researched by others. To some, the accounts may seem scary. To others, they may appear far-fetched. Others still may have already heard them in lesser detail. Whether you choose to believe or disbelieve the information, the purpose of this chapter is not to scare you, but to inform you of theories that are the subject of growing discussion and debate. Moreover, to explore the nature of evil and to ask the question, "What if hidden forces are intentionally manifesting evil in the world, and if so, what can we do about it?" If you have come to read this book trying to make sense of why you feel anger, anxiety, or depression in your life, and it turned out that something was designing it, you would probably want to know about it. More specifically, you would want to know why. If the function of evil is to reverse nature by disconnecting you from spirit, meditation can keep you connected.

Evil in its darkest form involves a higher purpose, and the primary action is a psychological assault whereby the victim may have their weaknesses and motivations used against them. Through psychological actions, evil assaults the victim's ability to control his or her life. In the movie *The Usual Suspects*, Kevin Spacey says, "The greatest trick the devil ever pulled was convincing the world he didn't exist." We know that evil deeds exist by the actions of men and women, yet the presence of a hidden catalyst for evil not only remains the subject of great debate in some circles, but also of ridicule and scorn. Either way, if a higher form of evil were to succeed in its purpose, it would make sense to operate from behind a veil.

The Occult

What does it mean when we call something occult? The word "occult" derives from the same root as the word "ocular" which means "relating

to the eye." When something is occult, it is considered hidden from sight. Misunderstood by most people and misrepresented in popular culture, the word is often associated with some form of devil worship. In reality, occultism is simply a hidden body of knowledge, neither inherently good nor evil, but used by the wielder of that hidden knowledge to promote good or evil. A hammer, for example, is neither good nor evil;

it is simply a tool used to do something. If a person uses the hammer to strike someone in the head, they have committed an evil act, so the hammer becomes a tool of evil. If a person uses that same hammer to build houses for the homeless, the hammer becomes a tool of good. Drawn from these two distinctions are the actions of *white occultists* and *dark occultists*. If the white occultist uses the hammer to help others, the dark occultist uses the hammer to destroy them for personal gain. According to Mark Passio, radio host of whatonearthishappening.com, "Occult does not mean evil; is simply information about how consciousness works. Those with occult knowledge are practitioners of consciousness who belong to various secret societies with roots in the mystery traditions of ancient Egypt and Babylon." Passio, a former high priest from the Church of Satan, believes that many who inherited this knowledge from these mystery traditions have perverted the tools by taking its knowledge and using it to accrue vast amounts of power in the world. Says Passio, "A small number of occultists understand how consciousness works and are using that knowledge against the bulk of humanity to control and manipulate their consciousness into a vibration of chaos and fear."

The secret societies derived from the mystery traditions are pyramidal, hierarchical, and compartmentalized in nature. Within this pyramid scheme, those at the top possess the higher levels of occult knowledge, and descending toward the bottom of each hierarchy are larger numbers of people, but with lower levels of occult knowledge. In these secret societies, there are also levels of initiation. For example, in the Freemason mystery tradition, a third degree mason sits at the bottom of the pyramid, and a thirty-three degree master mason sits near the top. Even when it comes to the hierarchical pyramids within mystery traditions, different levels of knowledge means those at the lower-levels are less informed of both occult knowledge and the intentions of those who reside at the top. If occult knowledge is a tool for individual or spiritual empowerment, and those who possess that knowledge do not share it with people freely, then those who keep the secrets hidden are more likely to pervert the knowledge into a form of control over others. In this case, lack of esoteric knowledge then becomes a form of individual or spiritual *disempowerment*. Over the last decade or so, this has become the central thesis of many conspiracy theories, ranging from an occult connection to the September 11th terrorist attacks to a New World Order government resembling the dystopian nightmare of books like *Brave New World* and *1984*. Embedded within these connections, conspiracy theorists claim, are the various symbols and numerologies that earmark the work of dark occultism.

In books such as Bill Cooper's *Behold a Pale Horse* and Albert G. Mackey's *Revised Encyclopedia of Freemasonry*, various connections exist between the Freemason mystery tradition and the founding of the United States. In fact, some of the most notable founding fathers of this time, including George Washington and Benjamin Franklin ,were well-known initiates of the mystery tradition. Washington, a 1752 initiate whose letters on Freemasonry are available at the Manuscript Division at the Library of Congress, noted that, "the great object of Masonry is to promote the happiness of the human race." Though George Washington presumably considered himself a white occultist, conspiracy theorists claim the numerology embedded within the year 1776 equates to something more sinister. According to occult researchers Bill Cooper, David Ike, Fritz Springmeier, Jordon Maxwell and others, the numbers 3, 7, 9, 11, 13, 33, 39 (and any multiple of these numbers) have special meaning to the mystery traditions. Thus, adding up the Roman numerals in 1776 (DCLXVI), and combining them in three base pairs (D = 500 + C = 100 + L = 50 + X = 10 + V = 5 + I = 1) creates the hidden numerical value 600 + 60 + 6, which equals 666. While the "M" is noticeably missing in this conversion, conspiracy theorists point to the fact that the Roman numbering system did not use this numeral until much later in time. Moreover, conspiracy theorists argue that anyone looking for occult numerology will find the meaningful numbers embedded in many significant world events of the past century.

Freemasonry and the Illuminati

In the words of politician Judith Moriarty, "The greatest conspiracies are not actually hidden, just fragmented in to different pieces, like a puzzle, right before our eyes." According to conspiracy theory, most of the mystery school secret societies fall under the umbrella called The Illuminati. At the top of the Illuminati pyramid are elite billionaires belonging to thirteen of the wealthiest families in the world. The secret societies allegedly connected to the Illuminati include the Freemasons, Skull and Bones, the Rosicrucians, the Golden Dawn, The Knights Templar, and The Bilderberg Group. Although the existence of the current Illuminati remains in debate, its roots trace back to the well-documented Bavarian sect founded by Adam Weishaupt in the 1700s. However, the Bavarian Illuminati as a new secret society was not new; rather, it was believed an incarnation of a secret society in existence for thousands of years under different names. The Freemasons, under the influence of the Bavarian Illuminati, started Freemasonry of the Scottish Rite, which began the 33 degrees of initiation that exist in Masonic Lodges today. At the 33rd level in Freemasonry is illumination. Freemasons under the Scottish Rite also included esoteric knowledge from the Knights Templar. It is believed that the Bavarian Illuminati, considered a benevolent masonic (or white occult) organization, helped start the French, Russian, and American revolutions.

In his book, *The Secret Destiny of America*, former Freemason Manly P. Hall cites the pyramid on the back of the U.S. dollar as the symbol of Illuminati influence and purpose. "On the reverse of our nation's great seal," writes Hall, "is an unfinished pyramid to represent human society itself, imperfect and incomplete. Above the pyramid floats the symbol of the esoteric orders, the radiant triangle with the all-seeing eye. There is only one possible origin for these symbols, and that is the secret societies which came to this country one-hundred-and-fifty years before the Revolutionary War....There can be no question that the great seal was directly inspired by these orders of the human quest, and that it set forth the purpose for this nation." The seal referred to by Hall appears on the back of the one dollar bill, featuring the pyramid with the removed capstone, and the word's *Novus Ordo Seclorum*, which translates from Latin as "New World Order."

The Esoteric Keys of Freemasonry

The word "esoteric" refers to knowledge known by only a few. When many people begin to gain esoteric knowledge, it then becomes *exoteric*. Freemasonry is a tradition that teaches natural law and morality through a system of symbols, allegories, and rituals interpreted to reveal hidden meanings. Because the tradition is hierarchical, authors like Albert Churchwood, who wrote, *The Ancient Origins of Freemasonry* believe the masonic lodges of today teach a watered down the version of the craft. As a result, the lower level Freemasons have far less esoteric knowledge than the higher-level masons, who keep their secrets guarded. In his book, *The Morals and Dogma of the Ancient and Accepted Scottish Rite of Freemasonry*, Albert Pike writes, "Masonry conceals its secrets from all except adepts and sages, or the elect, and uses false explanations and misinterpretations of its symbols to mislead those who deserve only to be misled. They conceal the truth from people, which they call 'light,' and draw them away from it." However, as philosopher Phil Rockstroh points out, the more people fall prey to believing in authoritarian rule, the more they believe what authority tells them. Does another human being have any right to judge what knowledge you do or do not deserve to have? What does your understanding about meditation tell you? The late Bill Cooper wrote, "They have placed themselves in an elitist attitude to tell us what we need, and they do not need to do that." Freemasons who reject Albert Pike's philosophy cite John J. Robinson's, *A Pilgrim's Path: Freemasonry and the Religious Right* as a more accurate representation of their beliefs. Regardless, the most widely recognized symbol in the Freemason mystery tradition is the compass and ruler, illustrated on the following page

The meaning of the Freemason symbol is straightforward. The ruler, placed on its point, represents lower consciousness. In lower consciousness, the base aspects of self—greed, lust, vanity, fear, anxiety, ego, anger, etc.—rules the individual. The compass, in an inverted form pointing upward, represents higher consciousness. Hence, Freemasonry as a tradition is about using craft for self-mastery to create a higher, unified form of consciousness and intellect. The number three is an important number in freemasonry because it represents the three aspects of consciousness, which include:

1. Thought
2. Action
3. Emotion

To put actions into harmony with natural law and promote self-rule, one must be upright and divine in all aspects of the self. While the square represents base instincts, the perfect circle drawn by the compass (angled at 33 degrees) represents the divine shape we must perfect. The presence of exoteric Freemasonry in popular culture also appears in some of the visual imagery presented in music videos produced by the progressive rock band *Tool*. In what hardly seems a coincidence, Tool's drummer, Danny Carey, claims his father was a Freemason. Toward the later years of the band's existence, *Tool*'s lead singer, Maynard James Keenan, helped form a super-group called *A Perfect Circle*, which released a follow up album titled *The Thirteenth Step*. Printed on the back of the U.S. dollar, the thirteenth level of the pyramid is the separated capstone featuring the all-seeing eye.

In Freemason symbolism, the "G" stands for *geometry*. When recalling the explanation of Sacred Geometry from Chapter 1, consider how the male generating principle creates the original genesis pattern, which eventually builds into the Flower of Life. In other versions of the Freemason symbol, the "G" radiates light which represents the solar mind, enlightenment, illumination, or Christ consciousness. The ruler in these same depictions runs horizontally through the "G" which represents a middle path or pillar of wisdom. Esoteric Freemasonry says that choosing the lower instincts over the higher way creates chaos. In order to get from the ruler (lower consciousness) to the compass (higher consciousness) one must pass through the middle of the "G" which also represents the third aspect of consciousness (emotion), a concept also repeated in the Kabbalistic Tree of Life. The "G" placed inside the ruler and compass represents the inner self and its creative aspects because the geometry of life is what we create by using thoughts, emotions and actions. In Shamanism, the "G" may also refer to the Gaian mind, which is the earth plane of existence, as well as the Gate to higher consciousness.

In this way, self-exploration is the common thread between meditative practice and the Freemason tradition. Through the male generating principle, what we get in life is the result of causal factors set into motion by the three pillars of consciousness (thought, emotion, action). What we care about (emotion), what we focus our attention upon (thought), and what we put our efforts toward (action) is what we are going to get in life. If we do not care, we continue to get results we do not want. Therefore, how we manifest our reality is entirely up to us. The goal of esoteric Freemasonry is to learn what creates certain things and to choose wisely. Love and fear are the underlying creative forces that work into the experience we collectively share. To manifest the reality we want, we need to understand how those polarities work. Says Mark Passio, "Dark occultists do not want you to understand how we are the creators of what we experience, but rather, to think we are powerless over what is created in the world. The generative principal is what Freemasonry is trying to teach people. Light freemasonry is building with light, the light of higher consciousness and love. Dark freemason builds with walls that it erects, seeing everything as separate. It builds through mind control, trying to get everyone to see authority as truth instead of truth as authority. This is why dark occultists are getting what they want, and why we seem to be running around not understanding why we are not getting what we want, which is true freedom."

In Freemasonry, the lower consciousness merged with the higher consciousness at the center of the "G" creates unity consciousness. You may recall a similar concept from an earlier discussion in Chapter 9 about Chinese Qi energy consisting of yin and yang. The yin (i.e., brain or higher consciousness) regulates the quality of energy. The yang (i.e., abdomen or lower consciousness) stores and supplies the body's energy quantity. When the martial artist combines these two energies, they draw the power of perfection. Similarly, when a downward triangle combines with an upward

triangle, the symbolic result in Freemasonry is unity consciousness, illustrated below.

Dark Occultism

In his book, *The Lost Keys of Freemasonry*, Manly P. Hall states, "When the Mason learns that the key to the warrior on the block is the proper application of the dynamo of living power, he has learned the mystery of his Craft. The seething energies of Lucifer are in his hands, and before he may step onward and upward, he must prove his ability to properly handle energy." Though popular culture often confuses the difference between Satan and Lucifer, the two biblical characters are quite different. The name Lucifer, derived from the Latin world *Lucis*, means light. According to astrotheology expert Jordan Maxwell, Lucifer is the Sun God, or Bringer of Light, worshipped by the ancient Phoenicians. Having studied astrotheology for over fifty years, Maxwell claims these astrotheological symbols and customs spilled over into Freemasonry and are identical to some of the symbols and customs found in Catholicism. To this end, Mark Passio contends there is a difference between Luciferianism and Dark Luciferianism, just as a difference exists between Freemasonry and Dark Masonry.

In Satanism, a dark occultist follows an antithetical moral code known as The Left Hand Path. Because Satanism worships the ego, the ego is therefore the God of that religion. Passio, appointed to the rank of Priest by the Church of Satan founder Anton LaVey, was also a member of an organization called The Order of the Evil Eye. Says Passio, "I began to understand the type of psychopathic individuals that were involved in these organizations, and the levels of power and influence they had in our society at higher levels, particularly in positions of influence, power, and responsibility. Realizing the nature of the people in these positions led me to my current work and a whole new spiritual awakening." According to Passio, The Church of Satan exists to sift through people who display the tendencies that higher-level dark occultist are looking for. Once brought into the secret societies, they enter the lower echelons of orders like Skull and Bones, societies with much more power and influence than The Church of Satan. "The Church of Satan was simply there to interface with the public," says Passio. "Dark Luciferianism is higher in the dark occult than Satanism. While Satanists are concerned with their own benefit, they are useful puppets for the Dark Luciferians who believe they are the enlightened ones and have the divine right to steer the course of humanity." According to Passio, all the tenets of Satanism flow from the identification with the ego mind, the barriers of true self-realization and spiritual awakening. Ego identification is the belief that the five senses are all that matters. The tenets of Satanism include:

1. Ego identification
2. Death as the permanent end of consciousness
3. The ego as God
4. The ego as the object of worship and strength

The Luciferians, according to Passio, know these tenets are false, so they propagate it because in reality, it is the religion of slavery and they want control. In this way, according to Passio, many Christians, Jews, Muslims, Buddhists and so forth, are living some of the satanic tenets without even knowing it. Because Satanism is the reversal of nature, the symbol of the religion, placing all the aspects of physical above the spiritual, is the reversed pentagram. Illustrated below, the pentagram places the four forces of the material world (earth, air, fire, water) above the fifth element (spirit) which points downward.

The purpose of this religion, says Passio, is to create an imbalance in consciousness that heavily favors the left hemisphere of the brain controlling rationalism and intellect (hence, The Left Hand Path). When the brain dwells in the rationality that only uses the five senses, the sacred feminine (or right brain) involving emotions of the heart, intuition, and compassionate become separate and dead. While you may not have access to secret teachings, you still have a meditative practice that will help keep the right and left hemispheres of your brain in perfect synchronization. If you continue to practice your meditation, you need not worry whether occult conspiracies are true or false. Since Freemasonry teaches unity consciousness, Passio contends that Luciferians practice and have unity consciousness because the Universe rewards the practice of unity. They care about what they want to achieve and have the will power to direct their actions into harmony with those two principles.

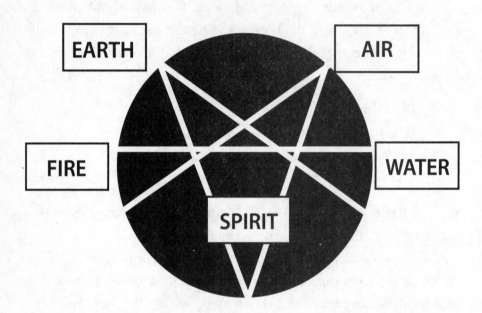

On this point, Jordan Maxwell contends that the Christian Bible misinterprets the role of Lucifer, and that Christ and Lucifer are really the same figure. While conspiracy theorists dispute the finer points, most agree that disinformation is part of the conspiracy. Some believe that even those who appear to be speaking out against dark occultists are really part of the disinformation network. People like Jordan Maxwell or Alex Jones, they claim, keep people in a state of fear, which is the part of the dark occult agenda. In *The Healing Begins Now*, Jonathan "Adampants" says, "You get people that pretend they are helping you when their goal is to hurt you, or they are being controlled to hurt you and they don't know it. If you read Fritz Springmeier's books, they are overwhelming you with fear. Some of the details are correct, but he is not enabling you...this is why if you are enabled, traumatic things will hardly even bother you."

Among the most disconcerting information in this conspiracy theory are the alleged firsthand accounts of the occult. In an interview on XTRACT Radio, Carolyn Hamlett, who claims to have grown up in an Illuminati family said, "I know that when I was four years old, I was told that there would be a man the organization they would choose to give a speech and start introducing our esoteric words. They called it 'making it exoteric.' They said it would be toward the end of the twentieth century, and it was going to mark a launching into the plan for what they called The New World Order. At that point, they would begin to work more blatantly before people and start using more mind control techniques to the masses. The man who gave that speech was George H.W. Bush, on September 11, 1990, which was exactly 11 years before September 11, 2001. The organization loves their numbers. He introduced several of the words that were esoteric, and my ears perked up right away. I knew exactly what that meant." Ms. Hamlett's remark about "choosing someone within the organization" is of interesting note considering George Bush (junior and senior) were both members of the Skull and Bones charter at Yale University.

Consequently, symbols in the form of pyramids, stars, and an all-seeing eye now appear frequently in film, television, and music videos. When celebrities exhibit strange behavior, mysteriously die in accidents, or have drug overdoses, conspiracy theorists point to a so-called mind control group known as *MK-Ultra*. This group allegedly creates and brands celebrities through trauma-based mind control techniques, and uses them as pawns to promote a satanic agenda. Those accused of promoting the symbolism include well-known rappers, athletes, billionaires, and politicians, all photographed while making Illuminati gestures in public. While different interpretations exist, conspiracy theorists also believe that director Stanley Kubrick's rumored involvement in the occult was the basis of such films as *Eyes Wide Shut* and *2001: A Space Odyssey*. Dan Brown's fictional book, *An-*

gels and Demons (produced into a 2009 film) makes the exoteric unveiling of the Illuminati appear more evident. Those who link the 9/11 terrorist attacks to dark occultism claim the destruction of the two towers in New York, including Building 7, symbolized the collapse of the three pillars of consciousness into unity consciousness. In other words, from the ashes of the old consciousness, a new one will arise. Ironically, the architectural façade of the new Freedom Tower features a triangle-shaped pattern projecting upward with another triangle-shaped pattern projecting downward. Years after the attack, people today still argue about the true nature of the event. Was it a terrorist attack that resulted from the friction of geopolitics, or is something evil operating from behind a veil? Just before 9/11, when the CIA lost track of Osama Bin Laden's whereabouts in Afghanistan, Bill Cooper predicted on his radio show, *The Hour of Our Time* that an Illuminati event was going to occur on U.S. soil in the near future. Two months following the attack, Cooper, who had been researching the occult since his days as a Naval Intelligence officer, died in a shootout with police after local authorities visited his home in Eagar, Arizona.

By appearance, it would seem that some occult rituals demonstrated in public might serve a purpose beyond symbolism. According to conspiracy theorists, that purpose is The Hegelian Dialect. In its most basic form, *The Hegelian Dialect* is a process of problem-reaction-solution (or thesis vs. antithesis = synthesis). In other words, by introducing two opposing forces, you create a desired outcome. Conspiracy theorists believe that dark occultists distort the Hegelian process as a way of creating chaos (ex: white + black = racism, men + women = feminism, liberal + conservative = social division, Jew + Muslim = terrorism). Others believe the Illuminati use the dialect to offer solutions to problems they secretly create. The philosophy of The Hegelian Dialect originated through nineteenth century German philosopher Georg Wilhelm Friedrich Hegel. Hegel reasoned that the individual only achieves consciousness of self by acknowledgement from another separate individual consciousness. In the aristocratic world, Hegel explained, the relationship between the lords and the lower classes prevented this mutual recognition of self and the attaining true self-consciousness. The slave denies his selfhood by failing to understand himself as more than an unfree object. The master denies his selfhood because he loses the physical act of working on things in the world.

Because both opposing forces lose themselves in each other, they must engage in a struggle to attain a new state of being. If the two forces meet in a struggle, the slave begins to recognize his free will by his willingness to brave death. The lord comes to realize he is not omnipotent and must deal with the slave on equal footing as another independent self. In this act, according to Hegel, both come to realize their combined freedom, and turn their mutual lack of consciousness toward the unification they lack. Hegel's dual meaning is both a social commentary and a philosophical point.

In the same vein, Mark Passio argues that *the Matrix Trilogy* is a cipher for the invisible social controls and the causal factors that led to humanity's current condition, as well as an answer to the way out. "Each film asks a specific question," says Passio. "The first film asks, 'What is the Matrix?' The second film asks, 'Why are we in the Matrix?' The third film asks, 'How do we get out of the Matrix?'" The three main characters of the Matrix Trilogy represent the three aspects of consciousness. The character Neo, Passio argues, symbolizes the neo-cortex (or higher brain) and the human will to act. The character Trinity represents the sacred feminine (emotion). Morpheus, also the name of the Greek god of dreams, represents knowledge.

Neo's story is about self-sacrifice and giving oneself for others, the embodiment of Christ consciousness. In the final scene of the trilogy, The Oracle asks The Architect about the people still connected to the Matrix. The Architect says, "The ones that want out will be freed," implying that they must first have the desire to want out. Although the Matrix trilogy asks and answers three important questions, the final question left unanswered is, "Who is The One?" The answer to that question, says Passio, is very simple.

You are.

Kabbalah and the Tree of Life

As written in the Book of Genesis, "And out of the ground made the Lord God to grow every tree that is pleasant to the sight, and good for food; The Tree of Life, also in the midst of the garden, and the Tree of Knowledge of Good and Evil."

Derived from the Flower of Life, the ancient mystery practice of Kabbalah uses The Tree of Life as a tool to understand the nature of God and the world's creation out of the void. Based on the writings of the sixteenth century Kabbalist Isaac Luria, Kabbalah is not part of the Jewish religion although many who practice Judaism incorporate Kabbalah into their religious practice. The aim of Kabbalistic practice, according to British Occultist Dion Fortune, is to transform the life of the individual by creating synergy between the human body and the universal creative forces identified by the Kabbalah. Kabbalah is a type of meditative practice that relates to the healing and the development of human capability. Not surprisingly, Kabbalah and Freemasonry are interwoven traditions. Similar to Freemasonry, Kabbalah itself is a neutral science, independent of the intensions of the wielder. Consequently, the Tree of Life pattern incorporates all the elements contained in Metatron's Cube, which consists of the four Platonic solids (earth, air, fire, and water). The illustration below demonstrates the Tree of Life pattern embedded within the larger pattern, The Flower of Life.

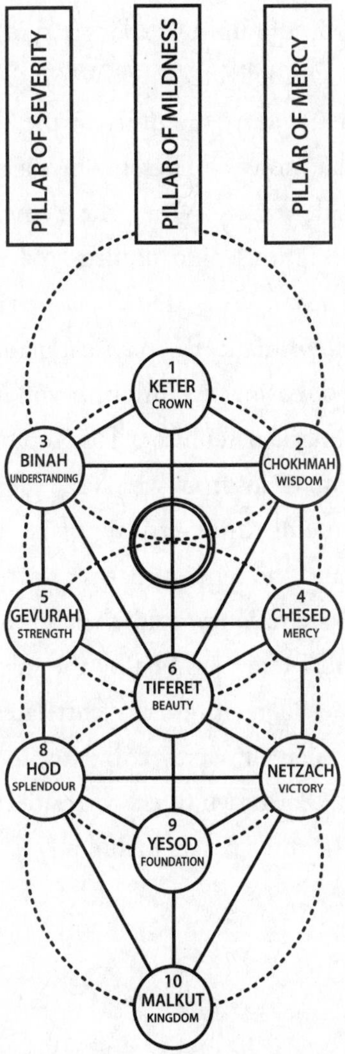

PILLAR OF SEVERITY

PILLAR OF MILDNESS

PILLAR OF MERCY

1
KETER
CROWN

3
BINAH
UNDERSTANDING

2
CHOKHMAH
WISDOM

5
GEVURAH
STRENGTH

4
CHESED
MERCY

6
TIFERET
BEAUTY

8
HOD
SPLENDOUR

7
NETZACH
VICTORY

9
YESOD
FOUNDATION

10
MALKUT
KINGDOM

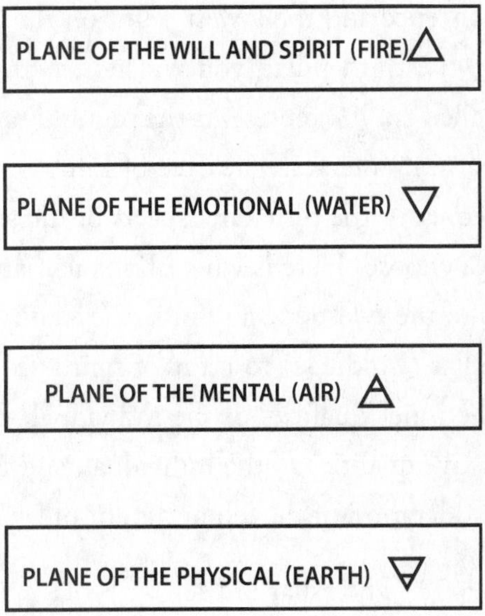

PLANE OF THE WILL AND SPIRIT (FIRE)

PLANE OF THE EMOTIONAL (WATER)

PLANE OF THE MENTAL (AIR)

PLANE OF THE PHYSICAL (EARTH)

The eleven spiritual emanations, called *sephirots*, describe the process of Sacred Geometry covered in Chapter 1 (To see the sephirots in their order, go to Appendix H.). The first sephirot, called *Kether*, is the limitless light that crystalizes at a fixed point to become the focus of the perfect circle. The limitless energy in the fixed point escapes into the infinite void to create a line, the second sephirot called *Chokmah*. *Chokmah* then births the idea of form¬ in the shape of a closed circle of energy, which births the third sephirot called *Binah*. The fourth and fifth sephirots, *Chesed* and *Geburah*, represent the elements of duality (the opposite of *Chokmah* and *Binah*). This duality appears represented by the upward triangle symbolizing fire opposing the downward triangle symbolizing water. When *Chokmah* and *Binah* conjoin with *Chesed* and *Geburah*, the unity of the sixth sephirot called *Tiferet* is born. From the harmony of Tiferet comes a pure elemental force, the seventh sephirot called *Netzach*. When the elemental force of *Natzach* meets the astral form, the eighth sephirot called *Hod*, they interact to create the ninth sephirot called *Yesod*. When *Yesod* develops into solid matter, the tenth sephirot called *Malkut* marks the physical plane of existence and the lowest point on the arc of cosmic evolution. If you look to the third pillar, you will notice an unmarked sephirot. This sephirot, called *Daath*, represents the point of random chaos from which the specific pattern emerges. The Tree of Life also contains three vertical pillars¬ that represent the different aspects of the self and the types of paths or actions we choose. Here is where Kabbalah and Freemasonry draw their similarities; the two opposing pillars (Serenity and Mercy) unified by the middle pillar (Mildness) to create a synthesis. The Pillar of Severity correlates to the inner qualities of the individual, the Pillar of Mercy correlates to the active qualities of the individual, and the Pillar of Mildness correlates to a moderation of the left and right pillars. The three pillars include:

1. The Pillar of Mercy
2. The Pillar of Mildness
3. The Pillar of Severity

The Tree of Life not only describes the process of creation, but it also correlates to human consciousness. The illustration below shows the Tree of Life pattern in alignment with the chakras.

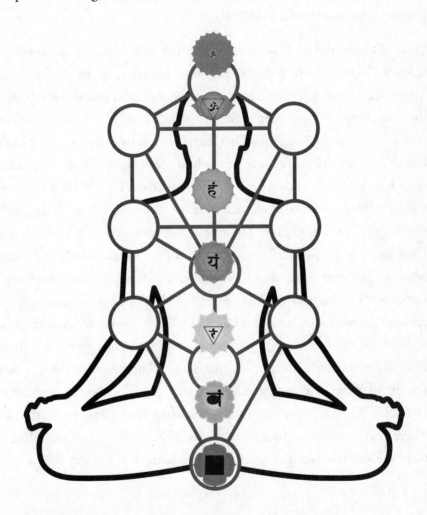

Malkut means kingdom because it correlates to our physical world connection, and thus, the root chakra. It is the physical consciousness of the five senses, the lowest level of awareness. *Yesod* means foundation because it represents the basis of initiation for which the individual begins to ascend into higher levels of consciousness. *Yesod* correlates to the sacral chakra of desire because when we meditate, the desire to ascend is how we begin to connect.

The bridge between *Hod* (under the Pillar of Severity, meaning splendor) and *Natzach* (under the Pillar of Mercy, meaning victory or willpower) correlates to the solar plexus chakra, which honors life force combining the internal and external will to ascend.

Once the internal and external will of life force unifies, the meditator reaches *Tiferet*, which means beauty and correlates to the heart chakra. Tiferet has the most connections of all the sephirots because it represents the love energy at the center of the universe. The bridge between *Geburah* (self-control) and *Chesed* (helping others) correlates with the throat chakra because it concerns influencing people in how we speak in order to invoke love or fear. *Binah* represents the understanding of knowledge and *Chokmah* represents the attainment and use of wisdom through the understanding of our knowledge. The bridge between *Binah* (knowledge) and *Chokmah* (wisdom) correlates to the third eye chakra because it concerns what we do with what we know. *Kether* (meaning crown) correlates to the crown chakra because it is the highest level of consciousness we can achieve. *Kether* stands atop the Pillar of Mildness because knowledge and wisdom combine in unity to meet in the middle. When you think of your meditative practice, consider how the Tree of Life describes the top-down process of Sacred Geometry and how unity consciousness creates life out of a void. When you meditate, you are starting from the bottom, the place where that generative process ended, with the intension of ascending toward the source of your creation. In every sense, it is the way back.

Conclusion

ur hope in writing this book is that you have come away with a better understanding of what it takes to reduce stress and anxiety through effective meditation. If you started with the assumption that the benefits of meditation were not possible, you are certainly wiser now. An experienced meditator uses many methods to quiet the mind and reduce stress. As you continue to practice the techniques outlined in this book, you will gain experience and become the kind of person with inner and outer balance. When the outside world becomes stressful, that is where your practice comes in. You will be a master of the balanced mind with the inner and outer power to harness positive energy. The way the world creates stress may change over time, but its changes will always create new opportunities for you to balance your life. Make it your mission in life to remain awake *and be the change you want to see in the world.* The road ahead is both challenging and rewarding. We wish you luck.

Before closing this book and heading off to employ these techniques, examine the questions at the end of this conclusion as they will help you determine just how ready you are to achieve effective meditation within ten minutes. As you set out in life, remember that true knowledge is knowledge of self, and true happiness means releasing yourself from ego-driven attachments, desires, and beliefs. As Bruce Lee once said, "Empty your mind. Be formless, shapeless...like water. If you put water into a cup, it becomes the cup. If you put water into a bottle, it becomes the bottle. If you put water in a teapot, it becomes the teapot. Water can flow, or it can crash. Be water, my friend."

Questions to ask after reading this book

1. Do I have a better understanding of meditation?
2. Do I feel comfortable using the strategies and protocols outlined in this book?
3. Do I feel it is feasible to support my meditative practice in the manners described?
4. Do I feel these strategies will reduce stress, eliminate anxiety, eliminate misunderstanding, reduce conflicts, and enrich my life?
5. Is there any information I am unsure about?
6. Where can I find information (in this book or otherwise) that will lead me to my answer?

Ten Grassroots Solutions for Consciousness Elevation

1. **Heal your individual worldview.** Get over apathy. Help alleviate the suffering of others instead of seeking personal comfort..

2. **Change the quality of info you give your attention to.** Information that creates depression of spirit is hypnosis and puts you into a negative trance state of mind. You are the product of the info you take in. Ignore mainstream media. Inform yourself through new alternative media and even the Internet.

3. **Develop true present moment awareness.** Do not focus on regret over the past or anxiety of the future. Avoid focusing on minutia of everyday living. Be in the moment but see the bigger picture around you from a global perspective, which encompasses all consciousness. Forget about repeating cycles of time.

4. **Change diet; eat healthy whole foods.** Avoid unnecessary drugs and detach from poisonous foods. Focus on organic local food production. Start an alkaline diet. Lower your intake of carbohydrates, sugars, and genetically modified foods. Eating right will help you focus your mind. You are what you eat.

5. **Detach from the current monetary system as much as possible.** Get off the debt system. You are largely at the mercy of other people controlling the monetary system; try to limit your dependency on it as much as possible. Look at alternative forms of currency. Look into strategies for self-sufficiency, trading on credits, borrowing online, or local systems of barter.

6. **Practice non-support of the ego-based dominator culture.** This culture continues to unbalance people more and more. Participants of this culture are people we know, even those we love. Try to bring the information to people to the extent that they are capable of understanding it. We think of them as contributors to the negative but they are the most in need of spiritual healing because their consciousness may be the most devastated. When enough people come to a level of consciousness that prevents manipulation by external influences, then local and global conflicts will end.

7. **Develop mindfulness by quieting the mind.** Empty your thoughts for a time to experience pure conscious awareness. But do not allow it to shut down critical thinking permanently. Different meditations, — sitting walking, stretching, binaural beat music, and scented candles — are helpful. Bathe in the quality of pure consciousness. Relinquishing control is the message you hear if you turn down the volume. The illusion of control is what is bringing your suffering upon you. Live in harmony with that which is. You are only in control of the way you think, feel, and act. Watch your actions.

8. **Learn to generate the divine within and use it for the correct reasons.** Recognize and develop consciousness. Natural, psychotropic compounds or meditative techniques can open up vistas of creativity because they open up consciousness and allow deeper connection with right brain consciousness.

9. **Practice positive thinking.** Keep a sense of humor even if your life is difficult. It is important to see the glass as half-full and recognize small steps in the right direction.

10. **Help others awaken.** So many people in the post-modern world have a poisoned worldview and need your understanding, not your hatred, contempt or resentment. They remain attached to egoism and want to stay in that state of disconnection. It is hard because you want to be angry that they do not understand. Work with them, and if they do not want to listen then you have to allow them to stay in that state. Eventually, they will discover the true nature of existence. It is a lesson that no one escapes, only delayed. Always examine yourself before you examine others. Remember that you have fallen from your higher self and acted in ways you are not proud to admit. A true teacher always remembers to enable the proper operation of the mind. Responsibility is "response ability," the ability to respond in a balanced way to the circumstances and the situation that you find yourself in. Understand that everything is connected. Every beings suffering is our own; we are all connected.

List presented by Mark Passio, 2012 Free Your Mind Conference.

The Seven Natural Laws of Nature

The law of perpetual transmutation — Directed energy always manifests into physical form. Ideas that we hold in our mind and give attention will manifest in reality.

The law of relativity — Nothing is good or bad, nice or ugly, smart or stupid. We have to relate all of it to something. If you think something is bad, relate your situation to something much worse, and it will become good. (Ex: saying, "This situation is bad, but I don't have cancer.")

The law of vibration and attraction — Nothing rests, everything vibrates. Feeling is conscious awareness. Vibrations in our mind dictate what we attract, so think positive to attract positive situations.

The law of polarity — Everything has an opposite: smart/stupid, good/bad, left/right.... You must look for the good in people and situations, and you will attract more good things in your life.

The law of rhythm — Good and bad things in life happen in rhythms and cycles. When you encounter a bad stretch in life, do not feel bad. The rhythm of life will not stay that way forever. Things will get better, so think of the good times that are coming.

The law of cause and effect — Whatever we think and feel will manifest in some way in the future. Action creates reaction. Think good thoughts, and treat every situation and everyone with respect; it will come back to you.

The law of gestation —Your goals and ideas are spiritual seeds that need time to incubate. They will manifest when the time is right.

The Twelve Laws of Karma

The law of cause and effect — Whatever we put out in the universe comes back to us.

The law of creation — Life does not just happen; it requires our participation. What we want to have in our life requires action.

The law of humility —If we refuse to see the good in people, but instead see them as enemies or possessing negative traits, we are not tuned into a higher level of existence.

The law of growth — Wherever we go, there we are. To grow in spirit, we must change ourselves, not the people, places, or things around us. When we change our heart, our life changes, too.

The law of responsibility — Nothing is ever wrong except what we need to change in ourselves. We mirror our environment, and our environment mirrors us. We must take responsibility for what we create in our lives.

The law of connection — No task, thought, gesture, behavior or intention is inconsequential because everything in the universe is connected. Past, present, and future are connected.

The law of focus — We cannot think of two things at the same time. When our focus is on spiritual values, it is impossible for us to have lower thoughts such as greed or anger.

The law of giving and hospitality — When we learn valuable life lessons, we must put into practice what we have learned.

The law of here and now — Dwelling in the past prevents us from being present. Hanging on to old thoughts, patterns, behaviors, and dreams prevents us from having new ones.

The law of change — History repeats itself until we learn the lessons that we need to change our path.

The law of patience and reward — All rewards require an honest effort. True joy is the process of doing rather than achieving.

The law of significance and inspiration — Whatever we put into life is what we get back. Weak efforts have no impact. Loving efforts lift up and inspire the whole.

Source: 12 Little Known Laws of Karma (That Will Change Your Life)
http://www.in5d.com/12-little-known-laws-of-karma.html

Inspirational Poem

Ithaca

As you set out for Ithaca
hope that your journey is a long one,
full of adventure, full of discovery.
Laistrygonians and Cyclops,
angry Poseidon — don't be afraid of them.
You'll never find things like that on your way,
as long as you keep your thoughts raised high,
as long as a rare sensation
touches your spirit and your body.
Laistrygonians and Cyclops,
wild Poseidon — you won't encounter them,
unless you bring them along inside your soul,
unless your soul sets them up in front of you.

Hope that your journey is a long one.
May there be many summer mornings when,
with what pleasure, what joy,

you come into harbors you're seeing for the first time;
may you stop at Phoenician trading stations
to buy fine things,
mother of pearl and coral, amber and ebony,
sensual perfume of every kind —
as many sensual perfumes as you can;
and may you visit many Egyptian cities
to learn and learn again from those who know.

Keep Ithaca always in your mind.
Arriving there is what you're destined for.
But don't hurry the journey at all.
Better if it lasts for years,
so that you're old by the time you reach the island,
wealthy with all you've gained on the way,
not expecting Ithaca to make you rich.
Ithaca gave you the marvelous journey.
Without her you would have not set out.
She has nothing left to give you now.

And if you find her poor, Ithaca won't have fooled you.
Wise as you will have become, so full of experience,
you'll have understood by then what these Ithacas mean.

—Constantine P. Cavafy

The Eight Stages of Yogic Practice

Sanskrit	English
1. *Yama*	Moral codes (what you should not do)
2. *Niyama*	Self-purification (what you should do)
3. *Asana*	Posture
4. *Pranayama*	Energy control
5. *Pratyahara*	Withdrawal from the senses
6. *Dharana*	Concentration
7. *Dhyana*	Deep meditation
8. *Samadhi*	Union with God

Source: "10 Minute Meditation for Deep Relaxation," by Dr. Alka Khurana

PH Level Food Chart

Your targeted acid/alkaline balance should be 7.2 (or slightly alkaline).

The body needs 20-30 percent acid-forming foods and 70-80 percent alkaline forming foods to maintain acid-alkaline balance.

Acid ratio should come from the acid-forming foods of grains, legumes, and nuts, not the other acid forming foods.

Healthy Alkaline Foods (Eat lots of them!)	Foods For Moderate Consumption	Unhealthy Acidic Foods (Try to avoid them!)
Vegetables	**Fruits**	**Meat, Poultry, And Fish**
Alfalfa Grass +29.3	**(In Season, For Cleansing Only Or With Moderation)**	Beef -34.5
Asparagus +1.3	Apples -8,5	Chicken (to -22) -18.0
Barley Grass +28.1	Apricot -9.5	Eggs (to -22)
Broccoli +14.4	Banana, Ripe -10.1	Liver -3.0
Brussels Sprouts +0.5	Banana, Unripe +4.8	Ocean Fish -20.0
Cabbage Lettuce, Fresh +14.1	Black Currant -6.1	Organ Meats -3.0
Cauliflower +3.1	Blueberry -5.3	Oysters -5.0
Cayenne Pepper +18.8	Cantaloupe -2.5	Pork -38.0
Celery +13.3	Cherry, Sour +3.5	Veal -35.0
Chives +8.3	Cherry, Sweet -3.6	

Healthy Alkaline Foods (Eat lots of them!)	Foods For Moderate Consumption	Unhealthy Acidic Foods (Try to avoid them!)
Comfrey +1.5	Coconut, Fresh +0.5	**Milk And Milk Products**
Cucumber, Fresh +31.5	Cranberry -7.0	Buttermilk +1.3
Dandelion +22.7	Currant -8.2	Cream -3.9
Dog Grass +22.6	Date -4.7	Hard Cheese -18.1
Endive, Fresh +14.5	Fig Juice Powder -2.4	Homogenized Milk -1.0
French Cut Green Beans +11.2	Gooseberry, Ripe -7.7	Quark -17.3
Garlic +13.2	Grape, Ripe -7.6	
Green Cabbage December Harvest +4.0	Grapefruit -1.7	**Bread, Biscuits (Stored Grains/Risen Dough)**
Green Cabbage, March Harvest +2.0	Italian Plum -4.9	Rye Bread -2.5
	Mandarin Orange -11.5	White Biscuit -6.5
Kamut Grass +27.6	Mango -8.7	White Bread -10.0
Lamb's Lettuce +4.8	Orange -9.2	Whole-Grain Bread -4.5
Leeks (Bulbs) +7.2	Papaya -9.4	Whole-Meal Bread -6.5
Lettuce +2.2	Peach -9.7	
Onion +3.0	Pear -9.9	**Nuts**
Peas, Fresh +5.1	Pineapple -12.6	Cashews -9.3
Peas, Ripe +0.5	Raspberry -5.1	Peanuts -12.8
Red Cabbage +6.3	Red Currant -2.4	Pistachios -16.6
Rhubarb Stalks +6.3	Rose Hips -15.5	
Savoy Cabbage +4.5	Strawberry -5.4	**Fats**
Shave Grass +21.7	Tangerine -8.5	Butter -3.9
Sorrel +11.5	Watermelon -1.0	Corn Oil -6.5
	Yellow Plum -4.9	Margarine -7.5
Soy Sprouts +29.5		**Sweets**
Spinach (Other Than March) +13.1	**Non-Stored Grains**	Artificial Sweeteners -26.5
	Brown Rice -12.5	Barley Malt Syrup -9.3
Spinach, March Harvest +8.0	Wheat -10.1	Beet Sugar -15.1
Sprouted Chia Seeds +28.5	**Nuts**	Brown Rice Syrup -8.7
	Hazelnuts -2.0	Chocolate -24.6
Sprouted Radish Seeds +28.4	Macadamia Nuts -3.2	Dr. Bronner's Barley
Straw Grass +21.4	Walnuts -8.0	Dried Sugar Cane Juice -18.0
Watercress +7.7		Fructose -9.5

Healthy Alkaline Foods (Eat lots of them!)	Foods For Moderate Consumption	Unhealthy Acidic Foods (Try to avoid them!)
Wheat Grass +33.8	**Fish**	Honey -7.6
White Cabbage +3.3	Fresh Water Fish -11.8	Malt Sweetener -9.8
Zucchini +5.7		Milk Sugar -9.4
	Fats	Molasses -14.6
Root Vegetables	Coconut Milk -1.5	Turbinado Sugar -9.5
Beet +11.3	Sunflower Oil -6.7	White Sugar -17.6
Carrot +9.5		
Horseradish +6.8		**Condiments**
Kohlrabi +5.1		Ketchup -12.4
Potatoes +2.0		Mayonnaise -12.5
Red Radish +16.7		Mustard -19.2
Rutabaga +3.1		Soy Sauce -36.2
Summer Black Radish +39.4		Vinegar -39.4
Turnip +8.0		
White Radish (Spring) +3.1		**Beverages**
		Beer -26.8
Fruits		Coffee -25.1
Avocado (Protein) +15.6		Fruit Juice Sweetened
Fresh Lemon +9.9		Fruit Juice, Packaged, Natural -8.7
Limes +8.2		Liquor -38.7
Tomato +13.6		Tea (Black) -27.1
		Wine -16.4
Non-Stored Organic Grains And Legumes		
Buckwheat Groats +0.5		**Miscellaneous**
Granulated Soy (Cooked Ground Soy Beans) +12.8		Canned Foods
		Microwaved Foods
Lentils +0.6		Processed Foods
Lima Beans +12.0		
Quinoa +		
Soy Flour +2.5		
Soy Lecithin (Pure) +38.0		
Soy Nuts (soaked Soy Beans, Then Air Dried) +26.5		

Healthy Alkaline Foods (Eat lots of them!)	Foods For Moderate Consumption	Unhealthy Acidic Foods (Try to avoid them!)
Soybeans, Fresh +12.0		
Spelt +0.5		
Tofu +3.2		
White Beans (Navy Beans) +12.1		
Nuts		
Almonds +3.6		
Brazil Nuts +0.5		
Seeds		
Caraway Seeds +2.3		
Cumin Seeds +1.1		
Fennel Seeds +1.3		
Flax Seeds +1.3		
Pumpkin Seeds +5.6		
Sesame Seeds +0.5		
Sunflower Seeds +5.4		
Wheat Kernel +11.4		
Fats (Fresh, Cold-Pressed Oils)		
Borage Oil +3.2		
Evening Primrose Oil +4.1		
Flax Seed Oil +3.5		
Marine Lipids +4.7		
Olive Oil +1.0		

Table: pH scale of alkaline and acid forming foods

*Table Reprinted with Permission from **www.balance-ph-diet.com**.*

Hip Opening Postures

ip Openers powerfully stimulate and balance the muladhara, or root and svadisthana, or sacral chakras. By physically rooting our pelvic floor and the base of our spine into the Earth, we plug ourselves into the vibrational current of the planet.

Hip openers work the epicenter of your body, where many old emotions can get stuck. Through creating balance in these chakras we can become grounded, comfortable within our own identity, and inherently creative.

Reclining Butterfly

Wide-legged Forward Bend

Warrior II

The Eleven Sephirots

Sephirot 1	KETER (Crown)	GOD, Infinite Light & Wisdom, Total & Supreme Consciousness
Sephirot 2	CHOHMAN (Wisdom)	Male Yang Energies, Pure Energy, Spiritual Force, Cosmic Father
Sephirot 3	BINAH (Understanding)	Yin Energy, Compassion, Pure Love & Understanding, The Cosmic Mother
Sephirot 4	CHESED (Mercy)	The Ruler, Majesty, Power & Authority, Consolidator Of Things
Sephirot 5	GEBURAH (Severity/Judgment)	The Warrior, Sphere Of Mars, Strength, Justice, Physical Power
Sephirot 6	TIPERETH (Beauty)	The Sun, Harmony, Beauty, Perfection, Unity, Creation
Sephirot 7	NEDZACH (Victory)	The Lover, Venus, Art, Creativity Inspiration & Erotic Spirituality
Sephirot 8	HOD (Splendor)	The Intellect, Mercury, Communication
Sephirot 9	YESOD (Foundation)	The Moon, Vision & Deep Memory, The Cycles In & Around Us, Illusion
Sephirot 10	MALKUTH (Kingdom)	Physical Reality, Death, Pain, Healing
Sephirot 11	DAATH	The Abyss, Random Chaos Of Thought & Conception

Glossary

acid — Any watery solution with a pH of less than 7, and thus a higher concentration of hydrogen ions.

alkaline — Any watery solution with a pH of more than 7, and thus a lower concentration of hydrogen ions.

alpha — The frequency range of brain wave activity that falls between 8 and 12 Hertz, or cycles per second.

ambient — A type of music that emphasizes tone and atmosphere.

asanas — The third path of Yoga. Postures for internal discipline.

ashtanga vinyasa Yoga — Form of Yoga focusing on strength building through the alignment of movement and breath. Also known as Power Yoga.

astral projection — An out-of-body experience that assumes the essence of spirit, which separates from the physical self during meditation to explore time and space.

aura — Vibratory energy that expands and contracts depending on the emotions and thoughts you emit.

beta — The frequency range of brain wave activity that falls between 12.5 and 30 Hertz, or cycles per second.

bikram Yoga — Form of Yoga that focuses on breathing techniques in a room set to 105 degrees Fahrenheit.

binaural beats — A sound with specific amplitude and frequency created by combining two different tones. Used for the purpose of altering brain waves and consciousness.

bodhicitta — Buddhist term for an awaked heart and mind.

bodhisattva — Buddhist term for person who seeks enlightenment with the goal of benefiting others.

cardiovascular system — The body's organ system responsible for transporting nutrients and removing gaseous waste from the body.

chakras — Energetic openings located at seven points along the body.

citta — Buddhist term for emotional and mental states, or mind and heart.

corpse pose — Yogic pose that requires lying down on your back with both arms and legs slightly spread apart, letting all the body's muscles relax.

dark occult — Occult used for evil purposes and self-benefit.

delta — The frequency range of brain wave activity that falls between 0.1 and 3 Hertz, or cycles per second.

dharma — Hindu term for behaviors considered to be in accord with life and the universe.

dhyana — The seventh path of Yoga. Meditation.

diksha — Sanskrit word for the preparation of a religious ceremony in Hindu and Buddhist religions.

dharana — The sixth path of Yoga. Concentration.

dodecahedron — The fifth (or spirit) element formed by sacred geometry.

ego — Latin or Greek term referring to the psychic apparatus that sees itself as "I."

ego drive — The impulse derived from the ego to protect and satisfy itself.

empty stance — A common standing meditation used in Qigong to relieve back pain whereby the meditator shifts weight off one leg and raises both arms.

energetic openings — Synonym for charkas.

energy body — Your surrounding vibratory energy known as the aura.

electroencephalogram (EEG) — A test that measures and records electrical brain wave activity by using sensors called electrodes.

esoteric — Knowledge known only by few people.

exoteric — Knowledge known by many people.

feng shui — The Chinese tradition of using colors to promote harmonization with the surrounding environment.

freemasonry — tradition that teaches natural law and morality through a system of symbols, allegories, and rituals interpreted to reveal hidden meanings.

Fruit of Life — The pattern in sacred geometry that serves as the template for the creation of all living things.

flow — An egoless state of consciousness characterized by effortless concentration and skilled execution of a task or challenge; also known as "being in the zone."

Flower of Life — The pattern in sacred geometry depicting the complete pattern of space and time.

fluoride — A chemical compound commonly added to water supplies, which has a calcifying or hardening effect on the pineal gland, rendering it inactive.

gamma — The fastest frequency range of brain wave activity, falls between 40 - 70 Hertz, or cycles per second.

gastrointestinal system — The body's organ system responsible for digestion.

golden ratio — Two quantities that are the same as the ratio of their sum.

gomden — A square meditation cushion.

hatha Yoga — Form of Yoga focusing on relaxation and stress reduction through exercises and postures.

hegelian dialect — The process of creating a synthesis between two opposite forces.

hertz — The unit of frequency in the International System of Units.

hexahedron — A six-sided cube representing the earth element formed by sacred geometry.

horse stance — A common standing meditation used in Tai Chi whereby the arms raise while the knees and hips bend as if the meditator is about to sit down.

hot Yoga — Form of Yoga practice in a room temperature of 105 degrees for the purpose of sweating toxins out through the pores.

hypercube — A three-dimensional square.

hypnotherapy — Therapy practiced by psychologists to create unconscious changes in patients' thoughts, attitudes, behaviors or emotions.

icosahedron — A 20-sided triangle representing the water element formed by sacred geometry.

illuminati — Secret society that incorporates all the organizational branches of mystery tradition.

immune system — Biological structures and processes within the body that protects against disease.

isochronic tones — A form of audio brainwave entrainment that combines two equal intensity pulses with intervals of silence while gradually increasing pulse speeds.

kabbalah — Meditative practice that relates to the healing and the development of human capability.

kundalini — The divine feminine "Shakti" or spiritual body energy released during in a state of deep meditation, which purifies the body and mind.

kundalini Yoga — Form of Yoga that focuses on raising the kundalini energy through the spine to produce a feeling of ecstasy.

left hand path — The satanic practice of worshipping the ego.

lymphatic system — The part of the circulatory system that serves an important function for the immune system.

luciferianism — High level dark occultism.

mantra — A sacred utterance that caries the vibratory energy of the cosmos. Used in Buddhism as a "mind tool."

mindful-based stress reduction (MBSR) — A secular form of meditation that combines medical research with traditional forms of meditation to improve chronic disorders and diseases.

Metatron's Cube — The geometric figure composed of 13 equal circles extending out to the centers of the other 12 circles. Otherwise known as The Fruit of Life.

metta — Buddhist term for lovingkindness or unconditional friendliness, especially toward the self.

musculature system — The body's organ system consisting of skeletal, smooth and cardiac muscles.

mystery tradition — Spiritual practices that originated in ancient Egypt and Babylon.

nervous system — Part of the body that coordinates the voluntary and involuntary actions and transmits signals.

niyamas — The second path of Yoga. Keeping the body and mind free of impurities, being austere, and studying the sacred texts.

occult — Hidden knowledge.

octahedron — An eight-sided cube representing the air element formed by sacred geometry.

orgonite — A solid material cured mold that combines fiberglass resin, metal shavings, and quartz crystal. Used by meditators for protection against negative energy.

pineal gland — Gland located in the midbrain which stimulates third eye perception.

Platonic solids — Named after the philosopher Plato, who identified five perfectly symmetrical shapes that meet at each vertex. Only five solids meet the criteria: octahedron, tetrahedron, hexahedron, icosahedron, and dodecahedron.

pH — The abbreviation for "power of hydrogen, " which measures is the level of hydrogen ion concentration in the human body.

Pillar of Mercy — The right pillar on the tree of life, indicating external action.

Pillar of Mildness — The middle pillar on the tree of life indicating moderation.

Pillar of Severity — The left pillar on the tree of life indicating internal action.

prana — Sanskit term for breath.

pranayama — The fourth path of Yoga. Regulation and control of the breath.

pratyahara — The fifth path of Yoga. Withdrawl of the senses in order to still the mind.

qi — Referred to in Chinese culture as the energy regulated by the yin and yang.

relaxation response — A physical state of deep rest that the body strives to achieve.

sacred geometry — Geometry used in the planning and construction of the universe.

samadhi — The eighth and final path of Yoga. Achieving unity of self with all things.

samsāra — Buddhist term for the continuous flow or repeating cycle of birth, life and death in reincarnation.

Satanism — Lower level dark occultism.

Seed of Life — The pattern in sacred geometry that lays the foundation for the creation of matter and the universe.

sephirot — A spiritual emanation on the tree of life.

shamatha — Sanskrit term for peacefully abiding.

seiza bench — Specially designed Japanese support for sitting in proper meditative position.

shakti — Sanskrit term for energy.

stress response — the body's transition from a resting state into a state of increased biological activity.

sun salutation — Yogic pose whereby the meditator raises both arms from each side of the body until both hands touch overhead.

sushuma — Sanskrit term for the meditator's body.

synchro-mysticism — An extraordinary coincidence that occurs in a way that has extreme meaning to the observer of the event, which leads the great insight or personal enlightenment.

systolic — The rate of blood pressure when the heart is contracting.

tantra — The meditative practice of channeling energy directly from the Universe.

tao — A metaphysical concept in Buddhism that signifies the formless and nameless energy of the universe.

tetrahedron — A four-sided triangle representing the fire element formed by sacred geometry.

theta — The frequency range of brain wave activity that falls between 4–7 Hertz, or cycles per second.

third eye — The brow chakra, or invisible eye which provides perception beyond ordinary sight.

Tree of Life — Spiritual pattern embedded within the Flower of Life that describes the process of creating physical matter from the void.

vesica piscis — That shape formed by the intersection of two circles.

vinyasa — Sanskrit term for practicing a series of poses.

white occult — Occult used for good purposes and helping others.

yamas — The first path of Yoga. Non-violence, truthfulness, moderation in all things, and non-covetousness.

yang — Referred to in martial arts as the part of the body (abdomen) which stores and supplies the body's energy quantity.

yin — Referred to in martial arts as the part of the body (brain) which regulates the quality of energy collected, stored, and released by a martial artist.

zabuton — Japanese cushion for sitting.

zafu — A round meditation cushion.

Bibliography

Allaboutspirituality.org. "Meditation and Contemplation." 2014. http://www.allaboutspirituality.org/meditation.htm.

Allen, Marc. *How to Quiet Your Mind: Relax and Silence the Voice of Your Mind, Today!* Empowerment Nation, 2011.

Amazing-green-tea.com. "Japanese Tea History: A Thousand Year Journey From China, Chanoyu to Sencha." 2014. http://www.amazing-green-tea.com/japanese-tea-history.html.

Askteal.com. How to Activate and Open Your Third Eye. 2013. http://www.askteal.com/videos/how-to-activate-and-open-your-third-eye.

Askteal.com. "Why are Spiritual Teachers so Contradictory?" 2013. http://www.youtube.com/watch?v=uCMBMQjjD7I.

Balance-ph-diet.com. "Acid Alkaline Food Chart." 2014. http://www.balance-ph-diet.com/acid_alkaline_food_chart.html.

Binauralbeatscenter.com. "Binaural Beats." 2012. http://www.binauralbeatscenter.com/index.html.

Binauralbeatsonline.com. "Experience Gamma Brain Waves with Gamma Binaural Beats." 2010. http://www.binauralbeatsonline.com/experience-gamma-brain-waves-with-gamma-binaural-beats/.

Bodhiactivity.wordpress.com. "Pitfalls in Meditation." 2013. **http://bodhiactivity.wordpress.com/2011/02/05/potential-pitfalls-in-meditation/**.

Bodian, Stephan. *Meditation for Dummies*. John Wiley & Sons, 2012.

Brainandspinalcord.org. Infections and Organic Brain Injury. 2013. **http://www.brainandspinalcord.org/brain-injury/infections.html**.

Breathing.com. "The Breathing or Breath Wave and The Speed Bump of Life." 2014. **http://www.breathing.com/articles/breathwave.htm**.

Buddhism.about.com. "Life of Buddha." 2013. **http://buddhism.about.com/od/lifeofthebuddha/a/buddhalife.htm**.

Christreturns.org. "Christ Returns, Speaks His truth." 2007. **http://www.christreturns.org/**.

Daringtolivefully.com. "How to Enter the Flow State." 2014. **http://daringtolivefully.com/how-to-enter-the-flow-state**.

Davich, Victor. *8 Minute Meditation: Quiet Your Mind, Change Your Life*. The Penguin Group, 2004.

Detoxsafely.org. "Herbs Commonly Used in Detox Programs." 2013. **http://www.detoxsafely.org/herbs_for_detox.html#detoxherbs**.

Eclecticenergies.com. "Opening the Chakras." 2014. **http://www.eclecticenergies.com/chakras/open.php**.

Energyopening.com. "Energy Medicine." 2013. **http://energyopening.com/index_files/Page483.htm**.

Ezinearticles.com. "Is it Easier to Learn to Meditate in a Group or Alone? The Pros and Cons of Group Meditation." 2009. **http://ezinearticles.com/?Is-it-Easier-to-Learn-to-Meditate-in-a-Group-Or-Alone?--The-Pros-and-Cons-of-Group-Meditation&id=2120516**.

Failzoom.com. "Interview with Carolyn Hamlett." 2011. **http://failzoom.com/ZzFVOERSVFJnOWsz**

Fluoridealert.org. "National Research Council (2006)." 2012. **http://fluoridealert.org/researchers/nrc/**.

Fluoridealert.org. "Pineal Gland." 2012. **http://fluoridealert.org/issues/health/pineal-gland/**.

Foxnews.com. "Was the Unibomber Correct?" 2013. **http://www.foxnews.com/opinion/2013/06/25/was-unabomber-correct-about-horrors-technology-combined-with-government/**.

Greatdreams.com. "Tree of life." 2014. **http://www.greatdreams.com/Qabalah/hod.htm**.

Greatergood.berkeley.edu. "Here's How Mindful You Are." 2011. **http://greatergood.berkeley.edu/article/item/heres_how_mindful_you_are/**.

Harrison, Eric. *Teach Yourself to Meditate in 10 Simple Lessons.* Ulysses Press, 2007.

Healingbeats.com. "Frequently Asked Questions." 2014. **http://healingbeats.com/faq.html**.

Helpguide.org. "How Much Sleep Do You Need?" 2014. **http://www.helpguide.org/life/sleeping.htm**.

Icwseminary.org. "Prayer and Fasting." 2013. **http://www.icwseminary.org/free_diploma/prayer.htm**.

Ijbs.com. "A Comparison of the Effects of Three GM Corn Varieties on Mammalian Health." 2009. **http://www.ijbs.com/v05p0706.pdf**.

Illuminati-news.com. "The Secret Order of the Illuminati." 1998. **http://www.illuminati-news.com/moriah.htm**.

Indiaprwire.com. "Avoiding Pitfalls of Yoga and Meditation." 2009. **http://www.indiaprwire.com/pressrelease/health-care/2009070128604.htm**.

Isochronictone.com. Binaural Beats, Pros and Cons. 2012. **http://www.isochronictone.com/articles/Isochronic-Tones-Vs-Binaural-Beats-Vs-Monaural-Beats.html**.

Kabbalah.info. "Kabbalah Revealed." 2001. **http://www.kabbalah.info/engkab/education-center/your-first-course-in-kabbalah**.

Khurana, Alka. *10 Minute Meditation for Deep Relaxation.* Dr. Alka Khurana all rights reserved, 2013.

Kripalu.org. "Balancing Act: An Interview with Jack Kornfield." 2011. **http://meditation.com/articles/Balancing_Act_An_Interview_with_Jack_Kornfield**.

Livestrong.com. "Core Muscle Stretches." 2013. **http://www.livestrong.com/article/355186-core-muscle-stretches/**.

Livestrong.com. "Exercises that Strengthen the Diaphragm & Abdominal Muscles to Help in the Breathing Process." 2013. **http://www.livestrong. com/article/113103-exercises-strengthen-diaphragm-abdominal/**.

Livstrong.com. "How Does Meditation Help Athletes. 2014. **http://www.livestrong.com/article/458411-how-does-meditation-help-athletes/**.

Livestrong.com. "Risks and Side Effects of Genetically Modified Food." 2013. **http://www.livestrong.com/article/417880-risks-side-effects-of-genetically-modified-food/**.

Livingenergyworks.com. "Strengthening Your Core." 2013. **http://www. livingenergyworks.com/meditation/strengthen-your-core/**.

Massgeneral.org. "Decreased Premature Ventricular Contractions Through Use of the Relaxation Response in Patients with Stable Ischemic Heart Disease." 1975. **http://www.massgeneral.org/bhi/assets/pdfs/ publications/Benson%201975%20Lancet.pdf**.

Martial-art-potential.com. "Meditation in Martial Art." 2013. **http://www.martial-art-potential.com/meditation.html**.

Mindfullivingprograms.com. "What is Mindfulness-Based Stress Reduction." 2014. **http://www.mindfullivingprograms.com/ whatMBSR.php**.

Ncbi.nlm.nih.gov. "An Update on Mindfulness Meditation as Self-Help Treatment for Anxiety and Depression." 2012. **http://www.ncbi.nlm.nih.gov/pmc/articles/PMC3500142/**.

Ncbi.nlm.nih.gov. "Brief Meditation Training Induces Smoking Reduction." 2013. **http://www.ncbi.nlm.nih.gov/pmc/articles/ PMC3752264/**.

Ncbi.nlm.nih.gov. "Generalized Anxiety Disorder." 2013. **http://www.ncbi.nlm.nih.gov/pubmedhealth/PMH0001915/**.

Ncbi.nlm.nih.gov. "Ultrastructure and X-Ray Microanalytical Study of Human Pineal Concretions." 1995. **http://www.ncbi.nlm.nih.gov/ pubmed/7645736**.

Nytimes.com. "Unibomber Manifesto." 1996. **http://partners.nytimes. com/library/national/unabom-manifesto-1.html**.

Onlinelibrary.wiley.com. "Acute Treatment with Pulsed Electromagnetic Fields and its Effect on Fast Axonal Transport in Normal and

Regenerating Nerve Vibration and Tissue." 2004. **http://onlinelibrary. wiley.com/doi/10.1002/jnr.490420512/abstract**.

Perry, Susan K. *Writing in Flow*. Writer's Digest Books, 1999.

Psy-flow.com. "Flow, the Psychology of the Optimal Experience." 2000. **http://www.psy-flow.com/sites/psy-flow/files/docs/flow.pdf**.

Reversespins.com. "George Washington's Masonic Collection." 2014. **http://www.reversespins.com/masons.html**.

Ritecare.com. "Implications of Adrenal Insufficiency." 2001. **http://www.ritecare.com/nutritional/natcell_adrenals.html**.

Salzberg, Sharon. *Real Happiness: The Power of Meditation*. Workman Publishing Company, Inc., 2011.

Sacred-geometry.com. "Ascension Through Sacred Geometry." 2013. **http://www.sacred-geometry.com/ascension.html**.

Sacred-geometry.com. "Introduction to Sacred Geometry." 2013. **http://www.sacred-geometry.com/bruce-rawles_ sacred_geometry.html**.

Sagemeditation.com. "Meditation Cushion." 2014. **http://www.sagemeditation.com/meditation-cushion/ meditation-cushion.html**.

Scribd.com. "Healing with Water." 2004. **http://www.scribd.com/ doc/47788640/Healing-With-Water-Emoto-2004**.

Scribd.com. "Yoga Anatomy." 2007. **http://www.scribd.com/doc/206643265/Yoga-Anatomy**.

Storylogue.com "How Do Writer's Unearth the Stories that Want to be Told?" 2010. **http://www.youtube.com/watch?v=TWxoTpINxxw**.

Swamij.com. "The Four Paths of Yoga." 2013. **http://www.swamij.com/four-paths-of-yoga.htm**.

Tapwithsusheela.com. "How to Actually Move up the Vibrational Scale." 2012. **http://tapwithsusheela.com/blog/wordpress/**.

Ted.com. "Four Scientific Studies on How Meditation can affect your Heart, Brain, and Creativity." 2013. **http://blog.ted.com/2013/01/11/4- scientific-studies-on-how-meditation-can-affect-your-heart-brain- and-creativity/**.

The-guided-meditation-site.com. "Meditation for Creativity." 2014. http://www.the-guided-meditation-site.com/meditation-for-creativity.html.

Theforbiddenknowledge.com. "The Illuminati/Freemason Signature." 2001. http://www.theforbiddenknowledge.com/hardtruth/13_33_freemason_sig.htm.

Totaltrainer.com. "Discover the Three Special Benefits of Good Body Alignment." 2010. http://www.totaltrainer.com/exercises/discover-the-three-special-benefits-of-good-body-alignment/.

Tripod.com "Physiological Aspects of Meditation." 2000. http://hanshananigan.tripod.com/meditation.html.

Wakeup-world.com. "Binaural Beats: A Meditative Gateway to Altered States of Consciousness." 2013. http://wakeup-world.com/2012/07/28/binaural-beats-a-meditative-gateway-to-altered-states-of-consciousness/.

Whatonearthishappening.com "Esoteric Freemasonry." 2011. http://www.whatonearthishappening.com/podcast?start=50.

Kabbalah and the Tree of Life with Mark Passio. 2011. http://www.whatonearthishappening.com/podcast?start=100.

Ymaa.com. "Why Meditation is Important in Martial Arts." 2011. http://ymaa.com/articles/why-meditation-is-important-in-martial-arts.

Young, Robert O., and Shelley Redford-Young. *The PH Miracle: Balance Your Diet, Reclaim Your Health*. Grand Central Life & Style, 2010.

Youtube.com. "Free Zone Interview on Satanic Evolution, with Mark Passio." 2011.

Youtube.com. "Satanism and Luciferiansim." 2013. http://www.youtube.com/watch?v=xaLTZwT9XQs.

Youtube.com. "Sovereignty, Natural Law, and Grassroots Solutions." 2012. http://www.youtube.com/watch?v=pWwPFw7Dk60.

Youtube.com. "The Healing Begins Now." 2007. http://www.youtube.com/watch?v=GUfk2QnUfQc.

Youtube.com. "The Matrix Decoded." 2012. http://www.youtube.com/watch?v=JvKEwr0iNA0.

Resources

Meditation-Supporting Dietary Supplements

*The following dietary supplements are available at most health stores. Herbal supplements are listed at the end of Chapter 3.

Liquid chlorophyll or concentrated green powder (wheatgrass, barley grass, kamut grass) — Fiber rich mixture of green grasses that help alkalize the body and remove toxins. Best brands include pHorever, World Organics, Innerlight, and DeSouza's.

Omega-3 and Omega-6 oils — Protection for the heart, lowers triglycerides, cholesterol, and high blood pressure

Alkaline Water — Water that has been ionized, filtered, and contains a high concentration of election energy (Look online for the nearest store that sells alkaline waterl)

Sodium Bicarbonate — Found in unprocessed mineral salt; reduces bone loss, irritation, and inflammation

Vitamin D — Most common deficiency in the human body, but important to overall health; for people with severe bone density loss, the most potent and effective supplemental form is Vitamin D_3

Glutathione — Antioxidant that binds to acids and allows them to excrete from the body; repairs body from damage caused by stress

N-acetyl cysteine — Controls negative microforms that result from toxic hazards such as cigarette smoke

Noni fruit concentrate — Antifungal that renews cells and helps rebuild blood and body tissue

Flavonoids — Supplement for fruits and vegetables; act as acid neutralizers

Rhodium and iridium — Increases cells ability to communicate with each other

List of Companies that Carry Meditation Supplies and Accessories

Source	Purchase	Contact
Wildmind	Music, courses, incense, jewelry, DVDs, meditation timers, and more	http://secure.wildmind.org/store/home.php?cat=
Carolina Morning	Meditation benches, cushions and mats, organic bedding, books, candles, meditation bells, and more	www.zafu.net/benches.html
DharmaCrafts meditation supplies	Clothing, cushions, benches, incense and burners, bells, and gongs	www.dharmacrafts.com/100xMS/DharmaCrafts-Meditation-Supplies.html

Most Popular Ambient Recording Titles

The Orb	A Huge Evergrowing Pulsating Brain that Rules From the Centre of the Ultraworld	1990
The Orb	Adventures Beyond the Ultraworld	1991
Global Communication	76:14	1994
Tetsu Inoue	Ambiant Otaku	1994
Monolake	Hongkong	1997

Biosphere	Substrata	1998
Future Sound of London	Lifeforms	1998
Tim Hecker	Radio Amor	2002
Aglaia	Three Organic Experiences	2003
Helios	Eingya	2006

List of Meditation Centers

Organization	Contact Information	About
Insight Meditation Center	Insight Meditation Center of the Mid-Peninsula 108 Birch Street Redwood City, California 94062 (650) 599-3456 **www.insightmeditationcenter.org** **insightmeditationcenter@gmail.com**	Based in Redwood City, California, IMC offers support for Vipassana or Insight Meditation. Practice is guided by Gil Fronsdal and Andrea Fella. The weekly schedule includes dharma talks, Yoga practice, discussions, sitting, and meditation instruction.
Shambala	Shambala 1084 Tower Road Halifax, Nova Scotia B3H 2Y5, Canada (902) 425-4275 **http://shambala.org**	A global community with more than 170 centers around the world, Shambala offers teaching and training. Shambala views every human as fundamentally good. Through meditation, each person's fundamentally good and intelligent nature extends outward to family, society, and community.
Chakrasambara Kadampa Meditation Center	Chakrasambara Kadampa Meditation Center 322 Eighth Ave, Suite 502, New York, NY 10001 (Entrance on 26th Street, between 8th and 7th Ave.) (212) 924-6706 **www.meditationinnewyork.org**	Offers meditation classes, talks, and retreats with guidance from qualified Western teachers. Weekly classes held in Manhattan, Bronx, New Jersey, Brooklyn, Queens, Long Island, and Westchester. Classes for kids also available.

Organization	Contact Information	About
Spirit Rock Meditation Center	Spirit Rock 5000 Sir Francis Drake Boulevard Woodacre, CA 94973 (415) 488-0164 Fax: (415) 488-1025 **www.spiritrock.org**	A Western dharma and retreat center offering classes and programs on Vipassana meditation.
Karuna Meditation Society	**www.karuna.ca**	Based on the teachings of Thich Nhat Hanh and Shunryu Suzuki Roshi, Karuna Meditation Society offers free, six-week meditation and discussion courses five times a year.
Austin Zen Center	Austin Zen Center 3014 Washington Square Austin, TX 78705 512-452-5777 **www.austinzencenter.org**	Based on the teachings of Shunryu Suzuki Roshi, Austin Zen Center offers classes, retreats, talks, seated meditation, and more.
Zen Center of Georgia	**www.zen-georgia.org**	Offering weekly Zazen and Okyo (chanting) meditation classes in the Zen tradition. Classes are offered in Avondale Estates and Alpharetta, Georgia.
Dahn Yoga	**www.dahnYoga.com**	Offering Yoga, meditation, and tai chi classes at centers around the United States. Instruction is also available through books and CDs sold on the website.
Sanatan Society	**www.sanatansociety.org/Yoga_and_meditation/hatha_Yoga.htm**	Offers education and instruction in Hatha Yoga.

Author Biography

ichael J. Cavallaro was born in New Hyde Park, New York, and was educated at Villanova University. Following his years as an editor with HarperCollins Publishers, he has worked as a freelance technical writer for commercial business. This is his fifth book.

Index